Cookery for all Occasions

Cookery
for all
Occasions

octopus

Contents

First published 1976 by
Octopus Books Limited
59 Grosvenor Street
London W1

© National Magazine Company Limited
ISBN 0 7064 0577 3

Produced by Mandarin Publishers Limited
22a Westlands Road
Quarry Bay, Hong Kong

Printed in Hong Kong

The recipes in this book were first published in Good Housekeeping
COOKING FOR TODAY and have since been revised, up-dated and metricated

Introduction

Who loves a party? Everyone, especially if the food's good. Yet planning the menus and finding the right recipes is often the hardest bit of organization. For this book we have selected recipes for all sorts of family and festive occasions. Thumb through it and you'll find menu plans for dinner parties and easy buffets, including christenings, weddings, and Christmas and Easter festive meals. There are ideas for informal entertaining, with barbecue and picnic menus, as well as plans for easy weekends and children's parties. All the recipes have been tested in the famous Good Housekeeping Institute kitchens and are presented in such a way that they can be followed easily. You can use them with confidence and be sure that the finished dish will taste and look delicious. We have used simple but effective decorations knowing that a busy hostess doesn't want too many fussy finishing touches. The size of casserole and dish is important too – the details you need are in the recipe. Look at the dishes used in the pictures – they'll give you serving ideas.

Mixing flavours is fun too but you can't afford to experiment when you're entertaining. In these recipes the experimenting has been done for you which means you can show off with new ideas and no worries. Try a Crown Roast of Pork with Orange Rice for a dinner party, Fennel and Gruyère Salad at a summer buffet, or Turkey Cranberry Salad on Boxing Day.

To make this book completely up to date metric and imperial measures are used. Use whichever set of figures you prefer – grams and litres or ounces and pints – it won't make any difference to the finished recipe. The Good Housekeeping experts have worked it all out for you.

Have fun planning your parties – may they all be successful.

Carol Macartney

Director, Good Housekeeping Institute

Perfect Dinner Parties

Boeuf Stroganoff

Menu
serves 4

Haricots verts a la tomate
Boeuf Stroganoff
Leaf spinach and boiled rice
Tranche aux fruits
Wine – Claret
(Haut Médoc or St. Emilion)

Timetable
for dinner at 8.00 p.m.
Day before: Make flan case.
5.00 p.m.: Collect ingredients and equipment. Fill flan. Beat and cut the steak and coat with seasoned flour. Prepare onions and mushrooms. Cook rice, drain and leave to cool. Wash and pick over spinach.
7.30 p.m.: Prepare first course. Put drained rice in a buttered casserole, cover tightly with a lid and place in warm oven to heat through.
Boil spinach, drain and refresh.
7.45 p.m.: Cook beef (add soured cream between courses); keep warm. Place roughly chopped spinach over a low light with a little butter.
8.00 p.m.: Serve first course.

Haricots verts à la tomate

½ kg (1 lb) French beans
¼ kg (½ lb) firm tomatoes
40 g (1½ oz) butter
1 bay leaf
sprig of thyme
salt and pepper

Top, tail and wash the beans. Plunge into boiling salted water, cover and cook for 5 minutes. Scald the tomatoes and remove the skins, then quarter them. Drain the beans in a colander, melt the butter in the pan over gentle heat and return the beans, with the tomatoes, bay leaf and thyme. Season with salt and freshly ground black pepper. Cover with a tightly fitting lid; if the lid is rather loose, place a buttered round of greaseproof paper under it to hold it tight. Simmer gently for about 15 minutes, shaking the pan occasionally. Remove bay leaf and thyme from beans before serving.

Boeuf Stroganoff

¾ kg (1½ lb) rump steak
3 × 15 ml spoons (3 level tbsps) seasoned flour
50 g (2 oz) butter
1 onion, skinned and thinly sliced
¼ kg (½ lb) mushrooms, sliced
salt and pepper
284 ml (½ pint) soured cream

Beat the steak, trim, cut into strips 0.5 cm by 5 cm (¼ in by 2 in) and coat with seasoned flour. Fry the meat in half the butter until golden brown – about 5–7 minutes. Cook the onion and mushrooms in the remaining butter for 3–4 minutes, season to taste and add the beef. Warm the soured cream and stir into the meat mixture. Serve with boiled rice and leaf spinach.

Tranche aux fruits

For pâte sucrée:
175 g (6 oz) plain flour
pinch of salt
40 g (1½ oz) caster sugar
75 g (3 oz) butter
2 × 15 ml spoons (2 tbsps) beaten egg

For pastry cream:
600 ml (1 pint) milk
100–125 g (4 oz) caster sugar
50 g (2 oz) plain flour
15 g (½ oz) cornflour
2 large eggs
50 g (2 oz) butter
icing sugar

For filling:
340-g (12-oz) can pineapple pieces
312-g (11-oz) can mandarin oranges
226-g (8-oz) can cherries

For fruit glaze:
2 × 15 ml spoons (2 level tbsps) apricot jam
15 ml spoon (1 tbsp) water

Sift the flour and salt on to a pastry board or marble slab. Make a well in the centre and into it put the sugar, butter and egg. Using the fingertips of one hand, pinch and work the sugar, butter and egg together until blended. Gradually work in all the flour and knead lightly until smooth. Put the paste in a cool place for at least 1 hour, return to room temperature until easy to roll out. Roll out the pâte sucrée and use to line a 35.5 cm by 11.5 cm by 2.5 cm (14 in. by 4½ in. by 1 in.) flan frame (if your oven is small, use a square flan frame), placed on a flat baking sheet. Line with greaseproof paper, fill with dried beans and bake blind at 200°C. (400°F.) mark 6 for about 25 minutes. Remove beans and bake for a further 5 minutes.
Heat the milk. Blend together the sugar, flour, cornflour and beaten eggs; stir in the milk. Return to the pan, heat gently, stirring until the mixture thickens and just comes to the boil. Stir in the butter. Cool. When nearly cold, spoon into the pastry case. Dust with icing sugar to stop a skin forming. Drain canned fruit thoroughly. Stone the cherries. Arrange fruit over pastry cream in tight panels. Bring jam and water to the boil. Bubble gently for 1 minute. Sieve and brush whilst warm over the fruit. Serve cold.

Tranche aux fruits, concealing a deliciously smooth pastry cream

Menu
serves 4

Pâté maison, French bread
Casserole of game
Braised celery and game chips
Pineapple and maraschino granito
Wine – Red Burgundy
(Côte de Beaune-Villages)

Timetable
for dinner at 8.00 p.m.
Day before: Make pâté and pineapple granito.
5.30 p.m.: Collect ingredients and equipment. Start birds cooking. Prepare potatoes for game chips. Slice pâté and put on individual plates.
7.00 p.m.: Scoop granito into pineapple shell and leave in coldest part of refrigerator. Cook game chips (or heat packet crisps) and celery; keep warm.
7.30 p.m.: Carve birds and complete casserole.
8.00 p.m.: Serve first course.

Pâté maison

¼ kg (½ lb) chicken liver
75 g (3 oz) lean pork or veal
50 g (2 oz) fresh white breadcrumbs
125 ml (4 fl oz) milk
salt and pepper
pinch of nutmeg
streaky bacon rashers, cut thinly and rinded
sprig of thyme
1 bay leaf
75 ml (⅛ pint) aspic jelly made from aspic jelly powder
10 ml spoon (½ tbsp) brandy

Mince the liver finely once and the pork or veal twice. Soak the breadcrumbs in milk. Season the liver and pork with salt, pepper and nutmeg. Stir in the breadcrumbs gently, otherwise the liver will lose its colour.
Line a 600 ml (1 pint) terrine with very thin slices of streaky bacon then put in the liver mixture. Top with more bacon and add the thyme and bay leaf. Cover with a lid and place in a roasting tin. Pour water into tin to a depth of 2.5 cm (1 in.). Place in the oven and cook at 170°C. (325°F.) mark 3 for about 1½ hours.
Add a little melted aspic jelly and the brandy 15 minutes before the end of the cooking time. Remove

from the oven. When beginning to cool, discard lid and place a plate and a weight on top. Allow to cool completely before covering with remaining aspic.
Serve with crusty French bread.

Casserole of game

2 partridges or pheasants (dressed)
25 g (1 oz) butter
2 × 15 ml spoon (2 tbsps) oil
1 small onion, skinned and chopped
100–125 g (4 oz) veal, minced
100–125 g (4 oz) lean ham, minced
1 small cooking apple, peeled and sliced
1 clove garlic, skinned and crushed
salt and pepper
1 bay leaf
4 × 15 ml spoons (4 tbsps) stock
142 ml (¼ pint) single cream
2 × 15 ml spoons (2 tbsps) brandy
lemon juice (optional)
100–125 g (¼ lb) button mushrooms
butter
watercress

Truss the birds and fry evenly in the butter and oil until well sealed and browned. Take out of pan and set aside. To the pan add the onion, veal, ham, apple and garlic. Cook gently for 5 minutes. Turn mixture into a casserole just large enough to take the birds, season and add the bay leaf. Place the birds on top, breast sides down, and pour over the stock.
Cook in the oven at 170°C. (325°F.) mark 3 for about 1 hour until showing signs of being tender. Remove from the oven, discard the bay leaf, turn birds over. Pour in cream. Warm the brandy, ignite it and add to casserole. Cover tightly and return to the oven for ¾ hour.
To serve, carve the birds and keep hot. Adjust seasoning in gravy and sharpen if necessary with lemon juice. Sauté the mushrooms in a little butter and add to the gravy. Reheat but do not boil. Spoon over the birds. Garnish with watercress and serve accompanied by game chips and braised celery.
Note: This method is also suitable for duck. Use a 1¾ kg (3½ lb) oven-ready duck, jointed into four; fry skin side down until brown and drain well on absorbent kitchen paper. Pour off nearly all the dripping from the pan, then continue as for game. Before adding the cream, again skim off as much fat as possible.

Saltimbocca alla romana is a traditional dish from Italy

Pineapple and maraschino granito

1 medium pineapple
sugar to dredge
150 ml (¼ pint) water
225 g (8 oz) caster sugar
rind and juice of 1 lemon
2 × 15 ml spoons (2 tbsps) maraschino liqueur
10 maraschino cherries

Split the pineapple down the middle and scrape the flesh and juice into a bowl. Discard centre core. Sprinkle the inside of the pineapple with sugar and chill. Make a purée of the fruit flesh and juice in an electric blender. Add water, sugar, lemon rind and juice and bring to the boil. Boil for 5 minutes. Cool, then turn into a freezing tray. Freeze until mushy. Turn the pineapple mush into a bowl, beat well and add the liqueur and cherries. Return to home-freezer or refrigerator and freeze until firm.
To serve, scoop the pineapple granito out of the tray and pile into the chilled shell. This dish looks particularly attractive on a silver or stainless steel dish, in a bed of ice cubes.

Menu
serves 4

**Pasta hors d'oeuvre
Saltimbocca alla romana
Petits pois à la française, croûtons
Praline bombe**
Wine – Red or white Chianti

Timetable
for dinner at 8.00 p.m.
Day before: Make bombe. Prepare mayonnaise for hors d'oeuvre.
5.00 p.m.: Collect ingredients and equipment. Prepare first course. Prepare veal rolls ready for frying. Fry croûtons; keep warm. Prepare vegetables.
7.45 p.m.: Cook main course and vegetables; keep warm. Unmould bombe on to chilled plate and return to freezing compartment.
8.00 p.m.: Serve first course.

Pasta hors d'oeuvre

100–125 g (4 oz) pasta shells
1 egg yolk
150 ml (¼ pint) corn oil
15 ml spoon (1 tbsp) vinegar
pinch of sugar
½ × 2.5 ml spoon (¼ level tsp) dry mustard
salt and freshly ground black pepper
15 ml spoon (1 tbsp) top of the milk
50 g (2 oz) onion, skinned and finely chopped
5 ml spoon (1 level tsp) tomato paste
100–125 g (4 oz) garlic sausage
100–125 g (4 oz) tongue, cooked
175 g (6 oz) crisp green apple, cored and finely diced
chopped parsley

Cook the pasta shells until tender in boiling salted water. Drain and rinse under cold running water. Make 150 ml (¼ pint) mayonnaise, using the egg yolk, oil, vinegar, sugar, mustard, salt and pepper. Blend in the top of the milk, onion and tomato paste. Cut garlic sausage and tongue into strips; toss with pasta and apple. Fork the mayonnaise through well.
Serve on individual plates garnished with chopped parsley.

Tomato jelly rings to serve as a first course at a dinner party

Saltimbocca alla romana

8 thin slices of veal
lemon juice
freshly ground black pepper
8 fresh sage or basil leaves or 5 ml
 spoon (1 level tsp) dried
 marjoram
8 thin slices prosciutto ham
butter
2 × 15 ml spoons (2 tbsps)
 Marsala
1 cm (½ in.) squares day-old
 bread, fried

Ask the butcher to bat out the veal to pieces about 10 cm by 12.5 cm (4 in. by 5 in.). Season with lemon juice and pepper. Place a little sage, basil or marjoram in the centre and cover with a slice of ham. Roll up and fix firmly.
Melt the butter to cover the base of a frying pan just large enough to take the rolls in a single layer. Gently fry the veal rolls until golden brown. Do not over-heat the butter. Add the Marsala. Bring to simmering point, cover the pan and simmer gently until the rolls are tender. Pour the juices over and surround with fried croûtons.

Petits pois à la française

¼ of a lettuce, washed and finely
 shredded
6 spring onions, halved and
 trimmed
a little parsley and mint, tied
 together
¾ kg (1½ lb) peas, shelled
150 ml (¼ pint) water
25 g (1 oz) butter
salt and pepper
10 ml (2 level tsps) sugar
butter for serving

Put all the ingredients except the extra butter in a pan, cover closely and simmer until cooked – about 20–30 minutes.
Remove the parsley and mint, drain the peas well and serve with a knob of butter.

Praline bombe

100 g (4 oz) sugar
150 ml (¼ pint) hot water
4 egg yolks, beaten
100–125 g (4 oz) almond toffee,
 crushed
5 ml spoon (1 tsp) vanilla essence
a pinch of salt
284 ml (½ pint) double cream,
 whipped
500–600 ml (1 pint) vanilla ice
 cream

Put the sugar into a saucepan and heat very gently until coffee-coloured. Add the hot water, dissolve the caramel and cool.
Put the egg yolks in the top of a double saucepan or in a bowl over a pan of hot water and pour on the caramel. Stir until the mixture thickens.
Cool, add the crushed toffee, vanilla essence and salt and fold in the cream. Turn into empty ice cube trays. Put in the ice-making compartment of the refrigerator set at coldest; freeze until half-set. Chill a pudding basin or bombe mould and line it to about 2.5 cm (1 in.) thickness with the vanilla ice cream. Fill the centre with the half-frozen praline mixture and finish off with more vanilla ice cream. Press on lid of mould, or cover basin with foil, and return to the freezing compartment.
Turn out just before serving.

Tomato jelly rings
Pork ragoût
Chocolate soufflé &
tuiles d'amandes
Wine – Alsace Gewürztraminer

Timetable
for dinner at 8.00 p.m.
In advance: Make the tuiles d'amandes and store in an airtight tin.
In the morning: Make tomato jelly rings and leave in a cool place to set.
Make soufflé but do not decorate with cream yet.
5.30 p.m.: Collect ingredients and equipment. Start pork cooking.
Make stuffing balls.
Prepare garnish for first course.
Decorate soufflé.
7.00 p.m.: Fry stuffing balls and keep warm.
Turn out jelly rings and garnish.
8.00 p.m.: Serve first course.

Tomato jelly rings

½ kg (1 lb) firm ripe tomatoes
2 small onions
1 small clove of garlic
1 bay leaf
5 ml spoon (1 tsp) peppercorns
5 ml spoon (1 level tsp) sugar
2.5 ml spoon (½ level tsp) salt
pinch of celery salt
pinch of grated nutmeg
15 ml spoon (1 level tbsp)
 powdered gelatine
15 ml spoon (1 tbsp) tarragon
 vinegar
3 × 15 ml spoons (3 tbsps) lemon
 juice
watercress

Scald the tomatoes, remove the skins, cut in quarters and remove the centres if tough. Chop the onions and crush the garlic. Put the tomatoes, onions, garlic, sugar, salts and nutmeg in a pan, add the bay leaf and peppercorns tied in muslin, and cook over a low heat until the onion is tender. Remove the muslin bag.
Dissolve the gelatine in 2 × 15 ml spoons (2 tbsps) water in a small basin over hot water. Work the tomato mixture in an electric blender, rub it through a sieve and turn into a measure. Add the vinegar and lemon juice and if necessary make up to 550 ml (1

pint) with water. Add the dissolved gelatine, pour into wetted individual ring moulds and leave to set.
To serve, turn out moulds and garnish with watercress.

Pork ragoût

2 onions, skinned and sliced
50 g (2 oz) fat or oil
1 kg (2 lb) shoulder of pork, boned
 and cubed
2 small green peppers (capsicums),
 de-seeded and sliced
2 cloves of garlic, skinned and
 crushed
150 ml (¼ pint) red wine
150 ml (¼ pint) stock or water
½ × 2.5 ml spoon (¼ level tsp)
 chilli powder
5 ml spoon (1 level tsp) celery salt
1 bay leaf
salt and pepper
40 g (1½ oz) long grain rice
75-g (3-oz) pkt. sage and onion
 stuffing mix

Cook the onions gently in the fat for about 5 minutes; remove from the pan and brown the meat in the remaining fat for 8–10 minutes; drain off any excess fat. Return the onions to the pan with the peppers, garlic, wine, stock, chilli powder (a little at a time according to taste), celery salt, bay leaf and seasoning. Cover and simmer for 1½ hours, or until the meat is tender. Meanwhile cook the rice in boiling salted water for 15–20 minutes and drain well. Make up the sage and onion stuffing according to the directions on the packet, shape into 12 small balls and fry until pale golden brown – 3–4 minutes. Add to the meat with the rice just before serving.

Chocolate soufflé

3 large eggs, separated
75 g (3 oz) caster sugar
2 × 15 ml spoon (2 tbsps) water
10 ml spoon (2 level tsp) powdered
 gelatine
2 × 15 ml spoons (2 tbsps) water
75 g (3 oz) plain (dark) chocolate
15 ml spoon (1 tbsp) brandy
300 ml (½ pint) double cream

Prepare a 12.5 cm (5 in.) soufflé dish by tying a double piece of oiled greaseproof paper around the dish extending 7.5 cm (3 in.) above the top. Whisk egg yolks and sugar with the water in a deep bowl over a pan of hot water, until thick and creamy. Remove from

10

Poularde farcie italienne

the heat and continue whisking until cool. Put the gelatine and water in a basin, stand this in a pan of hot water and heat gently until the gelatine is dissolved. Allow to cool slightly and pour into the egg mixture in a steady stream, stirring the mixture all the time. Melt the chocolate over a pan of hot water and stir the melted chocolate with the brandy into the egg mixture. Cool to the stage at which the mixture is nearly setting.

Lightly whip half the cream and fold into the chocolate mixture. Whisk egg whites in a clean bowl until stiff but not dry and quickly, lightly and evenly fold into the mixture. Pour the mixture into the soufflé dish and allow to set. Whip up the rest of the cream. When the soufflé is set, remove the paper and pipe 6–8 whirls of cream around the top and decorate with caraque or coarsely grated chocolate.

Note: To remove the greaseproof paper band, hold a knife in hot water then run it round the soufflé between the 2 layers of paper. This should loosen the paper sufficiently to allow you to peel it off easily.

Tuiles d'amandes

These biscuits are called 'tuiles' because they resemble the old-fashioned curved roofing tiles

3 egg whites
175 g (6 oz) caster sugar
75 g (3 oz) plain flour
75 g (3 oz) flaked or nibbed
  almonds
75 g (3 oz) butter, melted

Using a rotary whisk and a large basin, whisk the egg whites until stiff and fold in the caster sugar, sifted flour and almonds. Mix well. Fold in the cooled melted butter. Place teaspoonfuls of the mixture on a greased baking

sheet, keeping them well apart. Smooth out each one thinly with the back of a spoon, retaining the round shape. Bake at 190°C. (375°F.) mark 5 for 8–10 minutes, until lightly browned. Use a palette knife to lift each one from the baking sheet and place it over a rolling pin, so that it sets in a curled shape. Allow a moment or two for the wafer to harden and then remove to a wire rack to cool. Store in an airtight tin and serve in glasses.

Menu
serves 6

Avocado with cheese dressing
Poularde farcie italienne
Broccoli spears and new potatoes
Malakoff torte
Wine – Red or White Chianti

Timetable
for dinner at 8.00 p.m.
Day before: Bone and stuff chicken. Prepare torte but do not decorate; keep in refrigerator. Make chocolate squares.
5.45 p.m.: Collect ingredients and equipment. Put chicken to roast.
6.30 p.m.: Decorate Malakoff torte and return to refrigerator.
7.30 p.m.: Prepare avocados. Cook vegetables and keep warm.
7.45 p.m.: Dish up chicken and keep warm.
8.00 p.m.: Serve first course.

Avocado with cheese dressing

3 ripe avocados
a little lemon juice
50 g (2 oz) Roquefort or Stilton
  cheese
50 g (2 oz) cottage cheese

Halve each avocado lengthways with a stainless steel knife, making a deep cut through the flesh

11

Apfelstrudel is a universal favourite – serve them with cream

up to the stone and encircling the fruit. Separate the halves by gently twisting them in opposite directions and discard the stones. Brush the cut surface with lemon juice.

Dice the Roquefort cheese and mix with the cottage cheese. Carefully scoop out all the flesh from the pear skins, dice it and combine with the cheese mixture. Pile the mixture into the 'shells'.

Poularde farcie italienne

2 kg (4 lb) chicken (oven-ready weight)
1 large orange
¼ kg (½ lb) lean pork
¼ kg (½ lb) lean streaky bacon, rinded
1 large clove of garlic, skinned the chicken's liver
100–125 g (4 oz) onion, chopped
¼ kg (½ lb) pork sausage meat
2.5 ml spoon (½ level tsp) salt
freshly ground black pepper
2.5 ml (½ level tsp) dried thyme
50 g (2 oz) cocktail gherkins
25 g (1 oz) butter
2 × 15 ml spoons (2 tbsps) thin honey
½ × 2.5 ml spoon (¼ level tsp) powdered cinnamon

To bone the chicken, first cut off the wings at the second joint and the legs at the first. Then, using a small sharp knife, slit down the centre of the back and work the flesh from the bones, gradually turning it inside out and being careful not to break the skin. The ligaments of the wing and leg joints need to be severed and the leg joints broken before the flesh can be scraped off. Work round to the breast bone and, after separating the flesh from it, remove the carcass. (Most poulterers will bone the bird for you if you prefer). Boned, the bird should weigh about 1¼ kg (2½ lb).

Finely grate the rind of the orange. Mince the pork, bacon, garlic, liver and onion into a bowl. Blend in sausage meat, salt, black pepper, thyme and 2.5 ml spoon (½ level tsp) grated orange rind. Lay the boned chicken, skin side down, on a board. Turn the wings inside out. Spread half the stuffing over the bird and position 2 lines of gherkins along its length. Force a little stuffing into both legs and cover the gherkins with the remainder. Bring the sides together and sew them up using a trussing needle threaded with fine string. Sew legs flat against body.

Place the bird in a small roasting tin. Melt the butter in a small pan, add remaining orange rind. Brush over the chicken and season. Roast at 200°C. (400°F.) mark 6 for about 1½ hours. Meanwhile squeeze 6 × 15 ml spoons (6 tbsps) juice from the orange. Put this in the pan with the honey and cinnamon. Bring to the boil and bubble for 2 minutes. Pour juices from the chicken into the pan with the honey. Spoon orange and honey over chicken and return to the oven on the lowest shelf. Cook for a further 25 minutes, basting every 10 minutes so that it acquires a good glaze. Serve with broccoli spears and new potatoes.

Malakoff torte

225 g (8 oz) unsalted butter
175 g (6 oz) caster sugar
1 egg yolk
15 ml spoon (1 tbsp) coffee essence
50 g (2 oz) candied peel, finely chopped
25 g (1 oz) nibbed almonds
50 g (2 oz) ground almonds
100 ml (4 fl oz) rum
100 ml (4 fl oz) water
3 pkts Boudoir biscuits or sponge fingers
50 g (2 oz) plain (dark) chocolate
150 ml (¼ pint) double cream
2 × 15 ml spoons (2 tbsps) milk (optional)

Lightly oil a 20.5 cm (8 in.) cake tin. Cut 2 strips of greaseproof paper 2.5 cm by 40.5 cm (1 in. by 16 in.) and lay them across each other in the centre of the tin, or use a loose-bottomed tin. Line the base and the sides with paper. Cream the butter and sugar until pale and the sugar is only slightly gritty, beat in the egg yolk and coffee essence; fold in the candied peel and nuts. Blend the rum and water and pour into a flat dish. Crumple some kitchen foil and shape it into a collar to fit inside the base of the tin, leaving a small gap between the side of the tin and the foil to support the biscuits.

Soak the biscuits briefly in the rum but remove them before they soften. Place side by side round the outside of the tin in the gap left by the foil. Now carefully remove foil by easing it up the sides of the tin. The biscuits will remain in position if they have been firmly wedged.

Soak sufficient biscuits, one at a time, to line the base of the tin. Spoon half the creamed filling in small amounts over the biscuit-lined base. Spread the mixture in an even layer with a spatula. Briefly soak more biscuits in the rum and layer over the filling. Spoon remaining filling over the biscuit layer and place the few remaining rum-soaked biscuits over the top. Cut the tips of the biscuits off where they extend above the cake and embed the pieces into the surface. Chill the cake for at least 3 hours before serving.

Break the chocolate into a small bowl, place over a pan of hot, not boiling, water and allow to melt slowly. Ensure that no water bubbles into the chocolate. Line a baking tray with a sheet of non-stick paper (weighting down the paper at the corners if it comes off a roll). Pour the chocolate in a thin stream over the paper and spread to approximately 0.25 cm (¹⁄₁₀ in.) thickness with a palette knife. Leave to cool until firm but not brittle. To make the chocolate squares, dip a long knife into a jug of hot water, wipe dry and draw the knife through the chocolate at 2.5 cm (1 in.) intervals. Make cuts at right angles to the original cuts, 2.5 cm (1 in.) apart. Whip the cream with the milk until stiff but still of a slightly floppy consistency.

Ease the torte away from the tin by pulling the strips of grease-proof paper. Place a serving plate over the tin and invert the whole thing. Remove tin and paper or ease out from loose-bottomed tin. With a forcing bag and large star vegetable nozzle, pipe large whirls of cream over the cake and top alternate whirls with a chocolate square.

Menu
serves 6

Consommé
Tournedos Béarnaise
Potato sticks
Apfelstrudel
Wine – Beaujolais

Timetable
for dinner at 8.00 p.m.
Day before: Make apfelstrudel and parsley butter.
5.00 p.m.: Collect ingredients and equipment.
7.20 p.m.: Prepare béarnaise sauce and keep warm in a bain-marie. Fry bread croûtes lightly and keep them warm.
7.45 p.m.: Heat consommé and potato sticks. Reheat apfelstrudel at 180°C. (350°F.) mark 4.
Fry the tournedos, heat the artichokes and keep them warm without boiling. Garnish just before serving.
8.00 p.m.: Serve first course.

Consommé

1 × 425 g (2 × 15 oz) cans consommé
salt and lemon juice

Heat the consommé gently in a pan and add salt and lemon juice according to taste.

Tournedos Béarnaise

3 × 2.5 ml spoons (1½ tsps)
  chopped parsley
350 g (12 oz) butter, softened
3 × 210 g (3 × 7½ oz) cans
  artichoke bottoms
6 slices of bread, 7.5 cm (3 in.)
  square
6 × 15 ml spoons (6 tbsps) white
  wine vinegar
5 × 5 ml spoons (1½ tbsps)
  chopped shallot
6 peppercorns
1 bay leaf
sprig each of fresh tarragon and
  chervil
3 egg yolks
salt and pepper
2.5 ml spoon (½ level tsp) dried
  tarragon
2.5 ml spoon (½ level tsp) dried
  chervil
3 × 15 ml spoons (3 tbsps) cooking
  oil
6 tournedos, about 1 cm (½ in.)
  thick

Blend the parsley with 75 g (3 oz)
butter. Work into a pat, wrap in
waxed paper and chill until firm.
Drain the artichokes and rinse in
cold water. Simmer for about 7
minutes. Drain and keep warm.
Melt 75 g (3 oz) butter in a pan
and fry the bread on both sides
until golden. Drain on absorbent
kitchen paper and keep warm.
Put the wine vinegar, shallot,
peppercorns, bay leaf, fresh tarragon and chervil in a saucepan.
Boil rapidly until reduced to
about 25 ml (1½ tbsps). Cream
the egg yolks with a knob of butter and a pinch of salt in a basin
standing over a pan of hot water.
Thicken slightly over a gentle
heat. Strain the herb vinegar on to
it and mix well. Add 125 g (4 oz)
butter, piece by piece as the mixture thickens, stirring continuously with a wooden spatula.
Increase the heat slightly to
thicken the sauce. When all the
butter is added, adjust seasoning
and add 1 × 2.5 ml spoon (½ level
tsp) each dried tarragon and chervil. Keep the sauce just warm (not
hot as it may separate).
Heat remaining butter with the
oil in a heavy frying pan. Season
the steaks with pepper and fry
quickly in hot fat for about 3
minutes on each side (less if you
like them rare). Place the fried
croûtes on a warmed serving dish
and place a steak on each.
Arrange the artichoke bottoms
between the steaks and fill each
with béarnaise sauce; just before
serving top each steak with a pat
of parsley butter.

Apfelstrudel

225 g (8 oz) plain flour
2.5 ml spoon (½ level tsp) salt
1 egg, lightly beaten
2 × 15 ml (2 tbsps) oil
4 × 15 ml (4 tbsps) lukewarm
  water
40 g (1½ oz) seedless raisins
40 g (1½ oz) currants
75 g (3 oz) caster sugar
2.5 ml spoon (½ level tsp)
  powdered cinnamon
1¼ kg (2½ lb) cooking apples,
  peeled and grated
40 g (1½ oz) butter, melted
100–125 g (4 oz) ground almonds
icing sugar

Put the flour and salt in a large
bowl, make a well in the centre
and pour in the egg and oil. Add
the water gradually, stirring with
a fork to make a soft, sticky
dough. Work the dough in the
bowl until it leaves the sides, turn
it out on to a lightly floured surface and knead for 15 minutes.
Form into a ball, place on a cloth
and cover with a warmed bowl.
Leave to 'rest' in a warm place for
1 hour. Add the raisins, currants,
sugar and cinnamon to the apples
and mix thoroughly.
Warm the rolling pin. Spread a
clean old cotton tablecloth on the
table and sprinkle lightly with
1–2 × 15 ml spoons (1–2 tbsps)
flour. Place the dough on the
cloth and roll out into a rectangle
about 0.3 cm (⅛ in.) thick, lifting
and turning it to prevent it sticking to the cloth. Gently stretch
the dough, working from the
centre to the outside and using
the backs of the hands, until it is
paper-thin (traditionally it is thin
enough to read through). Leave
to dry and 'rest' for 15 minutes.
Cut the dough into strips 23 cm
by 15 cm (9 in. by 6 in.). Take
each piece in turn, place it on a
damp tea towel, brush it with
melted butter and sprinkle with
ground almonds. Spread the
apple mixture over the dough,
leaving 1 cm (½ in.) border uncovered all round the edge. Fold the
pastry edges over the apple mixture, towards the centre. Lift the
corners of the cloth nearest you
up and over the pastry, causing
the strudel to roll up, but stop
after each turn to pat it into shape
and to keep the roll even. Slide
each completed roll on to a lightly
buttered baking sheet. Brush the
strudels with melted butter and
bake at 190°C. (375°F.) mark 5 for
about 40 minutes, until golden
brown. Dust with icing sugar.
Serve warm with cream.

Strawberries Romanoff, topped with feuilles royales

Menu
serves 6

**Cucumber Portugaise
Turbot au four
Broccoli spears
Creamed potatoes
Strawberries Romanoff**
Wine – White Bordeaux
(Pouilly Fuissé)

Timetable
for dinner at 8.00 p.m.
Day before: Make feuilles
royales. Prepare fish stock, strain
and refrigerate.
5.00 p.m.: Collect ingredients
and equipment.
Clean mussels. Bake fleurons,
prepare orange garnish and
prepare vegetables.
5.30 p.m.: Prepare cucumber
Portugaise.
6.00 p.m.: Start to prepare dessert
(decorate just before serving).
7.15 p.m.: Start to cook main
course. Leave fish and sauce to
keep warm separately.
7.50 p.m.: Finish off main course
and keep warm.
8.00 p.m.: Serve first course.

Cucumber Portugaise

2 large cucumbers (or 4 small
  ridge cucumbers)
100–125 g (4 oz) onion, skinned
  and finely chopped
4 × 15 ml spoons (4 tbsps) cooking
  oil
4 firm ripe tomatoes, skinned and
  seeded
10 ml spoon (2 level tsps) tomato
  paste
2 × 15 ml spoons (2 tbsps) garlic
  vinegar
pinch of dried thyme
salt and freshly ground black
  pepper

Thinly pare the cucumbers using
a potato peeler, then cut into
2.5 cm (1 in.) lengths. Cut each
piece into quarters along the
length. Remove the centre seeds
with the point of a knife and discard. Plunge into boiling salted
water for 5 minutes; drain and
refresh under cold running water.
Sauté the onion in the oil until
tender, add the diced tomatoes,
tomato paste, vinegar and thyme.
Blend the cucumber with the
tomato. Season well and turn into
a serving dish. Chill thoroughly.
Serve with crusty bread.

This starter is simple, but looks luxurious

Turbot au four

100–125 g (4 oz) cod or fish
  trimmings
100–125 g (4 oz) onions, skinned
  and chopped
1 bay leaf
6 peppercorns
1.1 litre (2 pints) mussels
100–125 g (4 oz) butter
4 × 15 ml spoons (4 tbsps) dry
  white wine
6 cutlets of turbot (or sole or
  whiting) about 1¼ kg (2½ lb)
50 g (2 oz) plain flour
225 g (8 oz) shelled shrimps
2 egg yolks
salt and freshly ground black
  pepper
15 ml spoon (1 tbsp) lemon juice
100–125 g (4 oz) Parmesan cheese,
  finely grated
1 orange
fleurons of puff pastry to garnish

Put the cod or fish trimmings in a saucepan with 50 g (2 oz) chopped onion, the bay leaf and peppercorns. Cover with water and bring to the boil. Put the lid on the pan and simmer for about 1 hour. Top up with more water if necessary.
Meanwhile place the mussels in a large bowl under running water and scrape off any mud, barnacles, seaweed and 'beards' with a small sharp knife. Discard any that are cracked, open or loose (unless a tap on the shell makes them close). Rinse until there is no trace of sand in the bowl.
Melt 25 g (1 oz) butter in a pan, sauté the remaining chopped onion until soft. Add the wine and the mussels; cover and steam, shaking often, for about 5

minutes until the shells are open. Strain. Remove the mussels from their shells and discard the shells. Add the mussels and onion to the liquid in which they were cooked. Lay the fish cutlets in 1 layer in a roasting tin or similar container and strain 400 ml (¾ pint) fish stock over them. Cover with a sheet of buttered kitchen foil and bake in the oven at 170°C. (325°F.) mark 3 for about 20 minutes.
The fish when cooked should offer no resistance to a skewer inserted into the thickest part of the flesh, close to the bone. Remove the cutlets from the stock and keep warm.
Strain the stock. Melt 75 g (3 oz) butter in a pan, stir in the flour and gradually add the strained stock. Stir in the shrimps and mussels in their liquid. Add a little of the hot liquid to the egg yolks, beat them and pour back into the sauce. Heat through, season to taste and add the lemon juice.
Coat the fish with the sauce, sprinkle with grated Parmesan and put under a hot grill until golden. Garnish with the fleurons and segments of orange.

Strawberries Romanoff

½ kg (1 lb) strawberries, hulled
4 × 15 ml spoon (4 tbsps) port wine
5 × 5 ml spoons (1½ level tbsps)
  caster sugar
5 × 5 ml spoons (1½ tbsps) milk
215 ml (7½ fl oz) double cream
vanilla sugar

For feuilles royales:
175 g (6 oz) icing sugar, sifted
1 egg white

Put aside 6 whole strawberries. Thickly slice the remainder and place in a bowl with the port and sugar. Turn lightly and leave to soak for at least 1 hour. Spoon the strawberries into individual glasses.
Add the milk to the cream with the vanilla sugar and whip until the cream just holds its shape. Spoon this mixture over the strawberries. Before serving, decorate with whole strawberries and feuilles royales.
To make feuilles royales, gradually stir the icing sugar into the egg white and beat well. Make a piping bag out of greaseproof paper, spoon in the royal icing and snip off the tip of the bag to allow the icing to flow through. Pipe the icing freehand into leaf shapes on kitchen foil, starting with the outline and then filling in the leaf itself. Allow to dry for about 1 hour then pipe in the centre vein.
Place the leaves on foil under a low grill for about 10 minutes, until dried out and tinged brown. The leaves should now come away from the foil easily. Turn them over and dry for a little longer. Cool on a wire rack. Wrapped in foil, feuilles royales will store for up to 2 weeks.

Menu
serves 8

**Fonds d'artichauts
Crown roast of pork
with orange rice
Buttered cauliflower
Fruit meringue**
Wine – Hock (Liebfraumilch)

Timetable
for dinner at 8.00 p.m.
In the morning: Prepare crown of pork and make stock; strain and cool. Prepare flavouring vegetables for orange rice. Make pastry base for dessert.
5.00 p.m.: Assemble ingredients and equipment. Marinade artichokes and boil eggs. Finish dessert. Prepare cauliflower and keep covered.
5.30 p.m.: Put pork to cook.
6.00 p.m.: Make up first course.
7.15 p.m.: Cook rice and keep warm.
7.45 p.m.: Dish up and garnish pork. Make gravy. Cook cauliflower.
8.00 p.m.: Serve first course.

Fonds d'artichauts

178 g (6¼ oz) can artichoke
  bottoms, drained
juice of 1 lemon
2 × 15 ml spoons (2 tbsps) salad oil
salt and pepper
8 small eggs, hard-boiled
150 ml (¼ pint) thick mayonnaise
pinch of sugar
paprika pepper
lemon slices and parsley for
  garnish

Marinade 8 of the artichoke bottoms for 1 hour in 5 ml spoon (1 tsp) lemon juice, the oil, salt and pepper. Drain and arrange on serving dishes. Shell the eggs and slice off the bottoms so that they will stand. Place an egg upright on each artichoke bottom. Add the remaining lemon juice and sugar to the mayonnaise, spoon it into a forcing bag fitted with a small star vegetable nozzle, and pipe round the base of the artichokes. Dust with paprika. Garnish with lemon slices and parsley.

Crown roast of pork with orange rice

2 joints, 7 ribs from each side of a
  loin of pork
50 g (2 oz) lard, melted
salt and pepper
50 g (2 oz) butter
100–125 g (4 oz) celery, scrubbed
  and finely diced
100–125 g (4 oz) onion, skinned
  and finely chopped
½ × 2.5 ml spoon (¼ level tsp)
  curry powder
350 g (12 oz) long grain rice
juice of 2 large oranges
175 g (6 oz) seedless raisins
15 ml spoon (1 level tbsp) finely
  grated orange rind
1 orange for garnish, sliced
15 ml spoon (1 tbsp) stock

For stock:
1 onion, skinned and stuck with 5
  cloves
1 carrot, peeled
1 stick celery, scrubbed
8 peppercorns

Ask your butcher to skin the meat, remove the chine bones and trim the rib bones to an equal length. Keep the bone trimmings for the stock.
Score across both joints 4 cm (1½ in.) down from the bone tips. Remove the fatty ends and carefully scrape the bone tips free of flesh. Place the joints back to back, with the rib bones outermost. Sew the joint ends together using a trussing needle and fine string. Tie the string.

Crown roast of pork with orange rice

Place the crown in a roasting tin and tightly pack the cavity with foil to maintain the shape while cooking. Brush the outside of the meat with melted fat. Season. Cover the tips of the bones with foil to prevent charring. Place in the oven and roast at 220°C. (425°F.) mark 7 for about 2¼ hours, basting frequently.

Meanwhile, place the bone pieces, meat trimmings, onion, carrot, celery and peppercorns in a pan. Cover with water and sim-mer for 2 hours, topping up with hot water when necessary. Strain and put aside.

Melt the butter in a large sauce-pan, add the diced celery and onion and sauté until tender. Stir in the curry powder and cook for 1 minute longer. Add the rice, 700 ml (1¼ pints) stock and the orange juice. Season well, cover and simmer for 20 minutes, until the rice is tender. Add raisins and orange rind, reheat gently.

Remove the foil from the pork

Grape delight – a light dessert after a rich meal

crown and transfer the meat to a serving plate.

Pour off the fat from the roasting tin. Add about 300 ml (½ pint) stock to the sediment and season well. Stir the sediment into the stock and add the sherry. Cook for 1 minute. Strain into a gravy boat. Spoon the orange rice into the centre of the crown and around the meat. Garnish with orange slices warmed in the oven.

Fruit meringue

350 g (12 oz) bought puff pastry, thawed
15 ml spoon (1 tbsp) milk or 1 egg, beaten
1 large juicy lemon
200 g (7 oz) caster sugar
2 pears and 2 apples, peeled, cored and sliced
2 peaches, skinned, stoned and sliced
2 oranges, peeled and segmented
100–125 g (4 oz) black grapes, halved and pipped
425 g (15 oz) can pineapple pieces, drained
312 g (11 oz) can red cherries, drained and stoned
3 egg whites
75 g (3 oz) granulated sugar
a few glacé cherries, halved
angelica
25 g (1 oz) toasted, flaked almonds
1 lemon, sliced, for decoration, optional

Roll out the pastry to a 23 cm (9 in.) circle and place it on a wetted baking sheet. Brush with milk or beaten egg and prick it well. Stand the pastry in a cool place for 15 minutes, then cook in the oven at 230°C. (450°F.) mark 8 for

about 15 minutes, until well risen and golden brown. Allow to cool. Thinly pare the rind from 1 lemon with the potato peeler. Put it in a small pan with the juice of the lemon and 300 ml (½ pint) water. Bring to the boil and continue boiling until the liquid is reduced by half. Strain, return to the pan and add 100–125 g (4 oz) caster sugar. Dissolve the sugar over gentle heat then bring back to the boil and continue boiling until the syrup is reduced by half. Allow to cool.

Place the pastry base on a baking sheet and top it with the fruit, arranged in layers to a height of 7.5–10 cm (3–4 in.). Flatten the top slightly. Spoon the lemon syrup carefully over the fruit, allowing it to run through to the pastry base.

Whisk the egg whites until stiff but not dry, then whisk in the granulated sugar a little at a time, making sure the mixture is stiff between each addition. Whisk in half the remaining caster sugar a little at a time, then fold in the rest. Spoon into a forcing bag fitted with a large star vegetable nozzle. Pipe the meringue in circles over the fruit and pastry until both are completely covered; smooth with a flat-bladed knife. Place in the oven at 120°C. (225°F.) mark ¼ for 2–2½ hours until the meringue is firm but not coloured. Cool, then transfer to a serving dish. Decorate the meringue with halved glacé cherries, strips of angelica and toasted almonds. Cut the lemon slices in half and arrange neatly round the base of the meringue.

Menu
serves 8

Champignons Marie
Roast stuffed veal
Braised celery hearts and creamed potatoes
Grape delight
Wine – Claret
(Château Haut-Brion)

Timetable
for dinner at 8.00 p.m.
In the morning: Stuff veal and return to refrigerator. Prepare potatoes, keep under water. Halve and pip grapes; store in refrigerator.
5.00 p.m.: Assemble ingredients and equipment. Prepare all ingredients for first course but do not start to cook.
5.30 p.m.: Start to cook veal.
7.00 p.m.: Start to braise celery. Make up grape delight.
7.30 p.m.: Cook mushrooms and make toast. Dish up mushroom mixture at the last minute. Cook potatoes. Keep vegetables hot.
7.45 p.m.: Dish up veal and make gravy.
8.00 p.m.: Serve first course.

Champignons Marie

¾ kg (1½ lb) button mushrooms, wiped and stalks removed
6 × 15 ml spoons (6 tbsps) cooking oil
4 shallots, skinned and finely chopped
4 × 15 ml spoons (4 level tbsps) fine, dry breadcrumbs
salt and pepper
2 × 15 ml spoons (2 tbsps) lemon juice
4 × 15 ml spoons (4 tbsps) chopped parsley

Quarter the mushroom caps and half of the stalks. Heat the oil in a thick frying pan and fry them for 10 minutes, until brown. Chop the remaining stalks finely, mix with the chopped shallots and add to the mushrooms in the pan. Fry for a further 2–3 minutes. Drain any excess fat from the pan and add the breadcrumbs. Stir over gentle heat. Season and stir in the lemon juice and chopped parsley. Spoon into individual dishes to serve. Serve with fingers of hot buttered toast.

Roast stuffed veal

1¾ kg (3½ lb) boned shoulder of veal
salt and freshly ground black pepper
¼ kg (½ lb) thin rashers streaky bacon, rinded

For stuffing:
75 g (3 oz) onion, skinned and finely chopped
100–125 g (4 oz) mushrooms, wiped and chopped
2 cloves of garlic, skinned and crushed
5 ml spoon (1 tsp) grated lemon rind
3 × 15 ml spoons (3 tbsps) chopped parsley
100–125 g (4 oz) fresh white breadcrumbs
175 g (6 oz) pork boiling ring, skinned and chopped
salt and freshly ground black pepper
1 egg
2 × 15 ml spoons (2 tbsps) melted butter

Cut through the veal and open it out flat. Beat it lightly with a heavy knife or meat bat until it is a fairly even thickness. Season lightly.

Mix together the onion, mushrooms, garlic, lemon rind, parsley, breadcrumbs, chopped pork ring, salt and pepper. Add the egg and butter and bind the stuffing together. Pile it into the centre of the veal and fold each flap over it. Tie with string.

Stretch the bacon rashers with the back of a knife, cover the meat completely with bacon and tie the rashers in place with string. Wrap loosely in foil, weigh, and then place the joint in a roasting tin. Place in the oven and roast at 220°C. (425°F.) mark 7 for 35 minutes per ½ kg (1 lb). Remove the foil for the last 30 minutes, to allow the meat to brown.

Serve with braised celery hearts and creamed potatoes.

Grape delight

¼ kg (½ lb) black grapes, halved and pipped
¼ kg (½ lb) white grapes, halved and pipped
400 ml (¾ pint) apricot yoghourt
3 egg whites

Turn the yoghourt into a bowl. Whisk the egg whites until stiff and fold into the yoghourt.
Layer the yoghourt and grapes into glasses. Decorate with a few grapes on the top.

Menu

serves 10

Smoked trout with lemon wedges
Lamb en croûte
Courgettes and carrots
Rum glazed pears
Crème St Valentine
Wine – Loire (Pouilly-Fumé)

Timetable
for dinner at 8.00 p.m.
Day before: Marinade, stuff and cook leg of lamb; cool and store in refrigerator.
In the morning: Roll out pastry and wrap lamb; return to refrigerator. Prepare carrots.
6.30 p.m.: Assemble ingredients and equipment. Start to cook pears, when cooked keep warm. Skin trout if wished (leave on the head and tail) and serve on individual plates. Make crème St. Valentine.
7.15 p.m.: Put lamb en croûte in oven and make gravy.
7.45 p.m.: Cook carrots; when ready, keep hot. Cook courgettes for about 10 minutes.
8.00 p.m.: Serve first course.

A leg of lamb, stuffed and served 'en croûte' serves 10 easily

Lamb en croûte

2¼ kg (4½ lb) leg of lamb, boned
150 ml (¼ pint) red wine
½ kg (1 lb) pork sausage meat
100–125 g (4 oz) bacon rashers, rinded and chopped
15 g (½ oz) pistachio nuts, blanched and peeled
salt and freshly ground black pepper
25 g (1 oz) butter
225 g (½ lb) onions, skinned and sliced
sprig of fresh thyme or a little dried thyme
1 bay leaf
3 parsley stalks
1 clove of garlic, skinned and crushed
425 g (15-oz) can consommé
450 g bought puff pastry, thawed
2 eggs, beaten
5–6 × 5 ml spoons (1½–2 tbsps) cornflour

Marinade the lamb in the wine for 2–3 hours, turning occasionally.
Combine the sausage meat, bacon and nuts and season well. Take the meat out of the wine and dry on absorbent paper. Stuff the bone cavity with the sausage meat mixture. Sew up both ends of the joint with fine string.
Melt the butter in a large frying pan and brown the meat quickly on all sides. Transfer to a large casserole. Reheat the fat, add the onions, sauté and add to the casserole with the herbs, the marinade and the consommé. Cover and cook in the oven at 170°C. (325°F.) mark 3 for 2 hours. Remove the meat from the casserole and cool quickly, reserving the juices.
Roll out the pastry to an oblong 51 cm by 25·5 cm (20 in. by 10 in.). Brush the meat surface with beaten egg and dust with flour. Place it in the centre of the pastry and make a parcel by folding the short pastry ends into the centre. Trim off the excess and brush the pastry with beaten egg. Bring together the long edges and seal with beaten egg. Place the croûte, join side down, on a baking sheet.
Roll out the pastry trimmings and cut some leaves to decorate. Place these on the croûte and brush again with egg. Place in the oven and bake at 230°C. (450°F.) mark 8 for about 45 minutes. Cover with foil if the pastry is in danger of over-browning.
To make the gravy, remove the fat from the cooking juices from the lamb by pressing a sheet of absorbent kitchen paper on to the surface. Heat the gravy, thicken with 5–6 × 5 ml spoons (1½–2 tbsps) cornflour and adjust seasoning. There should be 550–700 ml (1–1¼ pints) of gravy.

Crème St Valentine
serves 6

175 g cream cheese
4 large eggs, separated
150 ml (¼ pint) double cream
2–3 × 15 ml spoons (2–3 tbsps) coffee essence
75 g (3 oz) caster sugar
milk chocolate

Whisk together the cream cheese, egg yolks and cream until thick. Stir in the coffee flavouring. Whisk the egg whites until they stand in peaks, gradually adding the sugar. Pour the coffee cream over the whites, and fold through. Pour into 6 small glasses or sundae dishes and chill.
Decorate with curls of milk chocolate, pared from a block with a potato peeler.

Rum glazed pears
serves 6

6 large firm eating pears
juice and finely grated rind of 1 lemon
150 g (5 oz) granulated sugar
15 ml spoon (1 tbsp) rum
15 ml spoon (1 level tbsp) arrowroot
2 × 15 ml spoons (2 tbsps) cold water

Peel the pears thinly, keeping the stems intact. Dip in lemon juice to prevent discoloration. Sit the pears in a single layer in a saucepan. Pour over the lemon juice, the grated rind and sufficient water to cover the pears to a depth of 2·5 cm (1-in.). Cover, bring to the boil and simmer for about 20 minutes until pears are tender. Meanwhile, place the sugar in a heavy based pan. Place over a medium heat and cook without stirring until the sugar caramelizes. Cool slightly. Remove the pears from the pan; gradually stir the poaching liquid and the rum into the caramel. Work with a wooden spoon to remove the caramel sediment from the base

17

of the pan. Blend the arrowroot with the water and gradually add it to the sauce, stirring all the time. Bring to the boil.
Replace the pears in the sauce, cover and simmer for a further 15–20 minutes. Serve warm with whipped cream.

Menu
serves 12

Chilled cream of spinach soup
Spiced orange gammon
Broad beans, carrots and rice
Coffee cream ring
Fresh fruit salad
Wine–Claret (Pauillac)

Timetable
for dinner at 8.00 p.m.
Day before: Make soup; store in refrigerator. Prepare orange caramel glaze; store in refrigerator. Make choux ring and store in an airtight tin. Soak gammon overnight.
In the morning: Make fruit salad. Prepare vegetables ready for cooking.
5.30 p.m.: Start gammon cooking.
Finish coffee cream ring.
7.15 p.m.: Glaze gammon and heat remaining glaze. Cook rice and keep hot. When gammon is cooked, keep hot. Make croûtons.
7.45 p.m.: Cook vegetables. Pour soup into individual cups and add cream.
8.00 p.m.: Serve first course.

Offer Crème St Valentine and Rum Glazed Pears as alternative desserts

Chilled cream of spinach soup

1 kg (2 lb) spinach
100–125 g (4 oz) butter
2 onions, skinned and chopped
1·7 litre (3 pints) chicken stock
2·5 ml spoon (½ level tsp) salt
Freshly ground black pepper
5 × 5 ml (1½ tbsps) lemon juice
2 bay leaves
25 g (1 oz) flour
150 ml (¼ pint) single cream
croûtons of fried bread
grated cheese

Wash and drain the spinach and discard the stalks. In a large pan, melt 50 g (2 oz) butter and sauté the onion until soft but not coloured. Add the spinach and sauté for a further 5 minutes, stirring frequently. Add the stock, salt, pepper, lemon juice and bay leaves. Bring to the boil, cover and simmer for about 20 minutes. Discard the bay leaves and sieve the soup or purée in a blender.
In a clean pan, make a roux with the rest of the butter and the flour. Slowly add the soup, stirring. Bring to the boil and simmer for 5 minutes. Adjust seasoning. Turn into a bowl and chill. Just before serving, pour into soup cups and add a little cream to each cup. Sprinkle grated cheese on the croûtons and melt it under the grill. Hand round separately.

Spiced orange gammon

3 kg (6-lb) middle gammon joint
175 g (6 oz) butter
150 g (5 oz) soft brown sugar
grated rind and juice of 3 oranges
5 × 15 ml spoons (5 tbsps) cider vinegar
2·5 ml spoon (½ level tsp) ground ginger
salt
freshly ground black pepper
2 whole oranges

Soak the gammon in cold water overnight. Drain and place skin side down in a large pan; cover with fresh water. Bring to the boil, skim off the scum, reduce the heat and cook for 55 minutes. Make sure that the joint is always covered with water, topping it up with fresh boiling water if necessary.
Drain the joint. Wrap it in foil and place in a roasting tin. Continue to cook in the oven at 180°C. (350°F.) mark 4 for about 50 minutes.

Meanwhile, prepare the orange glaze. Melt the butter and sugar over a low heat. When the sugar is dissolved, raise the heat and cook until golden. Remove from the heat and add the rind and juice of the oranges, vinegar and ginger. Continue to heat gently, uncovered, for 7–10 minutes. Adjust seasoning.
Slice the whole oranges and poach in water to cover until the rinds are soft. Drain and add to the orange caramel. Continue to heat gently for a further 5 minutes to infuse the flavours.
About 20 minutes before the end of the cooking time, remove the gammon from the oven, unwrap the foil and strip off the rind. Coat the fat with a little of the orange glaze. Return it to the oven and raise the temperature to 220°C. (425°F.) mark 7. Cook for a further 20 minutes.
Serve the gammon hot, with the rest of the glaze separately.

Coffee cream ring
make two

65 g (2½ oz) choux pastry i.e. made with 65 g (2½ oz) flour etc.

For decoration:
50 g (2 oz) flour
50 g (2 oz) soft dark brown sugar
50 g (2 oz) mixed nuts, roughly chopped
300 ml (½ pint) double cream
15 ml spoon (1 tbsp) coffee essence

Lightly grease a baking sheet and dredge with flour. Upturn a 19 cm (7½ in.) cake tin on to it and with one finger, mark around the tin. Remove tin, leaving the line.
Spoon the choux paste into a forcing bag fitted with a large plain nozzle and pipe it in a ring just outside the marked circle on the baking sheet. Bake in the oven at 230°C. (450°F.) mark 8 for 40 minutes then lower heat to 170°C. (325°F.) mark 3 and bake for a further 15 minutes. If the

ing starts to over-brown, cover with foil.

Cool the ring and split in half. In a small saucepan, melt the butter and sugar together over a low heat. When the sugar has dissolved, boil the syrup for 1-2 minutes and stir in the nuts. Drizzle the sauce over the top half of the choux ring.

Whisk the cream until it holds its shape; add the coffee essence. Spoon the cream inside the lower ring and top with the nut encrusted ring.

Fresh fruit salad

For syrup:
100–125 ml (4 oz) sugar
150 ml (¼ pint) water
× 15 ml (2 tbsps) lemon juice
5 ml (1 tbsp) orange liqueur

For salad:
eating apples, peeled and thinly sliced
pears, peeled and diced
oranges, peeled and segmented
large bananas, skinned and sliced

Dissolve the sugar in the water over a low heat, bring to the boil and boil for 2–3 minutes. Cool the syrup, then add the lemon juice and liqueur.

Mix all the fruits with the syrup. Serve chilled.

Menu
serves 12

Avocado, grapefruit and shrimp cocktail
Chicken with ginger
Boiled rice
Strawberry timbale
Norwegian cream
Wine – White Burgundy
(Chablis)

Timetable
for dinner at 8.00 p.m.

A few days before: Make meringue cases; store in an airtight tin.

In the morning: Prepare and cook custard for Norwegian cream. Hull strawberries. If wished fry chicken joints and get ready to put in oven; keep in refrigerator.

5.00 p.m.: Prepare grapefruit and dressing for cocktail. Start to cook chicken with ginger. Decorate desserts.

7.00 p.m.: Prepare avocados and finish cocktails.

7.30 p.m.: Boil rice; when cooked, keep hot.

8.00 p.m.: Serve first course.

Avocado, grapefruit and shrimp cocktail

2 grapefruit
8 × 15 ml spoons (8 tbsps) salad oil
4 × 15 ml spoons (4 tbsps) wine vinegar
salt and pepper
caster sugar
0·5 ml spoon (1 tsp) French mustard
3 ripe avocado pears
1 large lettuce, washed and well drained
600 ml (1 pint) thick mayonnaise
350 g (12 oz) shelled shrimps or prawns, fresh or frozen, and thawed

Peel the grapefruit with a sharp knife, removing all the pith, and divide into segments. Work over a bowl to catch the juice. Fork together the oil, vinegar, seasoning, a little caster sugar and the mustard.

Cut the avocados in half lengthwise, discard the stones and peel away the skin. Cut most of the flesh into small dice, but reserve half an avocado to cut 24 thin slices to garnish. Toss the avocado in the grapefruit juice to prevent discoloration. Drain.

Shred the lettuce and toss in the dressing together with the avocado. Arrange in the bases of 12 medium-sized glasses. Lightly fold the shellfish through the mayonnaise and spoon over the avocado and lettuce. Garnish with slices of avocado and grapefruit.

Chicken with ginger

6 × 15 ml spoons (6 tbsps) cooking oil
150 g (6 oz) butter
12 chicken joints
75 g (3 oz) seasoned flour
3 large onion, skinned and sliced
15 ml spoon (1 tbsp) powdered ginger
6 × 5 ml spoons (6 tsps) French mustard
1 litre 150 ml (2¼ pints) chicken stock
6 × 15 ml spoons (6 tbsps) medium sherry
salt and freshly ground black pepper
350 g (¾ lb) button mushrooms, wiped and stalks removed

Heat the oil and half the butter in a frying pan. Toss the chicken joints in seasoned flour to coat and fry until evenly browned.

Drain from the fat and place in a large casserole. Reheat the fat, add the onions and fry. Stir in any excess flour, ginger and mustard;

Baked gammon with an orange caramel glaze

cook for a few minutes. Off the heat, stir in the stock and sherry. Bring to the boil, stirring. Adjust seasoning and pour over the chicken.

In a clean pan, melt the remaining butter and quickly sauté the mushrooms; add to the casserole. Cover and cook in the oven at 170°C. (325°F.) mark 3 for about 1½ hours. If preferred, strain off the juices and reduce a little by boiling; return to the chicken before serving.

Strawberry timbale

4 egg whites
225 g (8 oz) caster sugar
284 ml (½ pt) double cream
142 ml (¼ pt) single cream
450 g (1 lb) strawberries, hulled and sliced

Draw a 20-cm (8-in.) circle on non-stick paper and place on a baking sheet. Whisk the egg whites until stiff and standing in peaks, add half the sugar, whisking continually until very stiff. Fold in the remaining sugar.

Spread some of the meringue mixture within the circle to form a base. Using a large star vegetable nozzle, pipe a circle of shell shapes to border the base. Pipe a circle of meringue just inside the shelled border, to form an interior wall. Pipe a similar double wall of shells in a circle on top, and complete the case by piping a final single border. This forms the timbale shape, with a deep hollow in the centre. Dry just below the centre of the oven at 160°C. (300°F.) mark 1–2 for about 3 hours until crisp. Leave to cool on a wire rack. Remove the paper.

Whip the creams together until they just hold their shape. Layer the cream and two-thirds of the sliced strawberries in the meringue case. Decorate with the remainder of the strawberry slices.

Norwegian cream
serves 6

150 g (6 oz) apricot jam
3 large eggs
15 ml spoon (1 tbsp) sugar
few drops vanilla essence
725 ml (¾ pt) milk
75 g (3 oz) plain dark chocolate
284 ml (½ pt) double cream, whipped

Cover the base of a 300-ml (2-pt) soufflé dish with the apricot jam. In a bowl, fork together 2 whole eggs, 1 egg yolk, the sugar and vanilla essence. Heat, but do not boil, the milk and pour on to the egg mixture, stirring. Strain on to the jam and cover the dish with foil. Stand the dish in a roasting tin with water to come half way up the dish and cook in the oven at 170°C. (325°F.) mark 3 for about 1¾ hours, until the custard is set. Lift the dish from the tin and leave until quite cold.

Pare the block of chocolate with a potato peeler so that it forms curls. Cover the surface of the custard with about half the chocolate curls.

Whisk the remaining egg white until stiff and fold into about a third of the whipped cream. Spoon on to the chocolate. Pipe the remaining cream round the edge of the dish and fill the centre with the remaining chocolate curls.

The wine to go with it

Draw the cork firmly but gently

If you are serving good food you owe it the justice of a good wine. Precisely which wine you serve with which food is largely a matter of personal taste and pocket; the suggestions we give with our dinner party menus are by no means the ultimate and some connoisseurs would doubtless have quite different ideas. There are, however, certain guidelines that it is as well to follow; just as some foods don't mix well, so some wines are better than others with certain foods.

Fish is always better with a white wine; for some reason, when fish is eaten with red wine both tend to take on a metallic taste which ruins them. Very oily fish can do this even to white wine and the only answer then is to stick to beer. Meats will take red, white or rosé. Beef and lamb tend to have the most pronounced flavours and do justice to the finest of clarets and Burgundies – but if mint sauce, garlic or other strong herbs are in the dish you are wasting your money if you drink anything too expensive, as the flavour will be drowned. A vinegary salad dressing will also kill any wine; if you wish to serve a dish accompanied by salad and wine, make the dressing with white wine or lemon juice in place of vinegar. Pork, veal or chicken are good with white wines (though not with a sweet Sauternes), but are equally good with a light red or rosé. The really sweet, heavy wines are best with desserts, especially cakes and pastries. Any dish cooked in wine should of course be accompanied by a similar wine. Most of our recommendations refer to French or the better known European wines because few of the better Australian, South African or Californian wines are exported at sensible prices. It is, however, well worth experimenting with these if you get the chance.

Food and wine

Clear soup, consommé, oxtail soup, smoked salmon or eel	Dry or medium dry sherry
Meaty and savoury hors d'oeuvre	Red Burgundy or Bordeaux or rosé
Other soups and most starters	Dry sherry or the wine chosen for the main course
Oysters, shellfish, fine fish plainly cooked	Chablis, Muscadet
Turbot, trout, bass, sole, salmon	White Burgundy, Moselle, Hock
Fish with sauces, cold meat	White Alsace
Pasta and pizza	Red Chianti Valpolicella, Bardolino
Paella	White Italian (e.g. Soave) or Spanish
Chicken, veal, pork	Red or white Bordeaux (dry), Alsace, hock, Graves or rosé
Lamb, beef, roast chicken, ham, game, pork, duck	Red Bordeaux or Burgundy, Côtes du Rhône (choose a fine wine for, say, a plain roast sirloin; something less demanding if there is a rich sauce with the meat).
Light sweets, gâteaux, ices	Sweet White Bordeaux
Cheese, nuts and dessert fruit	Port, Madeira, Marsala or cream sherry
	Champagne or a sparkling hock or Moselle can be served throughout a meal

Serving wine

There is a lot of nonsense talked about different glasses for different types of wine. To enjoy wine, your glass should be large enough to hold a generous helping without being more than half full, and the bowl should be roundish, cupping in towards the top so that the bouquet of the wine doesn't escape the instant it is poured out (that is also why you don't fill it more than half full). It should be stemmed so that the temperature of your hand does not affect the temperature of the wine, and it should be clear so that you can see the true colour of the wine. Tall stemmed hock glasses are very good for a chilled wine as they keep your hand well away from the bowl, and a long flute encourages Champagne bubbles to rise. But a glass that is right for one wine is just as right for any other and the range shown are all a good shape; 2–3 sizes could see you

through from sherry to port, whatever you serve in between.

The temperature at which wine is served i most important, as a fine wine can be ruined i it is over-heated; equally if it is too cold you will not be able to appreciate the full flavour Red wine should be drunk at room tempera ture and should be left standing in a warm room for several hours before serving. I should be opened an hour or so before serving to give it time to breathe. If you have left it too late for that, pour it into a warmed decanter, o warm the glass with your hands, but neve stand it in front of the fire, on a radiator, o hold it under a warm tap – the sudden warmth ruins the wine and it will never recover. When red wine has been brought to room tempera ture it is better to drink it all as it will probably spoil if allowed to go cold again. White wine i rather less sensitive – you just lie it down ir the refrigerator for half an hour or so, or if the refrigerator is full stand it in a bucket of col water and ice cubes for 20 minutes, until it i just chilled but not iced.

It may be a good idea to decant a red wine if i is more than 5–6 years old. Wine gradually forms a sediment which makes it cloudy if the bottle is shaken at all. A bottle that has lain or its side for a while will have all the sedimen lying along the one side of the bottle, so when you take it out of the rack, either keep it on it side in a cradle while you bring it to room temperature and open it, or stand it upright fo a few *days* so that the sediment can settle t the bottom of the bottle out of harm's way, o decant it carefully, leaving the sedimen behind.

Drawing the cork is not difficult. The easies way is to use a levered cork-screw. This wil enable you to do it without jerking the bottle particularly useful if you are trying to keep the bottle on its side in a cradle. If you use traditional cork-screw you will certainly have to raise the neck of the bottle a little, but if you keep it tilted as our expert has, the sedimen will remain together and just slide gentl down the side of the bottle. Don't panic if th cork breaks and you cannot get it out – jus push it through and if necessary strain th wine carefully into a decanter.

Choose stackable racks to store your wines s that you can add to them as your cellar grows. dozen or so bottles will meet the demands o most occasions if you choose a wide selection o wines. Our selection includes a light, sparklin French wine, red and white Burgundies, a goo red Chianti, a lighter white from Alsace an 2–3 cheap, lesser known wines to experimen with

Use glasses with a rounded bowl and a longish stem; 2–3 sizes will serve most occasions

Starting a cellar

People who do much entertaining, or like to open a bottle fairly regularly for family gatherings, will find it worth starting their own small cellars. If bottles are bought by the dozen they are, like most things, cheaper. You will also find that somehow the wine tastes better if you have kept it a while.

'Cellar' may sound a very grand word, but that cupboard in the spare room may be an ideal place for storing wine. Anywhere that is dark, has an even temperature (preferably on the cool side) and is not subject to vibration, will do. It needs to be deep enough to take the bottles lying down, and a store of a dozen will see most families through most occasions. Wine needs to be kept lying on its side, otherwise the cork will dry out and shrink, and there are many types of rack available. It is probably best to buy stackable racks, that you can add to as your stock increases; the traditional wood and galvanised metal racks as shown in our picture are as good as any.

If you are used to buying wine in single bottles, when required, you will have had some pleasant experiences and some nasty surprises. This is because very few wines are at their best when newly lugged home from the corner shop; they need time to settle again before you drink them. Another reason is that many wines are sold when freshly bottled and the merchant *intends* that you should keep them for 2–3 months at the very least before opening them – the trouble is unless you know him he probably won't tell you that! Merchants like to sell quickly because storage space is expensive and short term storing cannot affect the price they can charge to the customer; but wines suffer a sort of shock when transferred from barrel to bottle, almost like a bruising, which only time will heal.

If you have to buy in a hurry you are as well off with a brand-name wine; these are blended wines whose characters do not alter much with time and which will go down much the same as vin ordinaire does in France – enjoyable but not exactly select. Try several until you find one you like. Being less subtle in the first place, these wines also suffer less noticeably from being moved around. They are not meant for long term keeping.

When it comes to choosing wine, the novice often looks a bit blankly at the label. There is no need to be put off, though, if you are willing to admit your ignorance and let the wine merchant help you. The first thing you can tell from the label is whether you have a wine from a particular area, blended and bottled on the estate or by an established shipper; whether it is an out-and-out mix up, aimed simply at producing an acceptable drink with no pretensions (this usually applies to branded wines, which often are blends not only from different districts, but even from different countries); or whether it is from a single vineyard and a single year's growth – in which case the grower will have put his own name on it because he believes it is a wine to be proud of.

Nobody drinks fine wines every day, just as nobody eats fillet steak every day. Blended wines are often very good and are definitely not to be sneezed at (all except the most exceptional vintages of Champagne are blended, and nobody queries the quality then). If you decide to go for something better, though, ask your merchant for help.

The French laws of Appellation Contrôlée mean that French wine labels must tell you exactly what you're getting – which vineyard, what year and whether home bottled. Though not obliged to by law, the Germans often go into even more detail about whether they were early or late grapes, first pressing or second – all sorts of information which does mean something to an expert. Unfortunately other countries are less scrupulous and labels tend to be less helpful – you have to feel your way round and get to know those that are good from those that are not so good. From the label on a single vineyard French or German wine bottle, an experienced merchant can tell you whether the wine will be a full flavoured Burgundy or a lighter one, whether the white you are buying will be smooth, heavy and rich flavoured, or fresh and young tasting, and what degree of dryness or sweetness to expect. With these carefully labelled wines, it's not a question of good or bad, but a question of what you're after. At the other end of the scale, if you buy something labelled 'Spanish Chablis' or 'Australian Burgundy' you still know what you are getting – something that doesn't deserve a name of its own, but which vaguely resembles something else. Australian and Californian vineyards are now beginning to label their wines more carefully, to tell the customer in more detail what he is getting. The date on the bottle is not necessarily an indication of a good or bad vintage, more of the age of the wine. Wines of really poor vintages are rarely exported anyway, and many growers will sell off their poorer wine for blending rather than put their own label on it. There *are* special vintages for certain wines, but only a connoisseur could be expected to remember, or pay for, these.

What you do need to know is how old a particular type of wine should be before it is likely to reach its best. Most white wines are very good after as little as 3 or 4 years – some people will lay them down for longer but it is debatable whether it is worth the trouble. Rosés and a very few red wines are similar (the more recent the date on a Beaujolais bottle the better it should be; outside France it is rarely sold less than 2 years old, but beware of any that has more than 4 years under its belt).

The wines that are usually better for age are the red table wines (and port of course, but that's a subject in itself). No claret or red Burgundy will ever be bottled at much less than two years old. The best are then probably worth keeping in the bottle for 10 years to mature – if you pay a high price for a good single vineyard claret and then drink it while it is only 3–4 years old, you are wasting money; these are made to be kept and if drunk sooner are no better than a cheaper wine.

Financially it is sound to buy some young wines to lay down for a few years, as when they are ready to drink they will be much more expensive to buy – but do buy some for drinking sooner as well or you'll be miserable while you wait! Whatever you buy it will be a good investment in terms of enjoyment for yourself and your friends.

Setting the table is a gracious art that should not be allowed to die. Whatever anybody says about looks not counting, they most definitely do count when it comes to food. The look of the food itself somehow affects the way it tastes and an elegant or pretty table-setting, depending on the mood of the meal, will help your party off to a good start and maintain the atmosphere right through to the cheese.

If you are slightly nervous about the forthcoming meal (though you have no need to be if you follow our timetables!) a carefully planned table-setting can reassure you. This is the one place where nothing can go wrong at the last minute. You can set the table hours in advance if you wish and, provided you can keep the children out, it will still be perfect when guests arrive – leaving you free to give all your last minute attention to the food.

The basis for your table-setting will be the linen or mats you choose. Individual place mats can be right even for a formal occasion if you have a really super table to show off. A word of warning, though, to those with temperamental table surfaces – if you are going to supply enough mats to protect the table thoroughly from heat and scratches from all possible sources, the effect will be lost; you need to be able to leave large areas of wood exposed to achieve an uncluttered look.

To both protect your table and set off your best china and cutlery, the answer is an efficient heat-proof covering and a crisply laundered linen cloth. It is possible to buy to order protective cork mats that will exactly fit your table and fold away when not in use. This avoids the ugly lumps made by individual mats under a cloth. Alternatively, use a length of heavy green baize.

The traditional white damask cloth is still valid as a perfect formal setting for fine tableware, but if you prefer something a little more unusual, any plain colour to tone with your china will give the right effect; patterned cloths are better kept for informal occasions when plain earthenware plates and dishes are in use. And whatever your cloth, guests will appreciate really large linen napkins that properly cover even the most ample lap.

In general, keep your setting as simple as possible. Use colours sparingly and base them on the tones predominant in the china, bearing in mind that when the food arrives that should take the centre of attention. Silver, glass, candles (white or to match the china) and a few flowers will complete the picture. It would be so nice if we could all have a choice of china for different occasions. To have fine china for formal dinners and chunky earthenware for less formal occasions would be ideal (as would a choice of silver or stainless steel cutlery) – but of course we have to make do with what is available. The rule, though, is not to try to make your tableware do something for which it is not designed. If all you have is studio pottery, don't try to be formal with it.

Glasses add lustre to a table, and if you can provide two for each guest (one for wine, one for water) it will add luxury to the occasion. If you intend serving a second wine with the

Mix and match your tableware in style

dessert you absolutely *must* have fresh glasses for that.

Glasses go to the right of the place setting, above the knives. If you are putting out more than one glass, arrange them so that the one to be used first is on the right, and work inwards. Although it looks attractive to set out different shaped glasses, don't worry too much about having the correct glasses for each wine as the rules are much less strict now than they used to be. A large, stemmed glass with a rounded bowl, cupping in towards the top, is suitable for all wines.

Conventions about different glasses for different wines may have disappeared as irrelevancies, but those about arranging cutlery are still very much in existence. The principle of a place setting is that it should form a neat square, with the inside knife and fork the width of the plate apart and the dessert spoon and fork the same distance from the table edge. All the items should be as close together as possible without actually touching. This produces a much tidier result, especially if all the handles are lined up a consistent ½ in. from the edge of the table.

Knives (blades pointing inwards) and spoons always go on the right, forks on the left (left-handed people have to juggle for themselves – sorry). Exceptions are the dessert spoon and fork in neat alignment across the top (spoon handle to the right, fork handle to the left) and fruit knife, if it is needed, under the dessert fork, also with its handle to the right. These can just as correctly go to the sides, but it's a

matter of how much space you can afford – the more you build the setting sideways, the more widely you have to space the chairs.

The oft-quoted advice 'start at the outside and work your way in' should come out right with a properly laid table, which is doubtless why the rules have survived. A menu of soup followed by fish, then meat and finally the dessert, should have a left-to-right place setting as follows: fish fork, meat fork, space for plate, meat knife, fish knife, soup spoon. Dessert spoon and fork above the plate gap would logically be left to the end by anyone following this rule. The item that presents the most difficulty is the bread and butter knife, theoretically the last knife to be used but one that is needed throughout the meal. This may be placed either inside or outside the meat knife, or vertically across the side plate – the latter, incidentally is a good way of holding a springy linen napkin in position. Small spoons for starters or for desserts in glasses can be brought in with the dish.

For a buffet, even a formal one, the rules for positioning the tableware are thrown totally to the winds. The prevailing need at a buffet is to display the food to advantage and to put plates, cutlery and napkins where they will least hinder people coming to the table for serving. This usually means grouping them at one end of the table, where guests can collect them before moving on to gather their first course without getting in each other's way. Another solution, ideal if your room space will allow it, is a side table or trolley for these things. Positioning of utensils aside, the rules for setting a buffet table remain similar to those for any other table. Simplicity is again the key, the more so here as the display of all the food together at once imparts its own festive atmosphere. A plain cloth is the perfect background for elaborate trays of salads, cold joints and sumptuous desserts, and one big centrepiece of flowers, set well back where it can't be knocked over by reaching hands, will complete the scene.

For all the delights of displaying all the foods at once, it is better not to overcrowd the table. If you have a large number of guests and only an average-size table, it may be worth leaving the desserts off the table until most people have eaten their main course. You can then whisk away the empties and refurnish the table with desserts, refreshing the eye as well as tempting the palate.

Feel free to mix formal and informal styles. Any style followed through too precisely becomes stiff, and it is the unexpected touches that give individual flair. A formal table setting should logically have formal flowers, but simple garden flowers, like daisies or sweet peas, arranged casually in a pottery jug, may just bring the table to life. Conversely, an informal setting with pottery and multi-coloured linen could become magnificent with the help of a silver candelabra. 'Mix and match' is therefore the key. Bear this in mind when you are buying tableware and it will be much easier when you come to actually set the table. A little planning and imagination go a long way!

PLANNING A MENU

Planning daily menus for the family presents quite a problem for most people, without the extra thought of guests. There are the nutritional considerations to take into account, the personal likes and dislikes of the children, and the need for variety. You have to think of the time available for shopping and cooking, too. Cooking for guests takes just that little extra effort of planning. If anyone finds it no effort it is because her mind has learned to cope automatically with the groundwork, usually after much practice.

For a beginner it is important to accept your limitations, with regard to both cooking ability and circumstances. Unless you are lucky enough to have competent help for your dinner party, include only one course that is going to need serious on-the-spot concentration. Try to start with something that can either be bought or made a day or two in advance, like pâté. This will mean you can enjoy a pre-dinner drink with your guests and need vanish only at the last minute to prepare the toast. If the weather is cold, serve a hot soup made the day before and heated up at the last moment (a chilled soup in summer avoids even that!) Plan for a sweet that's simple too. There is no knowing how long the main course of a meal is going to take, and it is a pity to spoil it with worry about whether the next course is burning or boiling dry. Obvious dishes to avoid, unless you are absolutely confident of your skills and timing, are anything hit-or-miss like a hot soufflé, or anything fried. Mysterious pauses will have your guests every bit as worried as you are, wondering if they ought to offer to help.

For the inexperienced cook, the simplest solution is to choose as the main course a casserole that can be prepared entirely in advance. Potatoes baked in their jackets make a foolproof accompaniment, and you could offer a simple salad as a separate course. It is always best to choose vegetables that can wait happily for a few minutes while your guests catch up with them. Why sit wondering if the sprouts have gone soggy and yellow, when French beans, peas or carrots would have done equally well? And never risk trying out something new on an important occasion. If you want to branch into more exciting dishes, have a full 'dress rehearsal' with your family or some close friends who won't mind, the week before.

A good menu is a varied one. Give your guests cream of artichoke soup, veal à la crème and soufflé milanese and you'll have them all struggling to the sofa and falling asleep afterwards—the combined effect of a major assault on their digestive capacity and a certain boredom induced by cream in every course and a pale beigey colour predominating throughout. But if you serve a tomato salad before the veal and a tasty strawberry water ice with shortbread after, the effect will be quite different. If soufflé milanese remains your favourite dessert, serve steak and a fresh, green salad as the main course. The general principle is that a 'wet' course should follow a 'dry' one or vice versa and the same major ingredient should not feature in two courses. Texture is important and a menu that seems to be heading towards imbalance can often be redeemed by a simple touch, such as crisp croûtons with the soup or a salad instead of a cooked vegetable with the main course. A biscuit or a tiny helping of fresh fruit with a creamy dessert will often help. Flavour obviously needs considering because too much bland food is dull, whereas too much that is piquant is just impossible to eat. This is why a sharp hollandaise sauce is served with turbot, and a lemon sauce with a steamed sponge pudding. In reverse, it's why cream goes with a sharp flavoured apple pie, or rice is always served with curry.

Appearance, another vital factor, is one that is often overlooked. This can easily be improved by the moderate use of garnishes. A steak with chipped potatoes looks much more appetizing if set off with watercress and a grilled tomato, and avoid any really anaemic-looking combination—creamed fish with marrow and potatoes for instance; serve carrots instead of marrow and use chopped parsley and perhaps some paprika pepper to make it look more attractive. Consider the individual tastes of your guests and don't serve curry, tripe or any other fairly specialized taste without first checking that they're going to like it. Be considerate in less obvious ways too—if you know one of your guests is shy, don't serve something that needs to be eaten with blasé defiance of conventional table manners (corn-on-the-cob and spaghetti are prime offenders).

Having planned the menu, spend a little time working out a rough timetable. Give yourself time the day before to do any preparation that can be done in advance—however simple the menu, if you leave everything till 2 hours before the meal you will be rushed and flustered by the time the guests arrive. If you have chosen a simple menu, give yourself a treat by doing the absolute minimum of cooking on the day; you will enjoy the meal all the more.

Plan the shopping, too. Order anything like fresh fruit that you cannot buy in advance, to avoid disappointment, and let your butcher know if you want any special cut or boning out done for you. He will appreciate not having to tackle a whole side of beef when the shop is full on a Saturday morning.

All this planning is practical, and it has an additional psychological effect. A hostess who knows she has all the details under control and that the work is progressing to schedule will be calm and relaxed on the day, able to take a little more time over her own appearance. In the end she will win compliments from all angles!

Easy Weekends

Liver and bacon provencale

Make a change from every-day bacon and eggs

BREAKFAST

A good breakfast goes a long way towards keeping your guests happy for the rest of the day. It may be a meal they don't bother with at home, and the sheer luxury of having someone else prepare it is bound to make them appreciate your efforts. Most of the dishes in our menus can be prepared all at once, and then kept hot in the oven or on a hot tray.

Menu 1

Cereal or
Orange wake me up
Plain omelette
Prune and bacon rolls
Grilled tomatoes
Toast
Marmalade

Orange wake me up

For each person:
juice of 1 orange
15 ml spoon (1 tbsp) clear honey
1 egg

Place all the ingredients in an electric blender and switch on for 30 seconds. Alternatively whisk with a rotary whisk until thoroughly blended.

Prune and bacon rolls

prunes
streaky bacon rashers
prepared mustard

Soak the prunes (allow 2 prunes for each rasher of bacon) overnight in enough water to cover. Drain and stone them. (Alternatively, use well drained canned prunes.) Rind the bacon and stretch with a knife. Cut each rasher in half and spread with mustard. Roll one piece round each prune, place on small skewers and grill until the bacon is cooked.

Menu 2

Yoghourt
Mixed salad of dried fruits – prunes, apricots, apples, pears
Finnan haddie or bacon
Mushrooms
Rolls
Honey

Finnan haddie
serves 4

These are smoked haddock named after the Scottish fishing village of Findon, near Aberdeen.

2 finnan haddock (or smoked cod fillets) total weight approx. ¾ kg. (1½ lb)
550 ml (1 pint) milk
50 g (2 oz) butter
50 g (2 oz) flour
chopped parsley
salt and pepper
2 eggs, hard-boiled

Place the fish skin side up under a hot grill for a few minutes– this makes skinning very simple. Peel the skin off and cut the fish into 8 pieces. Poach in milk for about 15 minutes until tender. Drain off the milk into a measure and make up to 550 ml (1 pint) with more milk if necessary. Melt the butter in a pan, stir in the flour and gradually blend in the measured milk. Flake the fish, removing any bones, and add to the sauce with the chopped parsley, salt and pepper. Bring to the boil. Pour into individual serving dishes and garnish each with wedges of hard-boiled egg.

Menu 3

Fruit juice or
Honey muesli
Breakfast grill – kidneys, bacon, sausages, grilled tomatoes
Poached eggs
Toast
Bran muffins

Honey muesli
serves 4–6

4 oranges
grated rind of ½ lemon
4 eating apples, wiped
2 × 15 ml spoons (2 tbsps) sultanas
1 banana, peeled and sliced
2 × 15 ml spoons (2 level tbsps) ground almonds
2 × 15 ml spoons (2 level tbsps) rolled oats
15 ml spoon (1 tbsp) clear honey
4 × 15 ml (4 tbsps) single cream
1 red eating apple, cored
2 × 15 ml spoons (2 tbsps) lemon juice
black and white grapes, pipped

Squeeze the juice from 2 of the oranges into a large bowl. Add the grated lemon rind. Grate the apples into the juice, discarding the core. Add the sultanas, oats, banana, almonds, honey and cream. Turn into a serving dish. Divide remaining 2 oranges into segments. Slice the red apple and dip it into the lemon juice to prevent discolouration. Decorate the muesli with alternate slices of orange and apple and a few grapes. Serve chilled.

Bran muffins
makes 20

200 g (7 oz) plain flour
5 ml spoon (1 level tsp) salt
2 × 15 ml spoons (6 level tsps) baking powder
100–125 g (4 oz) ready-to-eat bran
450 ml (1 pint, less 6 tbsps) milk
4 × 15 ml spoons (4 tbsps) soft butter
4 × 15 ml spoons (4 level tbsps) caster sugar
2 eggs, beaten

Grease 20 6· 5 cm (2½ in.) diameter deep muffin tins. Sift the flour, salt and baking powder together. Soak the bran in milk for 5 minutes. Meanwhile, beat the butter and sugar until light; add the egg and stir until smooth. Add the bran mixture and stir. Add the flour and stir until only just mixed, no longer. Fill the muffin tins two-thirds full and bake in the centre of the oven at 200°C. (400°F.) mark 6 for 25 minutes, or until well browned. Turn out on a wire rack.
To serve, split rather than cut open, and butter.

Home-made muesli is wholesome and different from packet cereals

Bran muffins

Nobody expects a 3-course meal twice a day, but you probably feel you want to offer something a little more organized than your usual family Saturday lunch. These menus are quick and easy to prepare, even for a full house.

Menu
serves 4

Liver and bacon provençale
Buttered noodles
Green salad
Ice cream cake

Liver and bacon provençale

½ kg (1 lb) lambs' liver
50 g (2 oz) flour
2 × 15 ml spoons (2 tbsps) cooking oil
¼ kg (½ lb) lean streaky bacon rashers, rinded and chopped
½ kg (1 lb) onions, skinned and chopped
396 g (14 oz) can tomatoes
5 ml spoon (1 level tsp) dried marjoram
1 bay leaf
15 ml spoon (1 tbsp) Worcestershire sauce
400 ml (¾ pint) stock
salt and pepper

Slice the liver into long, thick strips, coat with flour and fry in oil until golden brown. Place in a casserole.

Add the bacon and onions to the frying pan and cook until golden. Stir in any flour left over from coating the liver. Add the tomatoes, marjoram, bay leaf and Worcestershire sauce. Stir in the stock, season well, place in the casserole. Cover with a tightly fitting lid and cook in the oven at 150°C. (300°F.) mark 2 for about 1½ hours. Serve with a green salad and noodles cooked in boiling salted water, drained and tossed in butter and pepper.

Ice cream cake

18 cm (7 in.) sponge sandwich cake
jam (e.g. cherry or blackcurrant)
a block of ice cream
142 ml (¼ pint) double cream, whipped

Split the sponge cake and spread one half with jam. Cover with ice cream, piling it up in the centre. Cut the other half of the cake into wedges and arrange round the

Double crust blackcurrant pie to finish a Saturday lunch

cake so that they open at the centre to show the ice cream. Fill the gaps between the wedges with cream, piping it in place.

Menu
serves 4

Devilled gammon with pineapple
Spinach, creamed potatoes
Double crust blackcurrant pie

Devilled gammon with pineapple

2 × 350-g (2 × 12-oz) gammon rashers
4 × 15 ml spoons (4 level tbsps) dry mustard
175 g (6 oz) light, soft brown sugar
226-g (8-oz) can pineapple rings
8 maraschino cherries

Trim the rind from the gammon rashers and snip the fat at intervals. Mix together the mustard, sugar and 8 × 15 ml (8 tbsps) syrup from the can of pineapple. Lay the gammon on the grill

rack, spread evenly with some of the sugar mixture and cook under a medium grill for 15 minutes. Baste with the pan drippings.

Turn the gammon, spread with remaining sugar mixture and cook for a further 15 minutes. Place 2 pineapple rings and 4 cherries on each rasher; baste, and cook for a further 5 minutes. If the fat shows signs of over-browning, cover the area with a piece of kitchen foil. Each rasher will serve 2 people. Serve with spinach and potatoes.

If the gammon tends to be salty, soak it in cold water for an hour before cooking, then pat it dry.

Double crust blackcurrant pie

For shortcrust pastry:
175 g (6 oz) plain flour
a pinch of salt
40 g (1½ oz) lard
40 g (1½ oz) margarine
6 × 15 ml spoons (6 tbsps) water (approx.)
milk, to glaze

½–¾ kg (1–1½ lb) blackcurrants
100–125 g (4 oz) sugar
15 ml (1 level tbsp) flour

First make the pastry. Mix the flour and salt together. Cut the fat into small pieces and add to the flour then, using both hands, rub the fat into the flour with the fingertips, until the mixture looks like fresh breadcrumbs. Add the water, stirring with a round-bladed knife until the mixture begins to stick together. With one hand, collect it together and knead lightly for a few seconds, to give a firm, smooth dough. Divide the pastry in 2, and use half to line an 18 cm (7 in.) pie plate. String, pick over and wash the fruit and mix it with the sugar and flour. Fill the lined pie plate with the fruit mixture and roll out the remaining pastry to form a lid. Damp the edges of the pastry on the dish and cover with the lid, pressing the edges well together. Scallop the edges, brush the top with milk and bake towards the top of the oven at 220°C. (425°F.) mark 7 for 10–15 minutes, until the pastry is beginning to brown. Reduce the temperature to 180°C. (350°F.) mark 4 and continue cooking for a further 20–30 minutes, or until the fruit is soft. Serve with cream, ice cream or custard made with cream.

Menu
serves 4

**Herring fillets
Normandy style
Grilled tomatoes,
Chip potatoes
Fresh fruit
Cheese board**

Herring fillets
Normandy style

*4 herrings (or ½ kg (1 lb) oily fish)
seasoned flour
2 × 15 ml spoons (2 tbsps) cooking
    oil
50 g (2 oz) butter
2 eating apples
juice of ½ lemon
pepper
chopped parsley*

Bone the fish and cut in halves down the centre. Dip fillets in seasoned flour and fry in the oil and 50 g (1 oz) butter until crisp and golden on each side; keep warm. Wipe pan out with absorbent kitchen paper.

Peel and core the apples and cut each into 8 pieces, then add the rest of the butter to the pan and sauté the apple until tender but still in whole pieces. Add the lemon juice and a dusting of freshly ground pepper (with a little more butter if needed). Arrange the fillets in a dish, overlapping each other, spoon the apple mixture over and sprinkle with chopped parsley.

TEAS

Teatime at the weekend may be anything from toast and muffins round the fire, to a quick mouthful in the kitchen. If you have guests, you may find they do not want tea, but something must be available for the hungry types. Even those who don't bother at home will probably develop a healthy appetite when they see some of your goodies.

TOASTED TEAS

Are ideal in winter, particularly if dinner is to be late. Your guests will be grateful for one of these snacks if they have spent the afternoon walking briskly in the snow – if they have just dozed in

front of the fire, try some tempting pastries instead! Toasted sandwiches usually need a knife and fork for eating. Apart from the recipes given here you can also serve traditional crumpets and muffins from your local bakery – toast these on a long fork in front of the fire.

Trident toasted
sandwiches
serves 4–6

*2 large eggs, hard-boiled
100–125 g (4 oz) strong Cheddar
    cheese, grated
198-g (7-oz) can tuna steak,
    drained and flaked
5 sweet pickled onions, chopped
4 × 15 ml spoons (4 level tbsps)
    mayonnaise
juice of ½ lemon
few drops Tabasco sauce
salt and freshly ground black
    pepper
40 g (1½ oz) butter
12 slices from a large, white,
    medium-sliced loaf*

Either chop the hard-boiled eggs or place in an egg slicer and cut in both directions. Combine the egg, cheese, tuna, pickled onions, mayonnaise, lemon juice, Tabasco, salt and pepper. Melt the butter in a small pan and brush it on to one side of each of the slices of bread. Place 6 of the slices, butter side down, on a board. Spread each with ⅙th of the filling, and top with another slice of bread, butter side up. Grill under a medium heat on both sides until golden. Cut in half and serve.

Smoked roe salad
serves 4

*1 lemon
150 ml (¼ pint) mayonnaise
few drops Tabasco sauce
salt and freshly ground black
    pepper
4 slices white bread from a
    medium-sliced white loaf
butter
1 small lettuce
3 large eggs, hard-boiled
225–350 g (½–¾ lb) smoked cod's
    roe
paprika pepper*

Blend the juice from ½ the lemon into the mayonnaise, add a few drops of Tabasco and adjust the seasoning.
Toast the bread until golden brown on both sides. Cool a little and butter liberally whilst still crisp. Lay 3 or 4 lettuce leaves on

Herrings Normandy style – cheap and quick to prepare

A huge toasted sandwich will satisfy tea-time appetites

each slice of toast and spoon the mayonnaise down the centre.
Slice the eggs and position overlapping down one side of the toast. Slice the roe and position down the opposite side. Take 4 slices from the remaining ½ lemon, make a cut into the centre of each slice, twist and place on top. Dust the egg with paprika pepper.

Pizza bambini
serves 4

*120 g (4½ oz) pkt mixed
    salami-cervelat-ham
6 anchovy fillets
100–125 g (4 oz) Lancashire
    cheese, grated
4 round soft rolls
butter
225 g (½ lb) firm tomatoes,
    skinned and thickly sliced
1 small green pepper (capsicum),
    seeds removed*

Roughly chop the meat and anchovy fillets. Combine with the grated cheese.
Halve the rolls and toast until golden on both sides, butter and spoon the cheese mixture on to each half. Spread evenly. Top each with a thick slice of tomato

and grill under a medium heat until the cheese bubbles and browns.
Garnish with thin rings of green pepper. Serve in paper napkins.

Beans and bacon
sandwich
serves 4

*113-g (4 oz) can baked beans in
    tomato sauce
8 rashers streaky bacon, rinded
horseradish sauce
prepared mustard
8 slices white bread, from a
    ready-sliced loaf
butter*

Heat the beans gently through in a small pan. Fry or grill the bacon until crisp, and then crumble on to a plate. When hot, mix the beans with a little horseradish sauce, to taste, and mustard, and stir in the crumbled bacon.
Toast the bread on both sides, butter and spread with the bean filling, as for an ordinary sandwich. Alternatively, butter the bread, untoasted, fill with the bean mixture and place each sandwich buttered side out in a special toasted sandwich cooker.

31

Cream horns are a real weekend luxury – make the horns in advance

SANDWICHES

Sandwiches are the easiest to eat if you don't want to sit down to a table with a knife and fork. Ring the changes with different types of bread – white, brown, wholemeal, granary, rye and so on – and slice it very thinly and butter it well. Fillings need to be well-flavoured; anything very delicate is muted to the point of tastelessness when encased in a double layer of bread.

For some unusual sandwich fillings, try the following mixtures:

Shrimp, chopped celery, shredded pineapple and mayonnaise.
Cream cheese, chopped walnuts and stoned raisins or dates.
Chopped tongue, chopped hard-boiled egg, mayonnaise and a pinch of curry powder.
Flaked, canned crabmeat, chopped avocado and mayonnaise.
Minced chicken, minced ham and finely chopped pineapple.
Cream cheese, chopped celery and chopped green pepper (capsicum).

CAKES

A large cake is always welcome at tea-time, either on its own or with sandwiches. These two are among our favourites.

Brandy, orange and sultana cake

This is a moist cake and keeps well for 2–3 weeks after baking.

675 g (1½ lb) sultanas
2 medium oranges
150 ml (¼ pint) brandy
225 g (8 oz) caster sugar
225 g (8 oz) butter
4 large eggs
225 g (8 oz) plain flour
50 g (2 oz) self-raising flour

The day before baking, place the sultanas in a deep bowl. Grate the rind from the oranges, add to the sultanas with the juice squeezed from the oranges (about 150 ml (¼ pint)) and the brandy. Stir well. Leave for at least 12 hours to plump up, stirring occasionally. Grease a 20·5-cm (8-in.) round cake tin and line with 2 layers of greased greaseproof paper. Tie a band of brown paper round the outside of the tin.

Cream the butter and sugar, beat in the eggs one at a time and lightly beat in the sifted flours. Fold in the fruit and all its juices. Turn the mixture into the prepared tin and bake in the centre of the oven at 170°C. (325°F.) mark 3 for about 3 hours. If the top of the cake appears to be getting too brown towards the end of the cooking time, cover with greased greaseproof paper. To test whether the cake is cooked, insert a hot skewer into the centre of the cake. It should come out perfectly clean. If any cake mixture is sticking to it, the cake requires longer cooking. Turn out and cool on a wire rack. Store in an airtight tin.

Walnut butter cake

75 g (3 oz) unsalted butter
50 g (2 oz) plain flour
15 g (½ oz) cornflour
3 large eggs
100–125 g (4 oz) caster sugar
100–125 g (4 oz) shelled walnuts, finely chopped
coffee butter cream or glacé icing, optional

Grease and flour a 23-cm (9-in.) diameter 1·8-litre (3¼-pints) tube cake tin.

Heat the butter gently until melted, remove from heat and let stand till any sediment settles. Sift the flour and cornflour together. Put the eggs and sugar in a large bowl, stand this over a saucepan of hot, not boiling, water and whisk until light and creamy. The mixture should be stiff enough to retain the impression of the whisk for a few seconds. Remove from the heat and whisk until cool.

Pour the tepid but still flowing butter round the edge of the mixture. Lightly fold in the butter until most of the fat is worked in. Re-sift half the flour over the surface of the mixture and fold in lightly. Fold in remaining flour and nuts. Pour the mixture into the prepared tin and bake in the centre of the oven at 190°C. (375°F.) mark 5 for about 20 minutes.

Serve plain or decorated with coffee butter cream or glacé icing.

Pastries

Introduce a touch of luxury into the weekend, without hard labour. The pastry cases can be made a day or two in advance and stored in an airtight tin. Fill them the day you intend serving them.

Tartlettes aux fruits
makes 6

For pâte sucrée:
100–125 g (4 oz) plain flour
pinch of salt
50 g (2 oz) caster sugar
50 g (2 oz) butter at normal room temperature
2 egg yolks

For crème pâtissière:
2 egg yolks
50 g (2 oz) caster sugar
20 g (¾ oz) plain flour
15 g (½ oz) cornflour
300 ml (½ pint) milk
1 egg white
vanilla essence
icing sugar for dredging

425-g (15-oz) can black cherries
150 ml (¼ pint) cherry juice
5 ml (1 level tsp) arrowroot
142 ml (¼ pint) double cream
4 × 15 ml spoons (4 tbsps) single cream

Sift together the flour and salt on to a pastry board. Make a well in the centre and into it put the sugar, butter and egg yolks. Using the fingertips of one hand, pinch and work the sugar, butter

and egg yolks together until well blended. Gradually work in all the flour and knead lightly until smooth. Put the paste in a cool place for at least 1 hour to relax. Have ready 11·5-cm (4½-in.) shallow patty tins. Roll out the pastry and use it to line the tins. Bake blind at the top of the oven at 190°C. (375°F.) mark 5 for 15–20 minutes. Turn out on a wire rack to cool.

Make up the crème pâtissière a day in advance to save time. Cream the egg yolks and sugar together until really thick and pale in colour. Beat in the flour and cornflour and add a little cold milk to make a smooth paste. Heat the rest of the milk in a saucepan until almost boiling and pour on to the egg mixture, beating well all the time.

Return the mixture to the saucepan and stir rapidly over a low heat until it boils. Whisk the egg white until stiff. Remove the custard mixture from the heat and fold in the egg white. Return the pan to the heat, add a few drops of vanilla essence and cook for a further 2–3 minutes. Leave to cool, dredged lightly with icing sugar to prevent a skin forming. Before serving, spread a layer of crème pâtissière over the base of each tart. Drain the cherries (reserving the juice) and stone them. Blend 150 ml (¼ pint) of the juice with the arrowroot, pour into a saucepan, bring to the boil and cook until it thickens (about 3 minutes). Allow to cool.

Whip the 2 creams together and pipe round the pastry cases. Arrange the cherries in the centre. Spoon the thickened juice over.

Cream horns
makes 8

225 g (8 oz) frozen puff pastry, thawed
1 egg, beaten
raspberry jam
142 ml (¼ pint) double cream
4 × 15 ml spoons (4 tbsps) single cream
icing sugar to dredge

Roll out the pastry to a strip 66 cm by 10 to 11·5 cm (26 in. by 4–4½ in.). Brush with beaten egg. Cut 8 × 1-cm (½-in.) ribbons from the pastry with a sharp knife. Wind each round a cream horn tin, glazed side uppermost. Start at the tip, overlapping 0·3 cm (⅛ in.) all the way and finish neatly on the underside. The pastry should not overlap the metal rim. Place on a damp baking sheet, with the joins underneath. Bake near the top of the oven at 220°C. (425°F.) mark 7 for 8–10 minutes, until golden. Cool for a few minutes.

Carefully twist each tin, holding the pastry lightly in the other hand, to ease off the case. When cold, fill the tip of each horn with a little jam. Whip together the two creams and fill the horns. Dust with icing sugar.

Informal dinners

Dinner when you have weekend guests has to be fairly informal, since you are not free yourself to make elaborate preparations in the shops or kitchen.

Menu
serves 4

**Avocado and melon cocktail
Rolled stuffed breast of lamb
Sauté potatoes and broccoli with browned almonds
Ananas glacé**

Avocado and melon cocktail

2 charentais (1 cantaloup) melons
4 avocados
lemon juice
¼ watermelon, optional
fresh mint, to garnish

Cut the charentais (or cantaloup) melons in half and discard the seeds. Scoop out as much of the flesh as is practical with a small vegetable baller and retain the skins. Cut the avocados in half lengthwise, remove the stones and scoop out the flesh with the same size baller. Sprinkle the avocado balls with lemon juice to prevent discoloration. Cut open the watermelon and cut out the flesh in the same way.
Pile the melon and avocado balls into the charentais melon skins and top with a sprig of mint. Chill for up to 30 minutes before serving.
Note: The melon balls can be prepared 1–2 hours in advance, but the avocado should be left as near as possible to the time of serving.

Rolled stuffed breast of lamb

1½ kg (3 lb) breast of lamb, boned
salt and pepper
100–125 g (4 oz) lean veal
75 g (3 oz) lean bacon
1 onion, skinned and finely chopped
25 g (1 oz) butter
75 g (3 oz) fresh white breadcrumbs
1 large mushroom, washed and chopped
5 ml spoon (1 level tsp) finely chopped parsley
cayenne pepper
ground mace
1 egg, beaten
milk, optional

Spread the boned out joint flat on a board, sprinkle with salt and pepper and rub the seasonings into the meat.
Pass the mixed veal and bacon twice through a mincer, then beat them well in a bowl. Lightly fry the onion in a little of the butter, until soft but not coloured. Add to the meat. Add the breadcrumbs, mushroom, remaining butter, and parsley; season with salt, pepper and a very little cayenne and mace. Lastly, bind with the beaten egg. Mix well, and if the mixture is too stiff add a little milk.
Spread the veal forcemeat over the lamb and roll the meat up loosely to allow the stuffing to expand during cooking. Tie the roll in several places with fine string, to hold its shape. Weigh it and calculate the cooking time, allowing 27–30 minutes per ½ kg (1 lb) plus 27 minutes. Place the meat in the roasting tin, putting it on a grill grid or meat trivet if it is fatty, and cook in the centre of the oven at 180°C. (350°F.) mark 4 for the calculated time.
Remove the strings and serve sliced fairly thickly, accompanied by a thickened gravy. Any stuffing left over can be cooked in a separate small dish and served with the joint.

Ananas glacé

2 small or 1 large pineapple
4 × 15 ml (4 tbsps) Kirsch
2 oranges
2 pears
2 × 15 ml (2 tbsps) lemon juice
12 glacé cherries
50 g (2 oz) piece crystallized citron peel, sliced
1 block vanilla ice cream

Refreshing and simple to make – avocado and melon cocktail

Cut the pineapple into halves lengthwise and scoop out all the flesh. Take care not to damage the shells. Remove the core and cut the rest of the flesh into cubes. Put these into a basin with the Kirsch. Chill the pineapple shells. Peel the oranges, removing all the white pith, and divide into segments, discarding the membrane. Add the oranges and any juice to the pineapple. Peel, core and slice the pears and dip them into the lemon juice before adding to the other fruit together with the glacé cherries and citron peel. Chill for at least 2 hours. Pile the fruit and juice into the pineapple shells and top with scoops of ice cream.

Menu
serves 6

**Florida cocktail
Carbonnade of beef
Runner beans,
Creamed potatoes
Pear and almond pie**

Florida cocktail

3 large juicy grapefruit
6 oranges
caster sugar
sherry, optional

Cut the grapefruit in half across the centre and divide them into segments using a small sharp knife or a curved grapefruit knife. Divide the pieces between 6 small sundae glasses, pouring

any juice over. Peel the oranges, removing all the white pith and again divide into segments, add to the grapefruit in the glasses, with their juice. Dust with caster sugar and add a dash of sherry for the adults. Serve chilled.

Carbonnade of beef

1½ kg (3 lb) lean stewing steak, cut into 1-cm (½-in.) cubes
salt and pepper
75 g (3 oz) fat or oil
100–125 g (4 oz) lean bacon rashers, rinded and chopped
50 g (2 oz) plain flour
400 ml (¾ pint) beer
400 ml (¾ pint) stock or water
3–4 × 15 ml spoons (3–4 tbsps) vinegar
¾ kg onions (1½ lb), skinned and chopped
2 cloves garlic, skinned and chopped
bouquet garni

Season the meat and fry a little at a time in the fat or oil until brown – about 5 minutes for each batch. Add the bacon and continue cooking for a few minutes. Remove the meat and bacon from the pan, stir in the flour and brown lightly. Gradually add the beer, stock and vinegar, stirring continuously until the mixture thickens. Fill a casserole with layers of meat, bacon, onion and garlic. Pour the sauce over and add the bouquet garni. Cover and cook at 150°C. (300°F.) mark 2 for about 4 hours. Add a little more stock while cooking, if the sauce seems very thick. Remove the bouquet garni before serving.

Pear and almond pie

375-g (13-oz) pkt frozen puff
    pastry, thawed
1 kg (2 lb) cooking pears
4 × 15 ml spoons (4 tbsps) brandy
50 g (2 oz) butter
175 g (6 oz) ground almonds
225 g (8 oz) caster sugar
5 ml spoon (1 level tsp) ground
    cinnamon
1 egg, beaten
a little sugar
284 ml (½ pint) double cream

Carefully peel and core the pears.
Cut them lengthwise into
eighths, and lay them in the base
of a round, shallow, 28-cm (11-in)
pie dish. Pour the brandy over
them and dot with the butter cut
into small pieces. Mix together
the almonds, caster sugar and
cinnamon and spoon evenly over
the fruit. Roll out the pastry and
cover the dish. Trim and crimp
the edges and decorate with pastry leaves cut from the trimmings.
Glaze with beaten egg and stand
the pie in a cool place for about 20
minutes, to prevent shrinkage
when cooking. Bake at 220°C.
425°F.) mark 7 for 15 minutes,
then reduce heat to 190°C.
(375°F.) mark 5 for a further
25–30 minutes, until the pastry is
well risen and golden brown.
Sprinkle with a little granulated
sugar 5 minutes before end of
cooking time and return to the
oven. Serve hot or cold with
lightly whipped cream.

Menu
serves 6

Hot stuffed tomatoes
Wiener beef braise
Blackcurrant
streusel

Hot stuffed tomatoes
6 even-sized tomatoes
40 g (1½ oz) ham, chopped
3 × 2·5 ml spoons (1½ tsps)
    chopped onion
20 g (¾ oz) butter
5 ml spoon (1 tsp) chopped parsley
3 × 15 ml spoons (3 tbsps) fresh
    white breadcrumbs
salt and pepper
3 × 15 ml spoons (3 level tbsps)
    grated cheese, optional

Cut a small round from each
tomato at the end opposite the
stalk, and scoop out the centres.
Lightly fry the ham and onion in
the butter for 3 minutes. Add the

Cheese topped gammon with peas lyonnaise for an informal dinner

parsley, breadcrumbs, salt and
pepper, cheese if used and the
pulp removed from the tomatoes.
Fill the tomato cases with this
mixture, pile it neatly on top, put
on the lids and bake at 200°C.
(400°F.) mark 6 for about 15
minutes.

Wiener beef braise
¾ kg (1½ lb) buttock steak (thick
    flank or topside) cut into 12
    slices
12 small frankfurters
75 g (3 oz) dripping
2 medium onions, skinned and
    chopped
4 carrots, peeled and cubed
1 large turnip, peeled and cubed
3 sticks celery, scrubbed and sliced
400 ml (¾ pint) beef stock, made
    with a cube
salt and pepper
¾ kg (1½ lb) potatoes, cooked and
    creamed
15 ml spoon (3 level tsps) cornflour

Beat the sliced beef with a rolling
pin. Roll each slice round a frank-
furter and tie with fine string or
cotton.
Melt half the fat and brown the
beef rolls on all sides. Remove the
rolls from the pan and add
remaining fat; sauté the vegetables until the fat is absorbed.
Place the beef rolls on top, pour
on the stock and season with pepper. Bring to the boil, cover,
reduce heat and simmer for about
2 hours until the meat is tender.
Lift the beef rolls out and arrange
in a ring of creamed potato. Keep
hot. Strain the cooking liquid,
thicken it with the cornflour and
check the seasoning. Pour sauce
over the beef rolls.

Blackcurrant
streusel
175 g (6 oz) plain flour
100–125 g (4 oz) butter
50 g (2 oz) caster sugar
½ kg (1 lb) blackcurrants
100–125 g (4 oz) sugar
284 ml (½ pint) double cream,
    whipped

For topping:
75 g (3 oz) plain flour
75 g (3 oz) butter
75 g (3 oz) caster sugar

Sift the flour, rub in the butter
and then add the caster sugar.
Knead the mixture until it forms
a dough. Press the dough out to fit
a cake tin 20·5 cm by 25·5 cm by
4 cm deep (8 in. by 10 in. by
1½ in.). Wash and top and tail the
blackcurrants, mix with the sugar
and strew over the base. To make
the topping, sift the flour, rub in
the butter very lightly. Add the
sugar but do not knead. Sprinkle
crumble mixture over the fruit.
Cook at 190°C. (375°F.) mark 5
for approximately 1 hour, until a
golden brown. Allow to cool a little then turn out of the tin. Serve
warm or cold, cut into squares
and topped with cream.

Menu
serves 4

Egg mayonnaise
Cheese topped
gammon
Lyonnaise peas, sauté
potatoes
Galette jalousie

Egg mayonnaise
4 eggs, hard-boiled and shelled
a few lettuce leaves
150 ml (¼ pint) mayonnaise
chopped parsley or paprika pepper

Cut the eggs lengthways into
halves or quarters. Wash and
drain the lettuce and put on individual plates. Serve the eggs on
the lettuce, cut side down; coat
with the mayonnaise and garnish
with parsley or paprika.

Cheese topped
gammon
4 gammon rashers (about 175 g
    (6 oz) each)
a little melted butter
2 green eating apples
175 g (6 oz) Cheddar cheese, thinly
    sliced

Rind the gammon and snip the fat
in four or five places on each
rasher. Line the grill pan with foil
and lay the rashers side by side on
the foil. Grill for 4–5 minutes,
turning halfway through cooking
time. Wipe and core the apples
but do not peel; slice thinly across
in rounds. Lay the apple slices
over the gammon.
Brush a little melted butter over
the apple slices and continue grilling for 2–3 minutes. Lay the
cheese slices over the apple and
return to the grill for a further 1
minute.

Lyonnaise peas
50 g (2 oz) butter
2 large onions, skinned and finely
    sliced
450 g (1 lb) pkt frozen peas
salt

Melt the butter in a small pan, add
the onion and cook over gentle
heat for 3 minutes. Meanwhile
bring a pan of salted water to the
boil, add the peas and cook for 3
minutes. Drain the peas and mix
with the onion.

Galette jalousie
225 g (8 oz) frozen puff pastry,
    thawed
1 egg, beaten
225 g jam or thick apple purée
1 egg white, beaten
caster sugar

Roll out the pastry into a strip
45·5 cm by 10 cm (18-in. by
4-in.). Cut into 2 portions, one

5 cm (2 in.) shorter than the other. Roll out the smaller piece to the same size as the larger. Place this piece on a dampened baking sheet. Brush a border 1 cm (½ in.) wide at the end of each strip with beaten egg. Spread the jam or purée over the centre of the pastry. Fold the thicker strip of pastry in half lengthwise. Using a sharp knife, cut across the fold at intervals to within 1 cm (½ in.) of the edge. Unfold the pastry and lift it carefully on to the portion on the baking sheet. Press the edges well together and knock up with a knife.

Bake in the centre of the oven at 220°C. (425°F.) mark 7 for about 20 minutes. Remove from the oven, brush with egg white, dredge with caster sugar and return to the oven for a further 5 minutes to frost the top.

Menu
serves 4

Steak and kidney pudding
Buttered cabbage
Sliced carrots
Creamed potatoes

Steak and kidney pudding

225 g (8 oz) suetcrust pastry – i.e.
225 g (8 oz) flour, etc.
225–350 g (½–¾ lb) stewing steak,
cut into 1-cm (½-in.) cubes
100–125 g (4 oz) kidney, skinned
and cored
2 × 15 ml spoons (2 level tbsps)
seasoned flour
1 onion, skinned and chopped

Half-fill a steamer or large saucepan with water and put it on to boil. Grease a 900-ml (1½-pint) pudding basin. Cut off a quarter of the pastry to make the lid. Roll out the remainder and use to line the basin.

Slice the kidney and coat both the steak and the kidney with seasoned flour. Fill the basin with the meat, onion and 2 to 3 × 15 ml spoons (2 to 3 tbsps) of water. Roll out the remainder of the pastry to around the size of the basin top and damp the edge of it. Place on top of the meat and seal the edges of the pastry well.

Cover with greased greaseproof paper or foil and steam over rapidly boiling water for about 4 hours, refilling the pan as necessary with boiling water.

The meat can be prepared and stewed with the onion for about 2 hours earlier in the day or the previous night before being used for the filling. In this case, reduce the steaming time to 1½–2 hours.

Menu
serves 6

Hot chicken pie
Green beans
Tomato salad

Hot chicken pie

2 kg (4 lb) oven-ready chicken
1 small onion, skinned and halved
1 carrot, peeled
1 leek, washed and trimmed or 1
stick celery, scrubbed
6 peppercorns
salt

For the sauce:

50 g (2 oz) butter

175 g (6 oz) onion, skinned and chopped

225 g (½ lb) sweet red peppers, seeded and finely chopped

50 g (2 oz) green chillies, halved and seeded

4 × 15 ml spoons (4 level tbsps) flour

550 ml (1 pint) chicken stock

100–125 g (4 oz) mature Cheddar cheese, grated

salt and freshly ground black pepper

175 g (6 oz) puff pastry (i.e. made with 175 g (6 oz) flour) or 375 g (13 oz) frozen puff pastry, thawed

1 egg, beaten

Simmer the chicken in sufficient water to cover with the vegetables – onion, carrot, leek or celery – peppercorns and salt, for about 2 hours. Remove chicken, reduce the liquor to 550 ml (1 pint) by rapid boiling and then strain. Melt the butter in a saucepan, fry the chopped onion, peppers and chillies for 10 minutes; if wished, the chillies may be removed at this stage.

Carve the chicken, cutting it into fork-size pieces, and discard the skin. Place the meat in a 1·7-litre (3-pint) pie dish with a funnel. Blend the flour into the fried vegetables and slowly add the strained stock, stirring continuously. Bring to the boil.

When the liquid has thickened, add the cheese and adjust the seasoning. Spoon over the chicken and allow to cool.

Roll out the puff pastry and use to cover the filled pie dish. Knock up and scallop the edge and score the top of the pastry into diamonds with a knife, glaze with beaten egg, place on a baking sheet and cook in the oven at 230°C. (450°F.) mark 8 for 30 minutes. Reduce heat to 170°C. (325°F.) mark 3 and cook for a further 30 minutes.

Hot, puff-topped chicken pie

Lasagne and jumbo prawn risotto

Top a vegetable fricassee with crisp fried crumbs

Lasagne
serves 4

2 × 396 g (2 × 14 oz) cans
  tomatoes, drained
15 ml spoon (1 level tbsp) tomato
  paste
5 ml (1 level tsp) dried marjoram
salt and freshly ground black
  pepper
½ kg (1 lb) lean minced beef
100–125 g (4 oz) lasagne strips
25 g (1 oz) butter
25 g (1 oz) flour
300 ml (½ pint) milk
175 g (6 oz) Cheddar cheese,
  grated
oil for glazing
100–125 g (4 oz) Mozzarella or
  Bel Paese cheese, sliced

Combine the canned tomatoes, tomato paste, marjoram, salt and pepper. Simmer in an open pan for 30 minutes. Add the mince and simmer for a further 25 minutes, still uncovered.
Cook the lasagne strips in a large pan of fast boiling, salted water for 10–15 minutes and drain.
In a small saucepan, melt 50 g (1 oz) butter, stir in the flour and gradually blend in the milk. Bring to the boil, stirring constantly. Remove from the heat. Add the Cheddar cheese and season.
Cover the base of an ovenproof dish (about 4 cm (1½ in.) deep) with strips of lasagne. Add alternate layers of meat and cheese sauce. Finish the final layer with strips of pasta placed diagonally across, with the sauces spooned

between. Lightly oil the pasta to prevent it drying. Bake in the oven at 190°C. (375°F.) mark 5 for about 30 minutes. Remove from the oven, add the slices of Mozzarella on top of the cheese sauce. Raise the temperature to 220°C. (425°F.) mark 7 and return the lasagne to the oven until the cheese is golden and bubbling.

Vegetable fricassee
serves 2

¼ kg (½ lb) courgettes
¼ kg (½ lb) firm tomatoes, skinned
  and sliced
90 g (3½ oz) butter
100–125 g (4 oz) onion, skinned
  and sliced
2·5 ml spoon (½ level tsp) dried
  thyme
2 × 15 ml spoons (2 level tbsps)
  flour
400 ml (¾ pint) milk
100–125 g (4 oz) Cheddar cheese,
  grated
salt and pepper
50 g (2 oz) fresh brown
  breadcrumbs

Slice the courgettes and blanch in boiling salted water for 3 minutes; drain. Arrange all but a few slices of courgette and tomato in the base of a 1·1-litre (2-pint) flameproof dish. Dot with 15 g (½ oz) butter. Cover with foil and keep hot under a low grill. Melt 50 g (2 oz) butter in a pan, add the onion and cook for about 2 minutes, until tender. Add the thyme and stir in the flour.

Remove the pan from the heat, blend in the milk, return to the heat and bring to the boil, stirring. Add the cheese and season well.
Melt the remaining 25 g (1 oz) butter in a frying pan and add the breadcrumbs. Cook until well browned. Remove the foil from the vegetables, cover with cheese sauce and top with the crisp crumbs. Garnish with the remaining slices of courgette and tomato.

Chicken ramekins
serves 2–4

100–125 g (4 oz) cooked chicken,
  minced
2 mushrooms, chopped
2 eggs, separated
2 × 15 ml spoons (2 tbsps) single
  cream
salt and pepper
15 g (½ oz) butter

Mix the chicken and mushrooms and bind with the egg yolks and cream; season to taste. Whisk the egg whites stiffly and fold into the chicken mixture. Divide between 4 buttered ramekins, place them on a baking tray and cook in the centre of the oven at 180°C. (350°F.) mark 4 for 15–20 minutes.

Oeufs à la maison
serves 2–4

100–125 g (4 oz) pkt frozen peas
1 onion, skinned and finely
  chopped
4 tomatoes, skinned and chopped
2·5 ml spoon (½ level tsp) garlic
  salt
salt and freshly ground black
  pepper
3 large eggs
300 ml (½ pint) milk
parsley

Cook the peas according to the directions on the packet. Just before the end of the cooking time, add the chopped onion and blanch for 1–2 minutes. Drain. Divide the peas, onion and tomatoes between 4 individual ovenproof soup bowls or soufflé dishes. Sprinkle the salt and pepper over the top.
Place the eggs and milk in a bowl, beat with a fork to mix then strain over the vegetables. Place the dishes in a roasting tin with water to come half way up, and cook in the oven 190°C. (375°F.) mark 5 for about 40 minutes. Garnish with parsley and serve with crusty bread.

Roquefort quiche
serves 4–6

100–125 g (4 oz) shortcrust pastry
  – i.e. make with 100–125 g
  (4 oz) flour, etc.
75 g (3 oz) Roquefort or other blue
  cheese
175 g (6 oz) cream cheese
2 eggs, beaten
142 ml (¼ pint) single cream
1–2 × 5 ml spoons (1–2 level tsps)
  grated onion or 15 ml spoon (1
  level tbsp) chopped chives
salt and pepper

Roll out the pastry and use to line an 18–20·5 cm (7–8 in.) flan case or metal pie plate. Place near the top of the oven at 220°C. (425°F.) mark 7 and bake blind for 10 minutes, until the pastry is just set.
Cream the 2 kinds of cheese together and stir in the eggs, cream, onion or chives and seasoning. Pour into the pastry case, reduce the oven temperature to 190°C. (375°F.) mark 5 and cook for about 30 minutes, until well risen and golden. Serve warm with a green salad.

Stuffed globe artichokes
serves 2–4

4 globe artichokes, trimmed
½ a small onion, skinned and
  finely chopped
2 mushrooms, washed and finely
  chopped
15 g (½ oz) butter
50 g (2 oz) cooked ham, chopped
10 ml spoon (2 level tsps) fresh
  white breadcrumbs
beaten egg to bind
salt and pepper

Cook the artichokes in boiling, salted water for 20–40 minutes, according to size, until the leaves will pull out easily. Drain and remove the inner leaves and the chokes.
Lightly fry the onion and mushrooms in the butter for about 5 minutes, then add the other ingredients, using enough beaten egg to bind the mixture. Season to taste, and spoon the mixture into the centres of the artichokes. Place them in a greased ovenproof dish, cover with greased greaseproof paper and bake in the centre of the oven at 190°C. (375°F.) mark 5 for 10–15 minutes.

Green bean and bacon flan

serves 4

For cheese pastry:
100–125 g (4 oz) self-raising flour
a pinch of salt
50 g (2 oz) butter, margarine or lard
50 g (2 oz) Cheddar cheese, grated
a little beaten egg or water

For filling:
4 × 15 ml spoons (4 tbsps) milk
50 g (2 oz) cheese, grated
4 eggs, beaten
salt and pepper
4 rashers streaky bacon, rinded
100–125 g (4 oz) cooked green beans

Sift together the flour and salt and rub in the fat until the mixture resembles fine crumbs. Stir in the cheese. Bind together with enough egg or water to give a firm but pliable dough. Roll out and use to line a 20·5 cm (8 in.) plain flan ring. Bake blind at 200°C. (400°F.) mark 6 for about 10 minutes. Remove from the oven and reduce the temperature to 190°C. (375°F.) mark 5.

Stir together the milk, cheese and eggs and adjust seasoning. Grill or fry the bacon until crisp, then cut into small pieces. Arrange half the bacon in the flan case and pour on a little of the egg mixture. Add the beans and the rest of the bacon and coat with the rest of the egg. Bake for about 30 minutes or until just firm. Serve hot or cold.

Jumbo prawn risotto

serves 4

15 ml spoon (1 level tbsp) dried onion flakes
50 g (2 oz) butter
175 g (6 oz) long grain rice
½ × 1·25 ml spoon (¼ level tsp) dried basil
400 ml (¾ pint) stock
198-g (7-oz) can jumbo prawns
3 large eggs
2 × 15 ml spoons (2 tbsps) chopped parsley

Soak the onion flakes in a little water for several minutes, then drain. Melt the butter in a saucepan, add the onion and fry gently for 3 minutes. Stir in the rice and cook, stirring occasionally, for several minutes until the rice appears opaque.
Add the basil, stock and liquor from the prawn can; bring to the boil, cover and simmer for 25 minutes or until the rice is cooked and the liquid absorbed.

Meanwhile, hard-boil the eggs, then chop. When the rice is cooked, stir in the prawns, egg and a 15 ml spoon (1 tbsp) parsley. Adjust seasoning. Turn into a serving dish and garnish with remaining parsley.

Tuna and spaghetti crisp

serves 4

100–125 g (4 oz) short-cut spaghetti
198-g (7-oz) can tuna steak, drained and flaked
300 ml (½ pint) white sauce
75 g (3 oz) cheese, grated
salt and pepper
25-g (1-oz) pkt, potato crisps

Cook the spaghetti in boiling salted water until tender, 8–12 minutes. Drain well and place in a bowl.
Add the drained and flaked tuna steak, the white sauce, cheese and seasoning. Mix well and transfer to a greased 1·1-litre (2-pint) casserole. Crush the crisps slightly and arrange on top. Bake for 20–30 minutes in the oven at 180°C. (350°F.) mark 4.

Stuffed eggs au gratin

serves 4

425-g (15-oz) can celery hearts, drained
4 rashers streaky bacon, rinded
4 eggs, hard-boiled
100–125 g (4 oz) cheese, grated
400 ml (¾ pint) white sauce
made mustard
4 slices white bread, crusts removed
butter, melted

Cut the celery hearts in thick slices and place in the base of a 1·1-litre (2-pint) casserole. Grill the bacon until crisp and crumble or chop it finely. Halve the eggs lengthwise and remove the yolks. Cream the bacon and egg yolks together, fill the mixture into the egg whites and pair up the halves again. Place them on the bed of celery.
Mix most of the cheese into the white sauce, adding a little mustard to taste. Pour over the eggs. Dice the bread, dip in a little melted butter and spoon in a ring round the outer edge of the dish. Sprinkle the remaining cheese in the centre.
Place the dish under a low grill until the bread cubes are brown and the sauce bubbling.

Stuffed artichokes are a luxury supper dish

Kromeski

makes 8

For fritter batter:
100–125 g (4 oz) plain flour
pinch of salt
15 ml spoon (1 tbsp) cooking oil
150 ml (¼ pint) warm water
1 egg white

For filling:
50 g (2 oz) butter
50 g (2 oz) plain flour
300 ml (½ pint) milk
1 egg yolk
15 ml spoon (1 tbsp) fruit table sauce
salt and pepper
100–125 g (4 oz) green peppers (capsicum), seeded and chopped
225 g (8 oz) cooked chicken, chopped
8 thinly cut rashers of back bacon, rinded
deep fat for frying

Sift together the flour and salt into a bowl. Make a well in the centre and pour in the oil and warm water; beat well. Allow to rest for 1 hour.
Melt the butter in a pan, remove from the heat, stir in the flour and cook for a few minutes without colouring. Gradually stir in the milk. Beat in the egg yolk and the table sauce and season well.
Blanch the chopped green pepper in boiling water for 1–2 minutes, drain and refresh in cold water. Drain again and add to the sauce with the chicken. Allow to cool. Divide the mixture into 8 and shape into cork shapes on a floured board. Wrap each portion in a rasher of bacon, securing with wooden cocktail sticks.
Stiffly whisk the egg white and fold the batter through the white. Dip the kromeski into the batter

Supper Russian style, with kromeski

Toast snacks are popular at supper time

and deep fry in fat or oil heated to 190°C. (375°F.) mark 5 for about 5 minutes until crisp and golden. Drain on absorbent paper. Remove the cocktail sticks. Serve really hot, with a savoury rice.

Savoury meringue slices
serves 4

4 eggs, separated
4 rounds buttered toast
salt and pepper
25 g (1 oz) Parmesan cheese, grated

Place an egg yolk on each round of toast. Whisk the egg whites until stiff, season the cheese and fold into the egg whites. Pile on to the toast and place under a low grill for about 10 minutes, until firm and golden brown.

Use up left-over vegetables in a Spanish omelette

Pick of the pantry pizza
serves 4

15 ml spoon (1 level tbsp) dried onion flakes
boiling water
225 g (8 oz) self-raising flour
15 ml spoon (1 tbsp) powdered stock
5 ml spoon (1 level tsp) baking powder
50 g (2 oz) butter or margarine
milk and water to mix
425-g (15-oz) can pilchards in tomato sauce
226-g (8-oz) can tomatoes, drained
75 g (3 oz) cheese, grated
freshly ground black pepper
chopped parsley, optional

Soak the dried onion in boiling water for 5 minutes. Sift together the flour, powdered stock and baking powder.
Rub in the fat and mix to a firm

scone dough with milk and water. Turn on to a floured board, knead lightly and roll to form a 23-cm (9-in.) round or, better still, press into a 23-cm (9-in.) flan ring. Drain the onions and spread over the dough. Arrange the pilchards on top with the drained tomatoes and sprinkle with cheese. Season with pepper.
Bake in the oven at 220°C. (425°F.) mark 7 for approximately 45 minutes. Cover with foil if necessary to prevent excessive browning. Serve hot from the oven, sprinkled with chopped parsley.

Chakchouka
serves 4

25 g (1 oz) lard
½ kg (1 lb) tomatoes, skinned and sliced
350 g (¾ lb) potatoes, peeled and sliced
100–125 g (¼ lb) green peppers (capsicums), seeded and finely chopped
1 clove of garlic, skinned and crushed
salt and freshly ground black pepper
4 eggs

Melt the lard in a saucepan and fry the tomatoes and potatoes slowly for 20 minutes. Add the peppers and garlic, season and simmer for a further 15 minutes. Poach the eggs in gently simmering water for 3–4 minutes.
Turn the vegetables into a hot serving dish, drain the eggs and arrange them on top of the vegetables.

Curried scramble
serves 2

1 small onion, skinned and chopped
fat for frying
3 × 2·5 ml spoons (1½ level tsp) curry powder
4 eggs
5 ml spoon (1 tsp) chopped parsley
3 × 15 ml spoons (3 tbsps) milk
salt and freshly ground black pepper
2 large slices buttered toast or 2–4 crumpets

Fry the onion in a little fat until soft but not coloured, then add the curry powder and fry slowly for 5 minutes.
Beat together the eggs, parsley, milk and seasoning. Add to the pan and cook gently, stirring constantly and lifting the egg from the bottom of the pan.
Serve on hot buttered toast or toasted crumpets.

Stuffed mushrooms on toast
serves 4

8 medium-sized mushrooms, wiped
1 small onion, skinned and finely chopped
15 g (½ oz) butter
3 × 15 ml spoons (3 tbsps) finely chopped cooked ham or bacon
5 × 15 ml spoons (5 level tbsps) fresh white breadcrumbs
25 g (1 oz) cheese, grated
5 ml spoon (1 tsp) chopped parsley
beaten egg to bind
salt and pepper
cooking oil
4 rounds buttered toast

Remove and chop the stalks from the mushrooms. Lightly fry the stalks and the onion in the butter for 3–5 minutes, until soft. Add the ham or bacon, breadcrumbs, cheese and parsley and enough egg to bind them all together. Stir until well mixed and hot, season to taste. Brush the mushrooms with a little oil and put in a greased baking tin. Pile the filling into the mushrooms, cover with greaseproof paper or foil and bake in the centre of the oven at 190°C. (375°F.) mark 5 for about 20 minutes. Serve on buttered toast.

Crab toasts
serves 4

a little butter
25 g (1 oz) fresh white breadcrumbs
99-g (3½-oz) can crab meat or fresh cooked crab meat
3 × 15 ml spoons (3 tbsps) top of the milk
salt and pepper
15 ml spoon (1 tbsp) sherry
4 slices toast

Melt 25 g (1 oz) butter in a saucepan, add the breadcrumbs and flaked crab meat, mix well and stir in the top of the milk. Stir for a few minutes over the heat and season well, then pour in the sherry. Cut the toast into triangles, removing the crusts, butter and pile high with the crab meat mixture.

Spanish omelette
serves 2

butter or oil for frying
1 small onion, skinned and chopped
2–3 mushrooms, wiped and sliced
1 cooked potato, diced
1 cap canned pimiento (sweet red pepper) chopped

small quantity cooked peas, beans
    or carrots
4 eggs
salt and freshly ground black
    pepper
chopped parsley

Put enough butter or oil into a
20·5-cm (8-in.) frying pan just to
cover the base. Add the onion and
sauté until soft but not coloured.
Add the mushrooms and cook
until tender. Add the potato,
pimiento and cooked vegetables.
Heat thoroughly.
Lightly mix the eggs, season and
pour over the vegetable mixture,
which should be bubbling. When
just set, turn upside down on to a
heated serving dish. Garnish
with chopped parsley and serve at
once.

Mushrooms in port wine
serves 2

40 g (1½ oz) butter
350 g (12 oz) button mushrooms,
    wiped and trimmed
4 thick slices of bread
2 × 15 ml spoons (2 tbsps) port
    wine
salt and freshly ground black
    pepper
50 g (2 oz) instant potato
2 × 15 ml spoons (2 tbsps) milk
142 ml (¼ pint) double cream
15 ml spoon (1 heaped tbsp) grated
    Parmesan cheese

Melt 25 g (1 oz) butter in a saucepan; add the mushrooms, shake
to coat them and sauté gently.
Toast 2 slices of bread and grate
the remaining slices into breadcrumbs. Cut the crusts off the
toast and cut each slice into 2
triangles. Add the port to the
mushrooms, season and continue
to simmer.
Meanwhile, make up the instant
potato with boiling water and stir
in the milk and remaining butter.
Spoon into a forcing bag and pipe
with a large star vegetable nozzle
round the edge of a flameproof
serving dish.
Stir the cream into the mushrooms and continue to cook gently, stirring until the sauce thickens. Lightly brown the potato
under the grill and spoon the
mushroom mixture into the
centre. Sprinkle with breadcrumbs and Parmesan and return
to the grill until the cheese is golden brown. Garnish with the
toast triangles and serve with a
salad of tomatoes and onion.

Saucisses au vin blanc

Kidney toasts
serves 2

¼ kg (8 oz) calf's kidney or 4
    sheep's or lamb's kidneys
100–125 g (4 oz) mushrooms,
    wiped
50 g (2 oz) butter
25 g (1 oz) flour
300 ml (½ pint) stock
4 × 15 ml spoons (4 tbsps) single
    cream
15 ml spoon (1 tbsp) sherry
2 large slices white bread
butter
salt and pepper
chopped parsley

Remove the fat and skin from the
kidneys, cut away the core. Cut
the kidney into small pieces.
Slice the mushrooms.
Melt the butter in a pan and sauté
the mushrooms and kidney for
about 5 minutes.
Stir in the flour and mix well.
Gradually add the stock, stirring
over gentle heat until thickened.
Bring to the boil, reduce the heat,
cover and simmer for about 20
minutes, or until the kidney is
cooked.
Add the cream, then the sherry to
the kidney mixture and reheat but
take care not to boil. Adjust seasoning.
Prepare 2 slices of fresh hot toast
and spread generously with butter. Stir some chopped parsley
into the kidney mixture and
spoon on to the toast.

Saucisses au vin blanc
serves 2

¼ kg (½ lb) pork chipolata
    sausages
40 g (1½ oz) butter
50 g (2 oz) onion, skinned and
    finely sliced
100–125 g (4 oz) lean back bacon
    rashers, rinded and diced
15 ml spoon (1 tbsp) flour
150 ml (¼ pint) chicken stock,
    made from a stock cube
2 × 15 ml spoons (2 tbsps) dry
    white wine
113-g (4-oz) pkt. instant potato
boiling water
salt and freshly ground black
    pepper
2 × 15 ml spoons (2 tbsps) milk
parsley for garnish

Twist each chipolata into two
and separate with scissors. Melt
15 g (½ oz) butter in a frying pan,
add the sausages and fry gently
for 2 minutes.
Remove the sausages from the
frying pan, add the onion and
bacon and fry for 2 minutes. Stir
in the flour, stock and wine and
blend well. Return the sausages
to the pan, cover and simmer for 6
minutes.
Make up the instant potato with
the boiling water, season well and
stir in the milk and remaining
butter.
Spoon potato into a forcing bag
fitted with a vegetable star nozzle
and pipe in whirls round a

flameproof serving dish. Place
under the grill to brown lightly.
Spoon the sausages and their
sauce into the centre of the potato
and garnish with parsley.
Serve with green beans or
asparagus tips.

Shrimp pancakes
serves 2

For filling:
1 small green pepper (capsicum),
    seeded and diced
15 g (½ oz) butter
113 g (4 oz) potted shrimps
15 g (½ oz) flour
142 ml (¼ pint) single cream
4 × 15 ml spoons (4 tbsps) milk
grated Parmesan cheese

For pancakes:
75 g (3 oz) plain flour
1 egg, beaten
150 ml (¼ pint) milk and water,
    mixed
salt and freshly ground black
    pepper
lard for frying

Blanch the pepper in boiling
water for 3 minutes; drain. Melt
15 g (½ oz) butter in a frying pan,
add the shrimps and heat gently.
Stir in 15 g (½ oz) flour, two-
thirds of the cream, the milk and
the pepper. Stir until thickened.
Keep hot.
Sift the flour into a bowl, beat in
the egg, milk and water and seasoning, and continue to beat well.
Heat a knob of lard in a frying

pan, spoon in 3 × 15 ml spoons (3 tbsps) batter, swirl round to coat the pan base and cook until golden underneath. Turn and cook the other side. Turn on to a hot tea towel and keep warm. Repeat with remaining batter, to make 4 pancakes.

Divide the filling between the pancakes and roll up each one carefully. Arrange on a hot flameproof serving dish. Pour the remaining cream over the pancakes, sprinkle with Parmesan cheese and brown under a hot grill.

Creamed ham and asparagus
serves 6

2 × 298-g (2 × 10½-oz) cans condensed cream of chicken soup
1 medium-sized onion, skinned and finely chopped
2 × 15 ml spoons (2 tbsps) dry sherry
salt and freshly ground black pepper
350 g (¾ lb) cooked ham or boiled bacon, diced
340-g (12-oz) can green asparagus tips, drained
100–125 g (4 oz) Emmenthal or Gruyère cheese, thinly sliced

Blend together the undiluted soup, onion and sherry. Adjust seasoning. Layer the ham and asparagus into a 1·1–1·4 litre (2–2½ pint) capacity ovenproof dish. Pour the soup mixture over. Top with slices of cheese and cook in the centre of the oven at 200°C. (400°F.) mark 6 for about 30 minutes. Serve with Melba toast or bread sticks.

Quiche Lyonnaise
serves 4

100–125 g (4 oz) shortcrust pastry – i.e. make with 100–125 g (4 oz) flour, etc.
1 large onion, skinned and chopped
2 × 15 ml spoons (2 tbsps) cooking oil
25 g (1 oz) butter
6 × 5 ml spoons (1½ level tbsps) flour
300 ml (½ pint) milk
100–125 g (4 oz) Cheddar cheese, grated
salt and freshly ground black pepper
2 eggs
parsley sprigs for garnish

Soup and a warm quiche for a casual supper party

Roll out the pastry and use to line a 20·5 cm (8-in.) flan ring or tin. Bake blind in the oven at 200°C. (400°F.) mark 6 for 15 minutes. Fry the chopped onion in the oil until soft and evenly coloured. Drain off the fat and spread the onion over the base of the freshly baked flan case.

Melt the butter in a small pan, blend in the flour and cook for 2–3 minutes, without colouring. Blend in the milk and most of the cheese, reserving a little; bring to the boil, stirring, and season. Keep this sauce warm.

Poach the eggs in gently simmering water for 3–4 minutes. Drain well and arrange them on the onion, in the flan case. Coat with the cheese sauce, and sprinkle with the reserved grated cheese. Place the flan under a pre-heated grill and brown quickly. Garnish with parsley sprigs and serve at once.

Use potted shrimps, peppers and cheese as a luxury pancake filling

Buck rarebit
serves 4

225 g (8 oz) Cheddar cheese, grated
25 g (1 oz) butter
5 ml spoon (1 level tsp) dry mustard
salt and freshly ground black pepper
3–4 × 15 ml spoons (3–4 tbsps) brown ale
4 eggs
4 large slices bread
butter

Place the cheese, butter, mustard, seasoning and ale in a thick-based pan and heat very gently until a creamy mixture is obtained. Meanwhile, poach the eggs and toast the bread.
Butter the hot toast generously. Pour the cheese mixture over the toast, put under a grill until golden and bubbling and top each slice with a poached egg.

Supper Menu
serves 10
for an informal evening at home

Cream of mushroom soup or chilled tomato juice
Onion quiche
Pineapple and pepper salad
French bread and butter
Cheese board

Timetable
for supper at 10.00 p.m.
Day before: Make the soup and refrigerate.
Fry the croûtons, cool and store in an airtight container.
Bake the shortcrust flan cases.
Same day: Slice the onions, sauté and keep in a covered bowl. Beat together the egg mixture and keep in a cool place. Prepare anchovies; keep covered.
Prepare the cheese board and keep it covered.
Early in the evening: Prepare the salad.
9.30 p.m.: Fill the flan cases, decorate and bake.
Put the soup to reheat. Refresh croûtons in oven for a short time.
Toss the salad.
10.00 p.m.: Serve supper.

Cream of mushroom soup

175 g (6 oz) butter
350 g (12 oz) onions, skinned and
    finely chopped
½ kg (1 lb) button mushrooms,
    wiped and chopped
75 g (3 oz) plain flour
1·7 litres (3 pints) chicken stock,
    made from 4 stock cubes and
    1·7 litres (3 pints) water
550 ml (1 pint) milk
salt and freshly ground black
    pepper
½ × 2·5 ml spoon (¼ level tsp)
    garlic salt
lemon juice
fried croûtons

Melt the butter in a large pan and
sauté the onions for 10 minutes,
until soft but not coloured. Add
the mushrooms, cover, and continue to cook for a further 5
minutes.

Swiss cheese fondue

Stir in the flour and cook for 3
minutes, then slowly add the
stock, stirring all the time. Bring
to the boil and simmer gently for
20 minutes.
Add the milk and seasonings and
lemon juice to taste. Simmer for a
further 10 minutes. Do not boil
after adding the milk. Garnish
with croûtons of fried bread just
before serving.

Pineapple and pepper salad

792 g (28 oz) can pineapple pieces
1 green pepper (capsicum)
    blanched, seeded and sliced
¼ cucumber (or ½ a small ridge
    cucumber) diced
50 g (2 oz) sultanas
1 lettuce, washed and shredded
4 × 15 ml (4 tbsps) French
    dressing

Drain the pineapple and reserve
the juice. Mix the pineapple
pieces with the pepper,
cucumber, sultanas and lettuce.
Combine the French dressing
and 2 × 15 ml spoons (2 tbsps)
pineapple juice, pour over the
salad and toss well.

Onion quiche

350 g (12 oz) shortcrust pastry –
    i.e. made with 350 g (12 oz)
    plain flour etc.
100–125 g (4 oz) butter
1 kg (2 lb) onions, skinned and
    sliced
4 eggs
50 g (2 oz) flour
400 ml (¾ pint) milk
salt and pepper
2 × 60-g (2 × 2-oz) cans
    anchovies, drained
stoned black olives

Use the pastry to line 2 plain
20·5 cm (8 in.) flan rings placed
on baking sheets. Bake blind at
200°C. (400°F.) mark 6 for 20
minutes.
Melt the butter in a frying pan and
fry the onions until soft, taking
care not to brown them. Divide
the onions between the flans.
Beat together the eggs, flour,
milk, salt and pepper, then pour
over the onions. Halve the
anchovies lengthwise and
arrange on top in a criss-cross pattern and place a black olive in
each space. Bake in the oven at
180°C. (350°F.) mark 4 for 20–30
minutes, until set.

Swiss cheese fondue

1 clove of garlic, skinned and
    crushed
150 ml (¼ pint) dry white wine
a squeeze of lemon juice
100–125 g (4 oz) Gruyère cheese,
    cut in thin strips
100–125 g (4 oz) Emmenthal
    cheese, cut in thin strips
10 ml spoon (2 level tsps) cornflour
1 liqueur glass of Kirsch
a little pepper and grated nutmeg
crusty bread, cut in cubes, for
    serving

Rub the inside of a flameproof
fondue dish with the garlic. Place
the dish over a gentle heat and
warm the wine and lemon juice
in it. Add the cheese and continue
to heat gently, stirring well until
the cheese has melted and just
begun to cook. Add the cornflour
and seasonings, blended to a
smooth cream with the Kirsch,
and continue cooking for a
further 2–3 minutes. When the
mixture is thick and creamy it is
ready to serve.
Traditionally, fondue is served at
the table in the dish in which it
was cooked, over a small spirit
burner. To eat, spear the cubes of
crusty bread on forks and dip in
the fondue.

FONDUE BOURGUIGNONNE

A meat fondue is a pleasant Swiss way of giving an informal dinner party for 6–8 people. It entails very little by way of preparation by the hostess, and what has to be done can all be done well in advance. In fact the guests cook their own meat in a pot at the table, which adds to the interest of the evening.

You need a fondue set consisting of a flameproof pot over a spirit burner, and a set of long handled forks. If you have no fondue set you could improvise with an electric table cooker – but the atmosphere won't be quite the same. The traditional meat fondue pots are copper or iron; there are also some attractive stainless steel pots available. Allow 175 g. (6 oz) good frying steak per person, cut into 2.5cm (1-in.) cubes. Fill the pot two-thirds full with cooking oil (corn oil is suitable) and heat on your ordinary cooker to 190°C. (375°F.) mark 5, using a frying thermometer for accuracy. Transfer the pot to the spirit burner or a table cooker that will keep the oil at just the correct temperature (the oil should not smoke or spit as this indicates a dangerous heat, but it must be hot enough to seal the meat quickly, so that the fat is not absorbed). It helps to have a second pot of oil heated so that the first can be replaced when the temperature of the oil begins to drop.

Place a plate of raw steak and a long handled fork in front of each person and equip them with a second fork with which to eat the meat (if they use the same forks as those on which the meat is cooked someone will get a nasty burn). Each person impales a piece of steak on the long handled fork and puts it into the oil until it is cooked. It is then transferred to the cold fork and dipped into one of the sauces on the table.

Hollandaise sauce

2 × 15 ml spoons (2 tbsps) wine or
*   tarragon vinegar*
15 ml spoon (1 tbsp) water
2 egg yolks
75–125 g (3–4 oz) butter
salt and pepper

Put the vinegar and water in a small pan and boil until reduced to about 15 ml spoon (1 tbsp); cool slightly. Put the egg yolks in a basin and stir in the vinegar. Put

Accompaniments for a meat fondue should be a mixture of colours and flavours

over a pan of hot water and heat gently, stirring all the time, until the egg mixture thickens (never let the water go above simmering point).

Divide the butter into small pieces and gradually whisk into the sauce and add seasoning to taste. If the sauce is too sharp add a little more butter – it should be slightly piquant, almost thick enough to hold its shape and warm rather than hot when served.

Tartare sauce

150 ml (¼ pint) mayonnaise or salad cream
5 ml spoon (1 tsp) chopped tarragon or chives
10 ml spoon (2 tsps) chopped capers
10 ml spoon (2 tsps) chopped gherkins
10 ml spoon (2 tsps) chopped parsley
15 ml spoon (1 tbsp) lemon juice or tarragon vinegar

Mix all the ingredients well, then leave the sauce at least 1 hour before serving, to allow the flavours to blend.

Tomato mayonnaise

Blend 150 ml (¼ pint) mayonnaise with tomato paste to taste.

Curry mayonnaise

Blend 150 ml (¼ pint) mayonnaise with a little curry powder to taste.

Horseradish sauce

Mix whipped double cream with horseradish relish to flavour.

Side dishes

Chopped banana
Sliced gherkins
Sliced olives
Green salad
Salad vegetables – tomato wedges, cucumber slices, whole small radishes, carrot sticks.

45

HOT SUPPERTIME DRINKS

Hot spiced tea
serves 6

3 whole cloves
1-cm (½-in.) stick of cinnamon
1·1 litre (2 pints) water
15 g (½ oz) tea
50 g (2 oz) sugar
75 ml (2½ fl. oz) orange juice
juice of 1 lemon
cinnamon sticks for serving

In a pan add the spices to the water and bring to the boil. Pour on to the tea in a bowl and allow to infuse for 5 minutes. Stir, add the sugar, stir again until dissolved and add the strained fruit juices. Place over a low heat and reheat but do not boil or even simmer. Strain and serve with cinnamon sticks.

Supper-time drinks are best served hot

Chinese orange tea
makes 1·3 litre (2¼ pints)

3 oranges
50 g (2 oz) flour
100–125 g (4 oz) sugar
1·1 litre (2 pints) water

Cut the oranges in half, scoop out the pulp and juice and place in a bowl. Gradually add some water to the flour to form a stiff dough, then roll into balls the size of tiny marbles and put on one side. Dissolve the sugar in 1·1 litre (2 pints) water in a large pan and bring to the boil, then drop in the flour balls and continue to boil until they float.
Add the orange pulp and juice, re-boil for 30 seconds and serve the tea very hot.

Borgia coffee
serves 3

pared rind of 1 orange
15 g (½ oz) finely ground coffee
300 ml (½ pint) water
300 ml (½ pint) milk
4 × 15 ml spoons (6 heaped tsps)
  drinking chocolate
4 × 15 ml spoons (4 tbsps) double
  cream, lightly whipped

Shred the orange rind into fine julienne strips and blanch in boiling water for a few minutes, until tender. Drain.
Use the coffee and water to make 300 ml (½ pint) black coffee (use an Espresso machine, filter, Cona, percolator or whichever method you prefer). Heat the milk in a small pan and whisk in the drinking chocolate.
Combine the black coffee and the chocolate, divide between 3 mugs and top each with whipped cream. Decorate with shreds of orange rind.

Egg nog
serves 1

1 egg
15 ml spoon (1 level tbsp) sugar
1 sherry glass of sherry or brandy
200 ml (⅓ pint) milk

Whisk the egg and sugar together and add the sherry or brandy. Heat the milk without boiling and pour it over the egg mixture; stir well and serve hot in a glass.

Hot spiced pineapple cup
makes about 900 ml (1½ pints)

2 × 400-ml (2 × 15-fl. oz) cans
  pineapple juice
4 × 15 ml spoons (4 level tbsps)
  sugar
2 × 15 ml spoons (2 tbsps) lemon
  juice
10 cm (4 in.) cinnamon stick
Simmer all the ingredients together for 10 minutes, remove the cinnamon and pour the juice into glasses.

Huckle-my-buff
serves 6

1·1 litre (2 pints) draught beer
6 eggs, beaten
50 g (2 oz) sugar
grated nutmeg
brandy to taste

Heat 600 ml (1 pint) beer with th[e] eggs and sugar, but do not boil. Remove from the heat and ad[d] the remaining beer, a generou[s] amount of nutmeg and brandy t[o] taste.
Serve in heatproof glasses.

Mulled cider
makes 6 servings

5 cm (2 in.) cinnamon stick
2·5 ml spoon (½ level tsp) whol[e]
  allspice
1·25 litres (2 pints) cider
225 g (8 oz) Demerara sugar
1 orange, sliced
1 lemon, sliced
whole cloves

Put the cinnamon stick and all[spice] spice in a muslin bag. Heat th[e] cider, sugar and spices in [a] saucepan and bring almost t[o] boiling point. Remove the spice[s.] Stud the centre of each fruit slic[e] with a clove, float the slices on t[op] of the mull and simmer gently fo[r] a few minutes.
Ladle the cider into tumblers o[r] mugs – a spoon in the glasses wi[ll] prevent them cracking.

Eating
Outdoors

Smoked trout is a new idea in outdoor eating

'Plenty of it and keep it simple' is the first maxim for outdoor eating. Appetites always seem to grow outside, and crockery and cutlery are usually fairly limited, but don't let this deter you from being a little imaginative with your menus. Whether picnic or barbecue is called for, both can provide the opportunity for delicious foods that you wouldn't normally eat inside.

Barbecues

A barbecue has its own particular advantage for a hostess in that the cooking is done out of doors too, and the men and the children are usually only too willing to help. There is the added satisfaction that if you are caught in a downpour, it is much nicer to be eating hot kebabs than a slice of cold veal and ham pie. Barbecues are internationally popular, America, South Africa and Australia all having their own special style.

Equipment

When choosing a barbecue, size must be top

priority. Any barbecue that is too small will have no variation of heat zones, and it is these that make for flexible cooking. As a rough guide, it takes a barbecue grid diameter of at least 45 cm (18 in.) to cook enough food for 8 people in one go. For open garden or hillside sites, it is wise to buy one with a windshield, and it's always worth choosing one that offers some control over the position of the grid. A rotisserie spit is useful but by no means essential, but if you do have one, make sure it is battery operated – turning is hard work.

If you're not prepared to spend money on such a seasonal extravagance but still fancy outdoor cooking, you can always build your own barbecue. Build it from used bricks that are already weathered, and either fix them with mortar or just lay them on top of each other and be careful how you treat it while you're cooking. For grids, use either scraper-type door mats or oven shelves with a covering of chicken wire.

Although many of the most popular American barbecues run off bottled gas or can even

be connected to the gas mains, the traditional fuel is charcoal. This does in fact impart a flavour of its own which it is a pity to forego. Most ironmongers or hardware departments stock charcoal and 2×3-kg (7-lb.) bags will give you ample fire for 4 hours. To light the charcoal you will need firelighters or methylated spirit – but do make sure these are fully burnt up before you put food on the grid or the food will taste of the lighting fuel. Get the fire going a good ½ hour before you start cooking, as well, so that the coals have had time to heat to a good red glow, without flames. A pair of bellows is invaluable for resuscitating a difficult fire. Once started, you'll also need thick oven gloves or some old leather gloves, long handled tongs and forks for turning the food and brushes or spoons for basting. Keep beside you a small table with plates to receive cooked food, a damp cloth to wipe your fingers and plenty of kitchen foil for cooking in. For eating, have a separate table and put out your old plates and dishes, kitchen cutlery and plenty of paper napkins. Plastic cutlery is all ght if you are doing kebabs, that don't need cutting, but can cause embarrassment if confronted with steak!

Choose your barbecue site with care. It should be far enough from the house for you to feel you are really outside, but near enough to make kitchen reinforcements practicable. It's no fun tripping through semi-darkness with a tray of glasses. The shelter of some vegetation is ideal so long as it is not too close, or if there is no natural shelter available it might be well to invest in a windbreak of Norfolk reeding or a canvas awning, because evening breezes can be chilly. A very popular alternative is to light a separate bonfire a little way from the cooking barbecue, simply for the purpose of generating heat. A bonfire can turn even a chill English evening into a balmy summer's night!

The food

Any food that you can grill on an ordinary cooker can be barbecued. Sausages are a little difficult because they tend to burst; bacon needs rolling and skewering; steak, chops, chicken portions and fish are all ideal. More fiddly to prepare, but easier to eat are the traditional shashlik, or kebabs. For these mix any tender cuts of meat – lamb, liver and bacon rolls are perhaps the most common, and if you suspect the meat may not be as tender as might be wished, marinade it overnight beforehand. Intersperse the meat with chunks of onion, bay leaves and tiny tomatoes. Most meats will need brushing with oil before cooking and basting with a barbecue sauce during cooking to prevent them drying out. Make large quantities of sauce for this purpose, as a lot will disappear into the flames; DON'T try to baste with oil, though, as this will flare and burn the meat – as well as the cook's hand.

Fish is excellent grilled on the barbecue, especially oily fish such as mackerel and herring. Clean the fish and dry on absorbent kitchen paper, score it 2–3 times to allow the heat to penetrate and season well.

Apart from the actual barbecued food provide lots of salads, potato crisps and jacket potatoes or French bread. If you anticipate a slow start to the cooking it might be a good idea to start with a big pot of hot soup, to keep people occupied. Otherwise drinks and plenty of appetizers will help.

Barbecue sauce

makes approximately 400 ml (¾ pint)

2 × 15 ml spoons (2 tbsps) malt or cider vinegar
150 ml (¼ pint) water
2 × 15 ml (2 level tbsps) sugar
15 ml (1 level tbsp) prepared mustard
2·5 ml spoon (½ level tsp) pepper
3 × 2·5 ml spoons (1½ level tsps) salt
½ × 2·5 ml spoon (¼ level tsp) cayenne pepper
1 thick slice of lemon
1 onion, skinned and sliced
50 g (2 oz) butter
150 ml (¼ pint) tomato ketchup
2 × 15 ml spoons (2 tbsps) Worcestershire sauce

In a saucepan, mix together the vinegar, water, sugar, mustard, pepper, salt, cayenne, lemon, onion and butter. Bring to the boil, reduce the heat and boil gently, uncovered, for 20 minutes. Add remaining ingredients and bring back to the boil. Use for basting meat during cooking and serve some extra in a sauce boat.

Smoking

Another pleasant method of outdoor cooking is smoking. This is usually done with specially treated oak sawdust, which lends a very pleasant flavour, and special smokers are on the market for this purpose.

The fish is well salted and placed on a grid over the sawdust in a pan with a ventilated lid. A small container of methylated spirit is put under the pan; the heat causes the wood to smoke, circulating it round the fish and out through the vents in the lid. It takes about 8 minutes to cook a medium-sized fish. The final flavour is delicate, and most people find it a distinct improvement on shop-bought smoked fish. The flavour can be varied by adding herbs such as rosemary to the smoking sawdust.

If you buy a smoker, it is also possible to use it for grilling, though the design of the pan still tends to encourage a somewhat smoky flavour. Grilling takes about 12–15 minutes.

Picnics

Picnics are less fraught with man-made hazards than barbecues, though they are still subject to weather complications. Because a picnic is usually away from home the food must be prepared in advance and there can be few last minute hitches on that score. If the 2-year-old falls into the butter, that's not your fault!

Planning is important. Count the people who are coming and allow a little extra for outdoor appetites. Except for purely utilitarian picnics, avoid the eternal sandwich. This not only lets you in for lots of preparation but is not very exciting to eat. Much more attractive are packs of cold meat and cheese, crusty French bread and cool butter, and fresh salads, all carried in polythene boxes or bags. Make use of vacuum jars for keeping cold drinks cold, or even for storing ice, and for keeping hot foods hot; if the weather turns a little chilly or damp, lots of people will be glad of a mug of hot soup.

For semi-vulnerable items, such as open fruit flans, quiches and pizza, use air-tight cake tins and remember to keep them upright. For liquids and jellies, soufflés and trifles, use screw-top jars or self-sealing plastic containers. Hard-boiled eggs and Scotch eggs travel well, so do savoury pies and patties and fruit pies. Cold cooked chicken pieces are always popular and so are cold lamb cutlets fried in egg and breadcrumbs. And always take plenty of fresh fruit.

The one thing that is often carried in vacuum flasks that is really better fresh-made is tea. A small spirit or gas burner that will boil a kettle means you can have as much fresh tea and coffee as you wish, leaving the flasks free for

Choose a large, round barbecue with a rotating grid to make the best use of the heat zones

more demanding foods. If you do carry tea in a flask, take the milk separately as it tastes much better if added at the last moment.

Finally, however much the children protest, do take as many home comforts as you can carry, otherwise you won't want to go again. This means a large waterproof groundsheet; fold-up chairs for all who are not of the spryest; a small table to work at, for buttering bread, dishing out, etc.; unbreakable crockery; paper napkins; a damp cloth for sticky fingers and a large box of tissues as well; a large spare bag for rubbish. Pack all the food and bits and pieces into as neat a container as you can manage, even if you don't have a specially designed picnic hamper. This will mean you can wander a little way from the car without having to make umpteen trips to and fro to collect everything. (Incidentally, if you're not taking a car, leave out this paragraph and concentrate on the food – you won't be interested in anything else!)

Barbecue Menus

Eating out of doors adds a zest to any appetite, and what better way to entertain friends on a summer evening than to have a barbecued meal in your own garden? Salads, sauces and vegetable accompaniments can all be prepared beforehand in your kitchen, and you'll find that most men enjoy being in charge of the barbecue – which leaves you free to enjoy yourself. Choose simple menus with desserts that can be cooked either in foil in the charcoal embers or in a pan on the grill.

Menu
serves 8

Tandoori chicken
Pappadums
Melon and banana salad
Sliced tomatoes and gherkins
Boiled rice
Peaches with Butterscotch sauce

Tandoori chicken

8 chicken joints
salt and pepper
212 ml (7½ fl. oz) plain yoghourt
3 × 2·5 ml spoons (1½ level tsps) chilli powder
pinch of ground ginger
pinch of ground coriander
1 large clove of garlic, skinned and crushed
juice of 1½ lemons
3 × 15 ml spoons (3 tbsps) melted butter

Remove any protruding bones from the chicken joints, wipe and season with salt and pepper. Combine the yoghourt with the chilli powder, ginger, coriander, garlic, lemon juice, 1 × 5 ml spoon (1 level tsp) black pepper and 10 ml spoon (2 level tsps) salt. Mix well and add the chicken pieces. Leave to stand for 3–4 hours, turning several times. Remove the chicken from the marinade, shaking off as much of the liquid as possible, then pour a little melted butter over each chicken joint. Place the joints on the barbecue grid and brown them quickly on all sides.

Remove the chicken and place each joint on a piece of kitchen foil, about 38 cm (15 in.) square. Fold over the sides of the foil, making a double join in the centre, and make a double fold in each end of the foil to seal. Place each packet on the grid and cook for a further 20 minutes, turning once during the cooking time. Heat the spicy marinade and serve separately.
Serve with pappadums and melon and banana salad.

Pappadums
These savoury wafer-like biscuits are usually bought, as they are not easy to make at home. Stored in an airtight tin they will keep for several months. White pappadums are fairly mild, red are very hot.

allow 1—2 pappadums per person

Choose a frying pan considerably larger than the raw biscuit. Heat a little fat to a high temperature, then fry the pappadums one at a time for about 20–30 seconds. Keep them flat by holding down with a flat draining spoon; when crisp, drain and serve hot.

Melon and banana salad

2 ripe cantaloup melons
8 bananas
lemon juice

Cut the melons in half, scoop out the seeds and discard. Remove the skin and cut the melon flesh into cubes. Peel the bananas and slice thinly. Turn in lemon juice to prevent browning, then mix the melon and bananas together.

Peaches with butterscotch sauce

50 g (2 oz) butter
2 × 425-g (2 × 15-oz) cans peaches, drained
soft brown sugar

Melt the butter in a frying pan over the barbecue and add the peaches, cut side up. Fill the centre of each with some soft brown sugar. Simmer gently until the sugar melts and runs into the butter to form a sauce. Serve with pouring cream.

Hamburgers and hot dogs are traditional barbecue fare

Menu
serves 12

Foil-roasted corn cobs
Hamburgers
Hot dogs
Jacket potatoes
Tomato sauce
Creamy mustard sauce
Hot weather green salad
Apple and tomato salad
Fruit and cheese

Foil-roasted corn cobs

12 corn cobs
100–125 g (4 oz) butter
freshly ground black pepper

Remove the husks and silks from the cobs. Mix together the butter and a generous amount of pepper. Spread some butter on each cob. Put the cobs on individual squares of kitchen foil, bring the sides together, with a double fold in the centre and make double folds at each end to seal.

Cook at the sides of the barbecue grid for 25–30 minutes, turning occasionally.

Hamburgers

1½ kg (3 lb) lean beef, finely minced
15 ml spoon (3 level tsps) mixed herbs
salt and pepper
melted butter or oil for coating
3 onions, skinned and sliced
12 soft round buns, split in half

Mix together the meat, herbs and seasonings. Shape into 12 flat rounds and brush with a little melted butter or oil. Grill over the barbecue for 6–10 minutes, turning them once (the cooking time depends on whether you like them rare, medium, or well done). Meanwhile, fry the onion rings in a pan in a little fat until soft and lightly coloured. Place the buns, split side down, on the grill and toast for 2–3 minutes.
To serve, top each hamburger with a few onion rings and put between 2 toasted bun halves. Wrap it in a paper napkin.
Serve various relishes separately.

Hot dogs

12 frankfurters
12 long soft rolls

Grill the frankfurters over the barbecue and put inside a split roll. Add some mustard, tomato sauce or relish. Wrap one end in a paper napkin and serve hot.

Tomato sauce

1 rasher bacon, rinded
½ kg (1 lb) tomatoes, chopped
2 onions, skinned and sliced
50 g (2 oz) butter
bouquet garni
500–600 ml (1 pint) stock
salt and pepper
10 ml spoon (2 level tsps) sugar
15 g (½ oz) flour
milk to mix

Dice the bacon and put the tomatoes, onions and bacon in a pan with the butter; cook with the lid on for about 10 minutes, shaking frequently.
Add the herbs, stock, seasoning and sugar and simmer gently, uncovered, for 30 minutes. The mixture should now be pulpy and well reduced.
Sieve the mixture, return it to the pan and bring to the boil. Blend the flour with a little cold milk, add to the pan and bring to the boil, stirring constantly. Cook for 2–3 minutes and adjust the seasoning.
Serve hot or cold with the hot dogs and hamburgers.

Creamy mustard sauce

142 ml (¼ pint) soured cream
2 × 15 ml spoons (2 level tbsps) prepared mustard
15 ml spoon (1 tbsp) minced onion
½ × 2·5 ml spoon (¼ level tsps) salt
¼ × 2·15 ml (⅛ level tsp) pepper

Mix all the ingredients together in a pan and heat gently for a few minutes.
Serve warm with the hot dogs and hamburgers.

Hot-weather green salad

1 lettuce
large bunch of watercress, optional
1 large cucumber (or 2 small ridge cucumbers), peeled
12–15 spring onions, skinned
French dressing
15 ml spoon (1 tbsp) white wine

Wash the lettuce and watercress, discarding stems and coarse outer leaves. Slice the peeled cucumber and spring onions very finely. Mix all the ingredients together in a bowl and add the French dressing and wine.

Apple and tomato salad

4 dessert apples, peeled and cored
½ kg (1 lb) tomatoes, skinned and sliced
French dressing
mustard and cress to garnish, optional

Dice the apples and put in a bowl with the tomato slices. Add enough salad dressing to coat and garnish with mustard and cress, if wished.

Menu
serves 8

Lamb chops
Sausages
Barbecue sauce
Rice
Layered coleslaw
Chicory and orange salad
Stuffed baked apples

Barbecue sauce

4 × 15 ml spoons (4 tbsps)
  Worcestershire sauce
4 × 15 ml spoons (4 tbsps) brown
  table sauce
4 × 15 ml spoons (4 tbsps)
  mushroom ketchup
10 ml spoon (2 level tsps) sugar
15 ml spoon (1 tbsp) vinegar
25 g (1 oz) butter, melted
cayenne pepper
salt
150 ml (¼ pint) water
1 small onion, skinned and thinly
  sliced

Blend all the ingredients
together, adding the onion last.
Be very sparing with the cayenne
pepper. Pour the sauce over the
meat to be cooked and baste frequently while it is cooking.

Layered coleslaw

1 small head of white cabbage
½ a cucumber (or 1 small ridge
  cucumber)
1 large green pepper (capsicum)
2 onions, skinned
bunch of radishes

For golden dressing:
300 ml (½ pint) mayonnaise
2·5 ml spoon (½ level tsp) salt
¼ 2·5 ml spoon (⅛ level tsp)
  pepper
¼ × 2·5 ml spoon (⅛ level tsp)
  paprika
10 ml spoon (2 level tsps) sugar
2 × 15 ml (2 tbsps) vinegar
2 × 15 ml (2 tbsps) milk
10 ml (2 level tsps) prepared
  mustard
2 egg yolks

Finely shred the cabbage. Score
the cucumber from end to end
with the prongs of a fork. Slice
the cucumber very thinly. Wash
and seed the pepper and cut into
fine rings; cut the onion into
wafer thin rings. Prepare and
wash the radishes. Slice thinly.
Arrange about a quarter of the
cabbage in a salad bowl; on this
arrange the cucumber in a layer,
cover with another quarter of the
cabbage, then a layer of green
pepper rings; next cover with
more of the cabbage, then a complete layer of onion rings. Finally, heap the remaining cabbage in
the centre. Arrange radish slices
round the outside of the salad.
Combine the mayonnaise for the
dressing with the remaining
ingredients and whisk until well
blended. Pour the dressing over
the salad.

Chicory and orange salad

3 large heads chicory (or 1 head
  celery)
3 large oranges
French dressing

Remove the root and outer leaves
of the chicory, wash (or scrub and
trim the celery) and cut into
chunks. Peel the oranges and
divide into segments. Mix the two
together in a bowl and sprinkle
with French dressing.

Stuffed baked apples

8 medium-sized cooking apples
6 × 15 ml spoons (6 tbsps) water
mixture of currants, sultanas,
  chopped dried apricots, mixed
  peel or glacé fruits
Demerara sugar
butter

Wipe the apples and make a shallow cut through the skin round
the middle of each. Core the
apples and stand them in an
ovenproof dish. Pour the water
round and fill each apple with the
fruit mixture. Sprinkle a little
sugar over the apples and top each
one with a knob of butter.
Bake in the centre of the oven at
200°C. (400°F.) mark 6 for ¾–1
hour until the apples are soft.
Alternatively, wrap individual
apples in foil (omitting the water)
and bake in the embers of the barbecue.

Menu
serves 12

Fish chowder
Mixed kebabs
Rolls and butter
Green salad
Bananes au caramel

Fish chowder

6 rashers of lean bacon, rinded and
  chopped
3 onions, skinned and sliced
1½ kg (3 lb) fresh haddock, cooked
  and flaked
3 × 396-g (3 × 14-oz) cans
  tomatoes
6 potatoes, peeled and diced
900 ml (1½ pints) fish stock
salt and freshly ground black
  pepper
3 bay leaves
6 cloves
400 ml (¾ pint) milk
chopped parsley

Stuffed apples, baked in the oven or in the embers

Fry the bacon until the fat runs,
add the onion and fry until clear.
Add the fish, tomatoes and
potatoes, with the stock and seasonings, and simmer gently for
about 30 minutes. Add the milk
and remove the bay leaves and
cloves, then reheat gently. Serve
in mugs, with a little chopped
parsley sprinkled on top.

Mixed kebabs

For the marinade:
2 parts olive oil
1 part wine vinegar
garlic, skinned and crushed
few peppercorns

lean, tender steak, cubed
sausages, halved
button mushrooms, wiped
small tomatoes, whole, or large
  tomatoes, quartered
rashers of lean bacon, rinded
button onions, skinned and
  par-boiled
a few bay leaves

Marinade the steak for a few
hours. Thread a selection of the
ingredients on to skewers (allow
2 skewers per person) and refrigerate them until required.
Brush them with melted butter
and grill over the barbecue, basting and turning regularly.

Bananes au caramel

350 g (12 oz) sugar
6 × 15 ml spoons (6 tbsps) water
12–15 bananas (according to size),
  peeled

Choose bananas which are
slightly under-ripe. Using a
strong, deep frying pan, dissolve
the sugar in the water over a low
heat. Bring to the boil and bubble
until the syrup is lightly coloured. Lay the bananas in the
sauce and spoon the caramel over
them until they are coated.
Cook for about 10 minutes on top
of the barbecue grill. Serve the
bananas with the caramel poured
over them.

Mix steak with sausages and bacon for tasty kebabs

SALADS

Serve crisp, cool salads for main courses, starters and accompaniments. Full of vitamins and minerals for your family, quick and easy to prepare for guests – salads are the answer to many a 'what shall we eat?' situation. Above: Dutch salad, based on cheese, apples and spinach.

Tivoli salad

serves 8

1 large crisp lettuce
2 × 340-g (2 × 12-oz) cans pork and ham, or equivalent in thickly sliced cooked ham
225 g (8 oz) Samsoe cheese
312-g (11-oz) can whole sweet corn kernels
3 × 15 ml spoons (3 tbsps) finely chopped onion
chopped chives to garnish

For dressing:
4 × 15 ml spoons (4 tbsps) mayonnaise
2 × 15 ml spoons (2 tbsps) cream
about 2 × 15 ml spoons (1½–2 tbsps) lemon juice
freshly ground black pepper

Wash and separate the lettuce. Cut the meat and cheese in thick slices, then into small cubes. Drain the corn and add to the meat and cheese, with the onion. Blend the mayonnaise and cream with lemon juice to sharpen; season with pepper. Fold this mixture into the meat and cheese. Arrange a bed of lettuce on a dish and pile the mixture on top. Garnish with chives.

Swedish chicken salad

serves 6

1¾ kg (3½-lb) oven-ready chicken, roasted
175 g (6 oz) long grain rice
1 green eating apple
1 red eating apple
2 bananas
lemon juice
142 ml (¼ pint) double cream
200 ml (7 fl oz) mayonnaise
5 ml spoon (1 level tsp) curry powder
salt and pepper
watercress for garnish

Allow the chicken to cool. Meanwhile cook the rice in boiling, salted water for about 12 minutes, drain and cool. Carve the chicken into slices and cut these into strips. Halve and core the apples and slice thinly. Peel the bananas and slice thickly. Sprinkle both with lemon juice. Whip the cream to the same consistency as the mayonnaise and fold it in. Add the curry powder. Fold in the chicken, apple and banana. Add more lemon juice and adjust the seasoning. Pile on a bed of rice, or combine with the rice. Garnish with watercress.

Tomato and anchovy salad

serves 6

rind of ½ a lemon
3 × 15 ml spoons (3 tbsps) lemon juice
3 × 15 ml spoons (3 tbsps) salad oil
½ × 15 ml spoon (½ level tbsp) caster sugar
salt and freshly ground black pepper
60-g (2-oz) can anchovy fillets, drained and finely chopped
40 g (1½ oz) shallots, skinned and chopped
¾ kg (1½-lb) tomatoes, skinned and sliced

Using a potato peeler, thinly pare the lemon rind, free of the white pith, and chop it. Whisk together the chopped rind, juice, oil, sugar and seasoning. Add the anchovies and shallots. Turn the tomatoes in this dressing and leave in a cool place for 1–2 hours.

Salad basque

serves 4

6 eggs, hard-boiled and sliced
198-g (7-oz) can tuna, drained and flaked
2 dill cucumbers, finely sliced
8 tomatoes, skinned and sliced
60-g (2-oz) can anchovy fillets, drained
3–4 × 15 ml spoons (3–4 tbsps) salad oil
15 ml spoon (1 tbsp) wine vinegar
5 ml spoon (1 level tsp) French mustard
2 × 15 ml spoons (2 level tbsps) tomato ketchup
5 ml spoon (1 level tsp) dried mixed herbs

Layer the sliced eggs, flaked tuna, cucumber and tomatoes in a salad bowl. Split the anchovy fillets in half lengthwise and arrange in a lattice over the tomato layer. Whisk the remaining ingredients together to make a dressing and pour over the salad. Chill.

Dutch salad

Juice of 1 large lemon
3 firm, green eating apples
225 g (8 oz) Edam cheese, rinded
200-g (7-oz) can pimientos (sweet red peppers), drained
350 g (12 oz) spinach

For dressing:
20 ml (1½ tbsps) cider vinegar
3 × 15 ml spoons (3 tbsps) corn oil
Salt and freshly ground black pepper
1·25 ml spoon (½ level tsp) dry mustard
1·25 ml spoon (½ level tsp) caster sugar

Put the lemon juice in a bowl. Dice the apples, discarding the core; turn at once in the lemon juice. Cut the cheese into dice the same size as the apples. Cut the pimiento into small strips. Carefully wash the spinach and remove all the stems; roughly break the drained leaves into manageable pieces.
Whisk together the dressing ingredients and toss the spinach in the dressing until it glistens. Drain, and arrange round the edge of the salad bowl. Toss the apple, cheese and pimiento in the remaining dressing and pile in the centre of the spinach.

Salami salad, served continental style on a wooden board

Bean and celery salad

225 g (½ lb) French beans, trimmed and halved
1 celery heart, scrubbed and finely sliced
½ dill cucumber, roughly chopped
212-g (7½-oz) can butter beans, drained
3–4 × 15 ml spoons (3–4 tbsps) well-seasoned French dressing
chopped chives to garnish

Cook the French beans in boiling salted water for about 5 minutes, drain and leave to cool. Toss the celery, dill cucumber, butter beans and French beans in enough dressing to moisten them.

Chill slightly and serve sprinkled with chopped chives.

Spinach Slaw

225 g (½ lb) fresh spinach
175 g (6 oz) white cabbage, washed and trimmed
50 g (2 oz) seedless raisins
4 × 15 ml spoons (4 tbsps) lemon juice
3 × 15 ml spoons (3 tbsps) salad oil
Salt and freshly ground black pepper
caster sugar
1 dessert apple, cored and chopped but not peeled

Remove any coarse stems from the spinach and wash thoroughly; pat the leaves dry on a clean cloth. Finely shred the spinach and cabbage. Soak the raisins in half the lemon juice until soft and swollen, then add to the spinach and cabbage.

Pork and bean salad

2 × 15 ml spoons (2 tbsps) chopped parsley
1 small onion, skinned and very finely chopped
5 ml spoon (1 level tsp) dry mustard
5 ml spoon (1 level tsp) French mustard
5 ml spoon (1 level tsp) paprika pepper
5 ml spoon (1 level tsp) salt
freshly ground black pepper
1·25 ml spoon (¼ tsp) grated nutmeg
2 × 5 ml spoons (2 tsps) caster sugar
juice of 1 orange
4 × 15 ml spoons (4 tbsps) salad oil
2 × 15 ml spoons (2 tbsps) tarragon vinegar
200-g (7-oz) can red kidney beans, drained
2 large cooked potatoes, diced
1 lb cold, cooked pork sausages
2 eating apples, cored and diced
2 tomatoes, skinned and seeded

Put the parsley, onion, seasonings, spices, sugar, orange juice, oil and vinegar in a lidded container, close and shake to make a dressing.

In a bowl, lightly toss together the beans, potatoes, sausages (cut into small chunks) apples and chopped tomatoes. Fold the dressing through and leave to marinade for 30 minutes, giving the mixture an occasional stir. Turn into a salad bowl for serving.

Salami salad

serves 4

100–125 g (4 oz) Danish salami, thinly sliced
100–125 g (4 oz) Samsoe cheese, diced
French dressing
small bunch of radishes, trimmed and sliced
1 clove of garlic, skinned and cut
1 lettuce, washed and roughly shredded
½ cucumber (or 1 small, ridge cucumber), thinly sliced
bunch of watercress, washed and trimmed
100–125 g (4 oz) Gruyère cheese, thinly sliced

Put 8 slices of salami to one side and cut the rest into strips, using scissors. Toss the Samsoe cheese in 2 × 15 ml spoons (2 tbsps) of the dressing, mix in a bowl with the salami and radishes. Add the garlic. Leave for a little time for the flavours to mellow.

Cut half way through each slice of the reserved salami and curl into cones.

To serve, remove the garlic, lightly toss the lettuce, cucumber and half the watercress in a little dressing. Arrange in a shallow flat dish. Tuck in the slices of Gruyère round the edge and pile the dressed cheese and salami mixture in the centre. Surround with salami cones and watercress sprigs.

SALAD DRESSINGS

French dressing

½ × 2·5 ml spoon (¼ level tsp) salt
¼ × 2·5 ml spoon (⅛ level tsp) pepper
½ × 2·5 ml spoon (¼ level tsp) dry mustard
½ × 2·5 ml spoon (¼ level tsp) sugar
1 × 15 ml spoon (1 tbsp) sugar
1 × 15 ml spoon (1 tbsp) vinegar or lemon juice
2–3 × 15 ml spoons (2–3 tbsps) salad oil

Put the salt, pepper, mustard and sugar in a bowl, add the vinegar and stir until well blended. Whisk in the oil gradually with a fork. The oil separates out on standing, so if necessary whisk the dressing again immediately before use. Alternatively, make a large quantity and store it in a salad cream bottle, shaking it up vigorously just before serving.

Note: The proportion of oil to vinegar varies with individual taste, but use vinegar sparingly. Wine, tarragon or other herb flavoured vinegar may be used.

Mayonnaise

1 egg yolk
2·5 ml spoon (½ level tsp) dry mustard
2·5 ml spoon (½ level tsp) salt
½ × 2·5 ml spoon (¼ level tsp) pepper
2·5 ml spoon (½ level tsp) sugar
150 ml (¼ pint) salad oil
15 ml spoon (1 tbsp) vinegar or lemon juice

Put the egg yolk into a basin with the seasonings and sugar. Mix thoroughly, then add the oil drop by drop, stirring briskly with a wooden spoon the whole time, or using a whisk, until the sauce is thick and smooth. If it becomes too thick, add a little of the vinegar. When all the oil has been incorporated, add the vinegar gradually and mix thoroughly.

Foamy mayonnaise

2 egg yolks
salt and pepper
150 ml (¼ pint) salad oil
2 × 15 ml spoons (2 tbsps) lemon juice
1 egg white, stiffly whisked

Cream the egg yolks and seasonings and add the oil drop by drop, stirring hard all the time, until the mayonnaise is thick and smooth, then stir in the lemon juice.

Put in a cool place until required; just before serving, fold in the egg white.

Thousand islands mayonnaise

150 ml (¼ pint) mayonnaise
15 ml spoon (1 tbsp) finely chopped stuffed olives
5 ml spoon (1 tsp) finely chopped onion
1 egg, hard-boiled and chopped
15 ml spoon (1 tbsp) finely chopped green pepper (capsicum)
5 ml spoon (1 tsp) chopped parsley
5 ml (1 level tsp) tomato paste

Mix all the ingredients together until evenly combined.

This is a popular American salad dressing.

Picnic Menus

Fried salami chicken is as good cold as hot

Garden Lunch
serves 6–8

Potted smoked salmon
Fried salami chicken
Italian cauliflower salad
Stuffed French loaf
Jellied beetroot and apple salad
Danish baked fruit salad

Potted smoked salmon

2 × 75-g (3-oz) pkts full fat soft cheese
finely grated rind of 1 lemon
2 egg yolks
284 ml (½ pint) double cream
salt and freshly ground black pepper
cayenne pepper
1 clove garlic, skinned and crushed
175 g (6 oz) smoked salmon trimmings
4 × 15 ml spoons (4 tbsps) finely chopped parsley
50 g (2 oz) fresh white breadcrumbs
50 g (2 oz) butter

Put the cheese, lemon rind, egg yolks and cream in a small bowl. Place the bowl over a pan of hot water and cook until smooth and thick. Remove from the heat. Season with salt, pepper, cayenne pepper and garlic.
Chop the smoked salmon finely and add to the cheese mixture with the chopped parsley and breadcrumbs.
Spoon into 6–8 individual soufflé dishes or ramekins until about two-thirds full. Melt the butter and pour a little into the top of each dish. Chill until firm.

Fried salami chicken

12–16 chicken drumsticks, skinned
100–150 g (4–5 oz) salami, skinned and sliced (2 slices per joint of chicken)
3–4 large eggs, beaten
⅔ large white loaf made into breadcrumbs
oil for deep frying
425-g (15-oz) can grapefruit segments, drained
¼ cucumber (or ½ small ridge cucumber) sliced

Make an incision to the bone along 1 side of each drumstick and loosen the flesh around the bone. Place 2 slices of salami around the bone, pull the chicken flesh together and secure with cocktail sticks.

Dip the salami-filled chicken fir into beaten egg, then brea crumbs and pat the crumbs well. Repeat the egg and brea crumb process to give a goo coating.
Deep fry in hot oil (182°C 360°F.) for 7–10 minutes, un golden brown and cooke through. Drain on absorbe kitchen paper and cool. Pack th drumsticks in several plast boxes with the drained grapefru segments and cucumber slices.

Stuffed French loaf

1 French loaf
5 sticks celery, scrubbed and chopped
a little butter
100–125 g (4 oz) cream cheese
milk
salt and freshly ground black pepper

Cut off the top of the loaf at slight angle, so that you remov the top and part of the inside Scoop out some of the inside t make room for the filling. Mix th celery, butter, cream cheese, mil and seasoning and pile this fillin into the loaf. Replace the top.
Wrap the stuffed loaf in foil unti required at the picnic. To serve cut the loaf into 5–7·5 cm (2–3 in. slices.

Italian cauliflower salad

1 medium-sized cauliflower
7 anchovy fillets, cut into small pieces
10 ripe olives, stoned and sliced
15 ml spoon (1 tbsp) bottled capers
15 ml spoon (1 tbsp) minced shallot or onion
freshly ground black pepper
3 × 15 ml spoons (3 tbsps) olive oi or salad oil
15 ml spoon (1 tbsp) vinegar

Wash and trim the cauliflower and break into small florets. Cook in a little boiling water for about 10 minutes, or until tender but still crisp.
Drain thoroughly, cool and chill. Place the chilled cauliflower, anchovy fillets, olives, capers and shallot in a bowl.
Shake the oil and vinegar together in a screw-top jar. Toss the salad very gently in the dressing and serve in a salad bowl.

This is an elegant salad for a garden lunch

Jellied beetroot and apple salad

1 pkt red jelly
300 ml (½ pint) boiling water
150 ml (¼ pint) vinegar
2 × 15 ml spoons (2 tbsps) lemon juice
450 g (1 lb) cooked beetroot
2 eating apples
50 g (2 oz) shelled walnuts

Break up the jelly tablet, place it in a basin and dissolve it in the boiling water.
When dissolved, mix together the vinegar and lemon juice, make up to 300 ml (½ pint) with cold water and add to the hot jelly liquid. Peel and slice or dice the cooked beetroot; peel, core and slice the apples. Place the walnuts in the base of a 1·1-litre (2-pint) ring mould and add the beetroot and apple in layers. Pour on the liquid jelly and leave in a cool place to set. To serve, unmould on to a flat plate and garnish.

Danish baked fruit salad

175 g (6 oz) dried prunes
175 g (6 oz) dried apricots
6 bananas, quartered
a few raisins, stoned
4 × 15 ml spoons (4 tbsps) thin honey
400 ml (¾ pint) fresh orange juice
grated rind of 1 lemon

Soak the prunes and apricots in warm water for several hours, or overnight. Butter a large, flat ovenproof dish and arrange the fruit on it. Add the honey to the orange juice and mix it well, then pour it over the fruit. Sprinkle the lemon rind over the fruit. Bake in the centre of the oven at 180°C. (350°F.) mark 4 for about 30 minutes. Cool. Serve with pouring cream.

Hamper Fare
for 8

Ham and cheese rolls
Curried kipper salad
Party chicken mould
Cabbage salad
Leek and tomato salad
Bread stick
Cherry and almond pie

Curried kipper salad

2 × 200-g (7-oz) pkts kipper fillets (or 425 g (15 oz) other smoked oily fish, boned)
8 × 15 ml spoons (8 tbsps) mayonnaise
10 ml spoon (2 level tsps) curry powder
10 ml spoon (2 sps) vinegar
100 g (4 oz) cooked long grain rice
½ kg (1 lb) tomatoes, skinned and sliced
8 sticks celery, scrubbed and sliced
salt and pepper
watercress for garnish, optional

Cook the kippers as directed on the packet. Skin them and cut into fingers. Mix the mayonnaise, curry powder and vinegar together. Stir in the kippers, rice, tomatoes and celery. Blend well and adjust the seasoning with a little salt and pepper. Pile into a plastic box. Take watercress sprigs along for a garnish, if wished.

Party chicken mould

½ a cooked chicken
2 eggs, hard-boiled
400 ml (¾ pint) well seasoned aspic jelly, made from aspic jelly powder and a dash of sherry
cooked peas

Cut the chicken into small pieces, removing all the bone and skin. Slice the eggs neatly. Wet a 1·1 litre (2-pint) ring mould with straight sides and coat with aspic jelly. Set the peas round the base. Dip each slice of egg in aspic jelly and position them round the side of the mould; leave in the refrigerator for a few minutes to set firmly. Fill up the mould with chicken and pour in the rest of the aspic. Leave in a cool place to set. Unmould just before leaving and carry in an insulated container.

Cabbage salad

1 small white cabbage
1 onion, skinned and chopped
3 × 15 ml spoons (3 tbsps) French dressing
5 ml spoon (1 level tsps) caraway seeds
2·5 ml spoon (½ level tsps) dried marjoram

Trim the cabbage, remove the outer leaves, then wash and shred it. Place it in a bowl and pour boiling water over it. After 10 minutes, drain and rinse under

---

A mixture of fresh and dried fruits for the Danish fruit salad

cold running water to cool. Drain the cabbage well and transfer it to a plastic box with a lid and add the chopped onion.
Make the French dressing, adding the caraway seeds and marjoram. Put the dressing into a screw-top jar and pour it over the salad at the picnic.

Leek and tomato salad

4 young tender leeks, washed
4 small tomatoes, skinned
1 lettuce
5 ml spoon (1 level tsp) chopped basil
5 ml spoon (1 level tsp) chopped chervil
3 × 15 ml spoons (3 tbsps) French dressing

Slice the white part of the leeks very finely. Cut the tomatoes into sections. Wash and drain the lettuce. Put the lettuce, leeks and tomatoes into a plastic container and sprinkle on the basil and chervil. Put the French dressing in a separate container and put the lid on firmly. Pour the dressing over the salad at the picnic.

Cherry and almond pie
make 2

350 g (12 oz) shortcrust pasty i.e. made with 350 g (12 oz) flour etc.
raspberry jam
50 g (2 oz) ground almonds
50 g (2 oz) caster sugar
1 large egg, beaten
350 g (¾ lb) cherries, stoned
caster sugar for dredging

Roll out the pastry and use half to line an 18-cm (7-in.) foil pie plate. Spread raspberry jam over the base.
Blend together the ground almonds, sugar and egg and

---

spread half this mixture over the jam. Add the cherries and cover with the remaining almond mixture. Cover the pie with a lid made from the remaining pastry and seal the edges. Decorate with leaves cut from the pastry trimmings.
Bake in the oven at 190°C. (375°F.) mark 5 for 30–40 minutes. Cool and dredge with caster sugar.

Picnic Menu
serves 8

Mixed meat pâté or meat loaf
Egg and vegetable flan
Golden slaw
Filled beetroots
French bread and butter
Pineapple soufflés

Mixed meat pâté

175–225 g (6–8 oz) bacon rashers, rinded
100–125 g (4 oz) lamb's liver, chopped
100–125 g (4 oz) lean raw pork, chopped
100–125 g (4 oz) sausage meat
25 g (1 oz) fresh white breadcrumbs
15 ml spoon (1 tbsp) milk
1 small onion, skinned and finely chopped
a little beaten egg
1 small glass brandy
salt and pepper
good pinch of ground nutmeg
225 g (8 oz) cold roast chicken, duck or game, sliced

A pâté covered with bacon rashers always looks attractive

Line an 18-cm (7-in.) round cake tin with kitchen foil leaving enough to cover the top later. Stretch the bacon rashers with the back of a knife and use them to line the cake tin. Mix together the liver, pork, sausage meat, breadcrumbs, milk, onion, egg, brandy and seasoning. Fill the tin, starting with a layer of sliced meat and alternating with layers of the forcemeat mixture. Cover with foil, place the tin in a roasting tin with water to come half way up and cook in the oven at 170°C. (325°F.) mark 3 for about 2½ hours.

Remove from the oven, cover with a plate, put a weight on top and chill overnight.

To pack, turn out of the tin, wrap the extra foil over the top and slip the pâté into a plastic bag.

Meat loaf

225 g (8 oz) stewing veal
225 g (8 oz) lean stewing beef
225 g (8 oz) lean bacon, rinded
100–125 g (4 oz) onion, skinned
50 g (2 oz) carrot, peeled and grated
100–125 g (4 oz) tomatoes, skinned and chopped
8 × 15 ml spoons (8 level tbsps) thyme and parsley stuffing mix
5 ml spoon (1 level tsp) salt
freshly ground black pepper
1 egg, beaten

Put the veal, beef, bacon and onion through the mincer twice. Combine this mixture with the remaining ingredients.

Place the mixture on a piece of kitchen foil and shape it into a loaf about 7·5 cm by 18 cm (3 in. by 7 in.). Wrap it neatly, place it in a baking dish or loaf tin and cook in the oven at 180°C. (350°F.) mark 4 for 1¼ hours: open the foil and cook for a further 1¼ hours. When cold, wrap in fresh kitchen foil or pack in a large plastic box. At the picnic, garnish with a few slices of tomato before serving.

Egg and vegetable flan

100–125 g (4 oz) shortcrust pastry – i.e. made with 100–125 g (4 oz) flour etc.
25 g (1 oz) butter
25 g (1 oz) flour
300 ml (½ pint) milk
75 g (3 oz) cheese, grated
salt and pepper
3 eggs, hard-boiled and sliced
1 pkt frozen mixed vegetables

Roll out the pastry and use it to line an 18-cm (7-in.) flan ring or case. Bake blind at 200°C. (400°F.) mark 6 until lightly browned. Cool. This can be done a day ahead.

Melt the butter, stir in the flour and cook for 2–3 minutes. Remove the pan from the heat and gradually stir in the milk. Bring to the boil and continue to cook, stirring, until the sauce thickens and is cooked. Stir in the cheese and season to taste.

Arrange the sliced eggs in the cooled flan case, retaining 2–3 slices for garnishing. Cook the frozen vegetables according to the directions on the packet, mix them with the cheese sauce, cool a little and spoon into the flan case. Leave until cold. Garnish with the remaining slices of egg just before packing.

Cover the flan with kitchen foil, but be careful not to stand anything on top of it. Slice it, as required, at the picnic.

Golden slaw

1 small Savoy cabbage
100–175 g (4–6 oz) Gruyère cheese, cut into thin strips
225 g (½ lb) red-skinned apples, cored and chopped
150 ml (¼ pint) mayonnaise
15 ml spoon (1 level tbsps) made mustard
5 ml spoon (1 level tsp) sugar
salt and pepper

Wash the cabbage well. Curl back the outer leaves, cut round the base of the heart and scoop out the heart, to leave a 'bowl'. Finely shred the cabbage heart and put in a basin with the cheese and apples. Combine the mayonnaise with the mustard, sugar and seasoning and toss the salad in this dressing until the ingredients are well coated. Spoon into the scooped-out cabbage and pack in kitchen foil or a plastic bag.

Filled beetroots

8 small cooked beetroots
salt and pepper
2 × 15 ml spoon (2 tbsps) lemon juice
8 sticks of celery, scrubbed and chopped
2 oranges, peeled and chopped
10 ml spoon (2 tsps) horseradish sauce
10 ml spoon (2 level tsps) sugar
French dressing

Peel the beetroots. Trim the base of each so that it will stand firmly and hollow out the centre to form a cup. Season with salt and pepper and sprinkle with lemon juice. Mix the celery and orange and fill the beetroot cups. Add the horseradish sauce and sugar to the French dressing, mix well and spoon over the beetroots. Wrap each one separately.

Pineapple soufflés

425-g (15-oz) can crushed pineapple
2 × 10 ml and 1 × 2·5 ml spoons (4½ level tsps) gelatine
4 large eggs, separated
75 g (3 oz) caster sugar
2 × 15 ml spoons (2 tbsps) whisky
142 ml (¼ pint) single cream
142 ml (¼ pint) double cream
frosted grapes for decoration

Drain the crushed pineapple. Reserve 2 × 15 ml (2 tbsps) juice and place it in a small bowl. Sprinkle over the gelatine and dissolve over a pan of hot water. Whisk the egg yolks, sugar and whisky in a large basin over a pan of hot water until they are thick and pale. Remove from the heat and add the crushed pineapple. Add a little of this mixture to the gelatine, mix well and pour it back into the soufflé mixture, whisking. Leave to cool, whisking from time to time.

Whisk the creams lightly together. Fold into the cool, but not set, pineapple base. Whisk the egg whites until stiff but not dry, pour the pineapple cream base over the whites and fold in lightly. Divide the mixture between the chilled soufflé dishes and put in a cool place to set. When set, decorate with frosted grapes.

Meat loaf and individual pineapple soufflés

A plastic mould is ideal for a picnic jelly

Tomato coleslaw

*350 g (¾ lb) white cabbage,
    quartered and washed*
1 red pepper (capsicum), seeded
4 tomatoes, skinned
*½ cucumber (or 1 small ridge
    cucumber)*
225 ml (8 fl oz) thick mayonnaise
*4 × 15 ml spoons (4 tbsps) soured
    cream*
10 ml spoon (2 tsps) clear honey
*10 ml spoon (2 tsps) tomato
    ketchup*
*salt and freshly ground black
    pepper*
juice of 1 lemon

Shred the cabbage finely and slice the pepper, tomatoes and cucumber. Beat the mayonnaise with the remaining ingredients and toss the salad ingredients in this dressing. Pack in a plastic container.

Summer pudding

make 2

*½ kg (1 lb) soft fruits (raspberries,
    currants, blackberries etc.)*
sugar
*thin slices white bread, crusts
    removed*

Stew the fruit gently with sugar and water as necessary, keeping it as whole as possible. Line a plastic pudding basin with bread and fill it with alternate layers of fruit and bread, retaining some of the juice. When the last layer of fruit is in the basin, pour the remaining juice over and cover the surface with a slice of bread. Cover the pudding with a plate and press this down with a heavy weight. Leave overnight, in the refrigerator.
Remove the weight and plate and cover the basin aith a lid or foil for carrying. Turn out before serving with cream.

*Picnic
Menu*
serves 12

**Courgette and
carrot soup or
Chilled vegetable
juice
Picnic sandwich box
Salmon rice
Fennel and
Gruyère salad
Coffee and vanilla
milk jelly**

Courgette and
carrot soup

*100–125 g (4 oz) butter or
    margarine*
*½ kg (1 lb) carrots, pared and
    thinly sliced*
*½ kg (1 lb) courgettes, trimmed
    and thinly sliced*
2·5 spoon (½ level tsp) dried thyme
2 bay leaves
2·3 litres (4 pints) chicken stock
*2 × 10 ml spoons (4 level tsps)
    tomato paste*
*6 × 15 ml spoons (6 level tbsps)
    instant potato powder*
*salt and freshly ground black
    pepper*
chopped parsley

Melt the butter in a large saucepan. Add the carrots and courgettes with the thyme and bay leaves. Cover and sauté, shaking the pan occasionally, for 10 minutes. Pour the stock into the pan, add the tomato paste and stir, bringing to the boil. Cover and simmer for about 30 minutes.
Add the potato, stir and bring back to the boil; adjust seasoning. Pour into a vacuum flask and garnish with chopped parsley when serving.

Picnic sandwich box
make 2

1 small uncut Bloomer loaf
75 g (3 oz) butter, melted
225 g (½ lb) pork sausage meat
*100–125 g (¼ lb) cooked ham,
    finely chopped*
*100–125 g (¼ lb) cooked tongue,
    finely chopped*
*50 g (2 oz) onion, skinned and
    chopped*
2 eggs
150 ml (¼ pint) milk
*salt and freshly ground black
    pepper*
2 eggs, hard-boiled and halved

Cut horizontally across the loaf, two-thirds of the way up. Remove the lid, gently ease away the bread from around the crust edge of both pieces and make 100–125 g (4 oz) of it into breadcrumbs. Brush the cavity of the loaf and lid with some of the melted butter. Combine the sausage meat, ham, tongue, breadcrumbs and onion. Beat together the raw eggs and the milk and combine with the forcemeat.
Place one-third of the mixture down the centre of the loaf. Arrange the halved hard-boiled eggs lengthwise on top and pack round with more forcemeat. Top with the lid.
Tie the loaf up like a parcel with string and brush all over with the remaining melted butter. Place on a baking sheet and bake in the oven at 200°C. (400°F.) mark 6 for 15 minutes. Cover with foil and continue cooking for another 45 minutes.
Unwrap, remove the string and cool on a wire rack. Pack in fresh foil. Cut the loaf into thick slices for serving.

Salmon rice
make 2

225 g (8 oz) long grain rice
*60 g (2 oz) can anchovy fillets,
    drained*
milk
3 × 15 ml spoons (3 tbsps) corn oil
15 ml spoon (1 tbsp) wine vinegar
15 ml spoon (1 tbsp) lemon juice
*5 ml spoon (1 level tsp) French
    mustard*
*salt and freshly ground black
    pepper*
*75 g (3 oz) onion, skinned and
    finely chopped*
*2 × 15 ml spoons (2 level tbsps)
    chopped parsley*
210-g (7½-oz) can pink salmon
1 small ripe avocado
extra lemon juice

Cook the rice in boiling salte water until tender and rinse it in cold water to cool it quickly Drain well.
Separate the anchovies, cove with milk and leave to soak for 30 minutes. Whisk together the oi vinegar, lemon juice and mus tard. Season well. Fork this dres sing through the rice with th onion, parsley and anchovies Discard the dark skin and bon from the salmon and flake th flesh. Lightly fold it through th rice, but take care not to brea down the salmon too finely. Pacl in a rigid plastic container.
Garnish with avocado slice tossed in lemon juice to preven discoloration.

Fennel and Gruyère
salad

2 fennel roots
225 g (8 oz) Gruyère cheese
freshly ground black pepper
lemon and oil dressing

Shred the fennel finely and cut the cheese into slivers.
Mix the fennel and Gruyère, season well with freshly ground black pepper. Pack in a plastic box.
Take the dressing separately and pour over the salad at the picnic.

Coffee and vanilla milk
jelly
make 2

50 g (2 oz) caster sugar
150 ml (¼ pint) strong coffee
400 ml (¾ pint) milk
*4 × 10 ml spoons (8 level tsps)
    powdered gelatine*
4 × 15 ml spoons (4 tbsps) water
vanilla pod

Add 25 g (1 oz) sugar to the coffee and 150 ml (¼ pint) of the milk. Dissolve half the gelatine in 2 × 15 ml spoons (2 tbsps) water in a basin over a pan of hot water. Add the coffee and milk mixture. Pour one third of this jelly into a picnic jelly mould and put in a cool place to set (keep the rest warm so that it does not set). Infuse the vanilla pod in the remaining milk for a short time, them make a jelly with this and the remaining sugar, gelatine and water. Pour half this vanilla jelly on to the set coffee jelly and put into a cool place to set. Repeat the layers, finishing with the coffee jelly. Transport the jelly in an ice-box, if possible, and unmould at the picnic.

Appetizer soup
Raised bacon and
egg pie
Pork loaf
Chicory salad
Tomato coleslaw
Green salad
Baps
Summer pudding

Appetizer soup

·4 litre (2½ pints) water
beef stock cubes
chicken stock cubes
× 425-g (2 × 15-oz) cans
  tomatoes
medium-sized onions, skinned
  and chopped
25 g (8 oz) carrots, peeled and
  thinly sliced
stalks of celery, scrubbed and cut
  into 1-cm (½-in.) lengths
peppercorns
·5 ml spoon (½ level tsp) dried
  sage
alt and freshly ground black
  pepper
ated Parmesan cheese to garnish

ut the water into a saucepan,
nen add the stock cubes,
matoes, onion, carrot, celery,
eppercorns and sage. Mix well,
ring to the boil, cover and sim-
er gently for 1 hour. Adjust sea-
ning. Pour while still hot into a
armed, wide-necked vacuum
g. Take the Parmesan in a sepa-
te container, to sprinkle on
ach serving.

Raised bacon and egg pie

or hot water crust:
50 g (1 lb) plain flour
0 ml spoon (2 level tsps) salt
00–125 g (4 oz) lard
00 ml (7 fl oz) milk or water
eaten egg to glaze

or filling:
kg (2 lb) bacon joint, cooked
egg, lightly beaten
× 15 ml spoon (2 level tbsps)
  tomato paste
× 15 ml spoons (3 tbsps) chopped
  parsley
reshly ground black pepper
eggs, hard-boiled
00 ml (½ pint) aspic jelly, made
  from aspic jelly powder

Use frozen mixed vegetables for this tasty flan

Sift the flour and salt into a basin and put in a warm place. Melt the lard and add the liquid. Bring to the boil and pour the mixture into the flour. Mix to a paste quickly, using a wooden spoon, turn it on to a floured board and knead until the dough is smooth and free from cracks.

Cut off a quarter of the dough and put aside. Use the rest to line an 18-cm (7-in.) round cake tin; take care to keep the pastry warm while it is being moulded or it will crack.

Divide the cooked bacon joint in half. Mince one half and mix the meat with the beaten egg, tomato paste, parsley and pepper to make a forcemeat. Chop and mix the remaining bacon and 2 of the cooked eggs.

Line the pastry with the force-meat. Fill the centre with the chopped bacon and eggs, placing the remaining hard-boiled egg in the centre.

Roll out the remaining piece of pastry to make a lid. Cover the pie and press the edges together to form a rim and scallop it. Make a cut in the centre to allow steam to escape and decorate the pie with leaves cut from the pastry trim-mings. Brush with beaten egg.

Bake the pie in the centre of the oven at 220°C. (425°F.) mark 7 for 30 minutes. Reduce the tempera-ture to 180°C. (350°F.) mark 4 and cook for a further 15 minutes. Carefully remove the pie from the tin and allow to cool.

Make up the aspic jelly and when it is on the point of setting, pour it into the pie through the hole in the centre of the lid. Chill to set the jelly completely. Pack in foil.

Pork loaf

½ kg (1 lb) raw lean pork, cubed
½ kg (1 lb) lean ham, cubed
15 ml spoon (1 tbsp) finely chopped
  onion
150 ml (¼ pint) thick white sauce
1 egg, beaten
salt and pepper
pinch of rosemary
thinly cut rashers of back bacon,
  rinded
vinegar

Mince the pork, ham and onion twice. Blend these very thoroughly with the white sauce, egg, seasoning and rosemary and place the mixture on a sheet of kitchen foil. Form it into a loaf shape and cover with the rashers of bacon.

Fold the foil over and seal the edges tightly. Place in a large pan of boiling water with a little vin-egar and salt added and boil gently for 2½ hours. (A saucer placed on the base of the pan will prevent the foil coming directly into contact with the metal.)

Remove the loaf from the pan, leave to cool and remove the foil. Pack in fresh foil for carrying.

Chicory salad

4 heads chicory (or 2 heads celery),
  trimmed
12 black olives, stoned
2 × 15 ml spoons (2 tbsps) vinegar
10 ml spoon (2 tsps) honey
2 onions, skinned and finely
  chopped
4 × 15 ml spoons (4 tbsps) salad oil
2 × 15 ml spoons (2 tbsps) lemon
  juice
pinch each of sugar and salt

Cut the chicory (or celery) into fine slices. Mix in the olives. In a screw-top jar, shake together the vinegar, honey, onions, oil, lemon juice, sugar and salt. Pack salad and dressing separately and toss together well just before serving.

COLD PUNCHES FOR SUMMER

On a warm summer's evening, what can be more refreshing than a delicious, cool punch with tangy pieces of orange or lemon floating in it. The word 'punch' is thought to be derived from the Hindu panch, meaning five, as the drink originally consisted of 5 ingredients – spirits (usually arak), sugar, spice, lemon juice and water. Introduced to England by the early traders with India, punches – both hot and cold – enjoyed great popularity during the 17th and 18th centuries. Nowadays, of course, the variations on this basic recipe are almost endless – hot or cold, spicy or mild, full of strong spirits or gently wine-based – and here we give you just a small selection of cold punches and wine cups which we think are perfect summer party drinks.

Make up the drinks well beforehand to give them plenty of time to chill really thoroughly, as well as allowing the flavours to blend. Serve punches and wine cups from a tall jug or – if you have one – a punch bowl. Garnish them well with fresh fruit and herbs such as mint or borage.

Kentish border punch
serves 25

For syrup:
400 ml (¾ pint) water
100–125 g (4 oz) sugar

juice of 6 oranges
juice of 6 lemons
600 ml (1 pint) tea, strained through muslin
1 medium sized fresh pineapple, peeled and coarsely grated
½ bottle gin
2·3 litres (4 pints) water, well chilled
chipped ice

Make the syrup by dissolving the sugar in the water and then bring to the boil. Boil for 10 minutes and allow to cool.

Mix together the syrup, fruit juices, tea, pineapple and gin and leave to stand for 1 hour. Add the chilled water and ice just before serving.

June cup
makes 2 litres (3½ pints) approx

1 bottle of Beaujolais, chilled
2 × 10 ml spoons (4 tsps) brandy
a few strawberries
1·1 litre (2 pints) fizzy lemonade, chilled

Pour the Beaujolais and brandy over the sliced berries and leave in a cool place for at least 30 minutes. Just before serving add lemonade.

Spicy fruit punch
makes 20 servings

600 ml (1 pint) fresh or canned orange juice
300 ml (½ pint) canned pineapple juice
juice and rind of 1 lemon
2·5 ml spoon (½ level tsp) ground nutmeg
6 cloves
2·5 ml spoon (½ level tsp) ground mixed spice
600 ml (1 pint) water
100–175 g (4–6 oz) sugar
700 ml (1¼ pints) ginger ale, chilled
crushed ice

Mix the fruit juices, lemon rind and spices in a large jug. Put the water and sugar in a saucepan and heat gently to dissolve the sugar; cool and add to the other ingredients in the jug. Chill. Strain the liquid and add ginger ale and crushed ice just before serving.

Wyndham's parachute
serves 15

2 bottles Burgundy-style red wine
2 bottles Burgundy-style white wine
1 bottle orange or lemon squash
orange flesh, diced
grapes, peeled and pipped
small can pineapple pieces, drained
peach slices
¼ bottle brandy
grapes for garnish

Mix the wines, squash and fruit in a large serving bowl and leave

Garnish these summer drinks with fruit and herbs, party-style

in the refrigerator for 2 hours. Just before serving, pour in the brandy, but don't stir, and garnish with a small bunch of grapes.

Aveleda wine cup
serves 6

¼ bottle dry sherry
1 bottle Portuguese Vila Real
15 ml spoon (1 tbsp) curaçao
1 'split' of soda water
borage, cucumber and unpeeled sliced apple to garnish

Mix the liquids well and chill in a jug for at least 1 hour. Garnish just before serving.

And for the children – whether it's an 'official' party, or half-a-dozen friends for tea after school – here are a few non-alcoholic drinks that they are sure to enjoy.

Frosted blackcurrant float
serves 4

600 ml (1 pint) milk
4 × 15 ml spoons (4 tbsps) sieved blackcurrant jam or 150 ml (¼ pint) fresh blackcurrant purée
sugar or honey to taste
few drops of carmine
vanilla ice cream

Whisk together the milk, jam or purée, with the honey or sugar and colouring in a blender and chill well. Pour into tall glasses and top each with a small spoonful of vanilla ice cream.

Diddy cup
serves 12

3 × 340-g (3 × 12-oz) cans orange juice
12 cloves
½ bottle French blackcurrant syrup (sirop de cassis)
1·1 litre (2 pints) soda water, well chilled
6–8 ice cubes
1 orange, cut into rings
283-g (10-oz) can blackcurrants, drained
sprigs of mint

Put the orange juice and cloves into a pan, bring slowly to the boil, strain and leave to cool. When cold, add it to the syrup and chill thoroughly. Add the soda water and ice and stir. Decorate with orange rings, blackcurrants and mint.

If you freeze the drained blackcurrants in ice-cubes they make a pretty garnish to float in the glass. *Note:* when the last of the small guests have gone, add some rum to this, for a delicious reviver.

Banana milk shake
serves 2

600 ml (1 pint) milk
1 banana, peeled and sliced thinly
5 ml spoon (1 tsp) honey
dash of lemon juice

Put the ingredients into an electric blender and switch to high speed for ½–1 minute, until frothy. Serve in tall glasses with a straw.

EASY BUFFETS

Strawberry meringue slice is a delicious way of making a little fruit go a long way

Menu
serves 30

Cheese and walnut dip
Celery
French bread and butter
Glazed baked gammon
Pressed tongue
Salmon cutlets in aspic with mayonnaise
Stuffed pepper salad
Green salad
Tomato and onion salad
New potatoes in French dressing
Strawberry meringue slice
Pineapple chiffon flan

Timetable

The ham and tongue may be prepared 2–3 days before. The meringue layers and mayonnaise may also be made well in advance. Prepare the salmon, salad dressings, dip and pineapple chiffon flans the day before. On the day, finish the sweets and make up the salads.

Cheese and walnut dip

½ kg (1 lb) Wensleydale or mild soft cheese
400 ml (¾ pint) top-of-the-milk
25 g (1 oz) onion, grated
tomato paste
salt and pepper
40 g (1½ oz) walnuts, finely chopped

With a fork, work the cheese until creamy, adding the milk a little at a time. Beat in the grated onion, tomato paste to taste and seasoning. Finally, fold in the chopped walnuts. Serve with crisps, crackers and pretzels.

Glazed baked gammon

gammon joint, approx. 2½ kg (5 lb)
2 onions, skinned and quartered
2 carrots, peeled and quartered
1 bay leaf
4 peppercorns
about 20 cloves
3–4 × 15 ml spoons (3–4 tbsps) brown sugar

Weigh the gammon, then calculate the cooking time, allowing 20–25 minutes per ½ kg (1 lb) plus 20 minutes over. Cover the joint with cold water and allow to soak for about 1 hour. Drain and place the gammon in a large pan, skin side down; cover with fresh cold water and bring slowly to the boil, skimming off any scum that forms. Time the cooking from this point.

Add vegetables, bay leaf, peppercorns and 3 cloves, cover the pan and simmer gently for half the cooking time, then drain and wrap in foil. Bake in the centre of the oven at 180°C. (350°F.) mark 4 until ½ hour before the cooking time is complete. Raise the oven heat to 220°C. (425°F.) mark 7. Undo the foil, peel away the rind from the gammon, score the fat into diamonds, stud with cloves and sprinkle the surface with brown sugar. Return the joint to the oven until the fat is crisp and golden.

Allow to cool for serving.

Pressed tongue

1 salted ox tongue, 1¼–1½ kg (2½–3 lb)
8 peppercorns
1 carrot, peeled and sliced
1 onion, skinned and studded with 3 cloves
1 bay leaf

Wash the tongue, and allow it to soak for 24 hours if highly salted. Put the tongue into a saucepan, just cover with cold water, cover and bring to the boil. Remove any scum with a spoon. Add remaining ingredients. Bring to the boil again, reduce heat and simmer the tongue until thoroughly tender. Allow about 1 hour of cooking time per ½ kg (1 lb).

When cooked, plunge the tongue briefly into cold water. Ease off the skin while tongue is still hot and remove the small bones from the back of the tongue. Return meat to the cooking liquid and allow to cool.

When cold, curl the tongue into a round soufflé dish or deep cake tin lined with foil. The container used should be large enough to take the tongue, leaving a few gaps.

Check that the cooking liquid will set when cold. If it does not set to a firm jelly, either reduce by boiling fast or add a little gelatine. Just cover the meat with cool, strained cooking liquid. Press either with a heavily weighted plate, or a tongue press. Chill until the juices have jellied and turn out.

Tomato and onion salad

Skin and slice 30 tomatoes and arrange in dishes. Sprinkle with finely chopped onion, season and pour over 300 ml (½ pint) French dressing. Sprinkle with chopped fresh parsley and marjoram.

Salmon cutlets in aspic

10 salmon cutlets – 175–225 g (6–8 oz) each
butter
2 lemons
5 bay leaves
salt and white pepper
600 ml (1 pint) aspic jelly made from aspic jelly powder
home-made mayonnaise
cucumbers and lemon for garnish

Liberally butter 10 pieces of kitchen foil large enough to envelop each cutlet. Lay a thin slice of lemon and half a bay leaf on each cutlet; season and seal in foil. Place on baking sheets and cook in the oven at 170°C (325°F.) mark 3 for about 20 minutes. Chill in the foil.

Unwrap and discard the bay leaves and lemon. Turn the cutlets upside down on a wire rack placed over a baking sheet. Meanwhile make up the aspic jelly. When on the point of setting spoon over the cutlets. Garnish with cucumber and lemon. Serve mayonnaise separately.

Note: A 225 g (8 oz) cutlet will give 2 portions. To serve one cutlet per person choose those cut from the tail end weighing 150–175 g (5–6 oz).

To make 600 ml (1 pint) mayonnaise: Mix 4 egg yolks with 10 ml spoon (2 tsps) each salt, dry mustard and sugar and 5 ml (1 level tsp) pepper. Add 600 ml (1 pint) salad oil drop by drop, stirring briskly all the time, until the sauce is smooth and thick. Gradually add 4 × 15 ml spoons (4 tbsps) white vinegar and mix.

Stuffed pepper salad

2 red and 2 green peppers
  (capsicums), approx. ½ kg
  (1 lb)
175 g (6 oz) cottage cheese
175 g (6 oz) cream cheese
chives, chopped
1 small onion, skinned and
  chopped
salt and pepper
parsley, chopped
watercress

Cut away a thin slice from the stem end of each pepper. Wash and remove seeds. Beat together the cottage cheese, cream cheese, chopped chives and chopped onion, seasoning and parsley. Stuff the seasoned cheese mixture into the peppers, press firmly and chill for about ½ hour. To serve, slice the peppers and arrange in rows. Garnish with watercress sprigs.

Strawberry meringue slice
make 2

6 egg whites from large eggs
350 g (12 oz) caster sugar
284 ml (½ pint) double cream
142 ml (¼ pint) single cream
350–450 g (¾–1 lb) strawberries,
  hulled

On each of 3 pieces of non-stick paper, mark with a pencil a rectangle 30·5 cm by 10 cm (12 in. by 4 in.). Place on baking sheets. In a deep bowl, whisk the egg whites until stiff. Add half the sugar and whisk again until stiff enough to stand in firm peaks. Fold in all but 3 × 15 ml spoons (3 tbsps) of the remaining sugar. Spread a thin film of meringue over one of the rectangles to cover well. Using a

plain 1 cm (½-in.) vegetable nozzle in a fabric forcing bag, pipe a trellis across the base. Divide the remainder of the meringue between the other rectangles and level off smoothly. Dust each layer with 5 ml spoon (a teaspoon) of caster sugar. Dry the meringues in the oven set on its lowest setting for about 4 hours. Peel the paper away. When cold, store in an airtight container. Whisk together the creams until just stiff enough to hold the shape of the whisk. Slice half the strawberries. Layer meringue with about two-thirds of the cream and the sliced fruit. Press the top lightly then pipe rosettes of cream over it and decorate with the remaining strawberries.

Pineapple chiffon flan
make 2

For flan crust:
225 g (8 oz) sweetmeal biscuits
100–125 g (4 oz) butter, melted
25 g (1 oz) caster sugar

For filling:
4 × 15 ml spoons (4 tbsps) water
10 ml spoon (2 level tsps)
  powdered gelatine
3 large eggs, separated
175 g (6 oz) caster sugar
425-g (15-oz) can crushed
  pineapple, drained, or fresh
  pineapple in season
grated rind and juice of 1 lemon
225 g (8 oz) full fat soft cream
  cheese
whipped cream for decoration

Crush the biscuits and blend the crumbs with the butter and sugar. Use to make a shell in a 25·5 cm (10-in.) loose-bottomed French fluted flan tin.
Pour the water into a cup and sprinkle the gelatine over. Beat egg yolks and 50 g (2 oz) sugar until pale, add pineapple, lemon rind and juice. Turn into saucepan and cook, without boiling, until thick. Blend in the soaked gelatine and then the cream cheese. Cool until on the point of setting.
Whisk the egg whites stiffly and gradually whisk in 75 g (3 oz) sugar. When it stands in firm peaks, fold in remaining 25 g (1 oz) sugar and the pineapple cheese. When beginning to set, pile into the biscuit shell and chill. To serve, remove flan ring, mark into portions and pipe a whirl of cream on each portion.

A biscuit crumb case and a cheesy filling make this unusual flan

Menu
serves 12

**Chicken mille
feuilles
Ham royale
Gala salad wheel
Jacket potatoes
Ginger cream trifles**

Timetable
Make the pastry layers and the chicken mixture for the mille feuilles the day before, also stuffing for ham royale. Finish off the savouries and salads on the day. The ginger cream trifles may be made early in the morning.

Chicken mille feuilles
make 2

225 g (8 oz) frozen puff pastry,
  thawed
225 g (8 oz) full fat cream cheese
10 ml spoon (2 tsps) lemon juice
2 × 10 ml spoons (4 level tsps)
  thick mayonnaise
½ × 2·5 ml spoon (¼ level tsp) salt
freshly ground black pepper
350 g (12 oz) cooked chicken flesh
3–4 lettuce leaves, finely shredded
100–125 g (¼ lb) firm tomatoes

Roll out pastry into a rectangle 30·5 cm by 28 cm (12 in. by 11 in.) 0·5 cm (¼ in.) thick. Prick well and place on a dampened baking sheet. Divide equally into 3 crosswise and separate slightly. Bake at 200°C. (400°F.) mark 6 for 20–25 minutes until well risen. Cool on a wire rack.
In a bowl, using either a rotary whisk or an electric blender, blend together the cheese, lemon juice, mayonnaise and seasonings. Cut the chicken flesh into small manageable pieces and add

two-thirds to the creamed cheese mixture. Spread lightly over the 3 pastry layers and sprinkle shredded lettuce on top. Slice the tomatoes thinly, cut in half again and arrange over the lettuce.
Layer up the pastry and chicken to form a loaf, top with remaining chicken and tomatoes. To serve, cut into thick slices, with a really sharp knife.

Ham royale

175 g (6 oz) long grain rice
1 sachet of saffron
1 bay leaf
10 ml and 15 ml spoons (1½ tbsps)
  olive oil
175 g (6 oz) cooking apple, peeled
  and cored
40 g (1½ oz) butter
175 g (6 oz) onion, skinned and
  finely chopped
10 ml spoon (2 level tsps) curry
  powder
6 × 15 ml spoons (6 tbsps) single
  cream
1 small lemon
salt and pepper
¾ kg (1½ lb) sliced ham
283-g (10-oz) can sweet red
  peppers (pimientos), drained
black olives, stoned
parsley

Cook the rice until tender in boiling salted water to which the saffron and bay leaf have been added. Rinse the cooked rice in cold water, drain and remove bay leaf. Tip rice into a basin, add the oil and fork it through the rice to coat the grains.
Chop the apple finely. Melt the butter in a saucepan and add the apple and onion. Cover with a lid and cook over gentle heat for 5 minutes. Sprinkle the mixture with the curry powder and cook for 1 minute longer. Remove from heat. Pour in the cream then blend it into the rice with the

grated rind of the lemon and 3 × 15 ml spoons (3 tbsps) juice. Season well with salt and freshly ground black pepper. Reserve 12 slices of ham. Dice the remainder with 3 of the red peppers and fork this through the rice. Leave the mixture to stand for an hour or so to 'marry' the flavours. Divide the mixture between the ham slices and roll them up. Decorate the rolls with the remaining peppers cut into strips, stoned black olives and parsley sprigs.

Gala salad wheel

For tomato cups:
12 even-sized firm tomatoes
142 ml (¼ pint) soured cream
150 ml (¼ pint) mayonnaise
350 g (¾ lb) hard white
  cabbage, finely shredded
12 black olives, stoned

For devilled eggs:
12 eggs, hard-boiled
3–4 × 15 ml spoons (3–4 tbsps)
  mayonnaise
1½–2 × 5 ml spoons (1½–2
  level tsps) curry powder

For mixed salad:
1 head of celery
2 eating apples, peeled and cored
1 onion, skinned and halved
300 ml (½ pint) French dressing
2 medium lettuces
1 kg (2 lb) cold cuts (e.g. ½ kg
  (1 lb) rare roast beef, ¼ kg
  (½ lb) garlic sausage, ¼ kg
  (½ lb) pork roll)
cress and ½ cucumber, sliced, or 1
  whole cucumber

Cut a thin slice from each of the tomatoes at the end opposite the stalk. With a teaspoon, carefully scoop out pips and core and discard. Drain the tomato cases upside down. Fold the soured cream into the mayonnaise. Stir in the shredded cabbage. Pile coleslaw mixture into the tomatoes and top each with an olive. Keep covered until required.

Cut the hard-boiled eggs in half lengthwise and remove the yolks. Cream the yolks with 3–4 × 15 ml spoons (3–4 tbsps) mayonnaise and the curry powder. Pipe back into the whites. Cover until required.

Finely chop the celery and apples and slice the onion very thinly. Mix with the French dressing. Just before arranging the wheel, add the lettuce, roughly torn.

Pile the celery salad in a pyramid on a large flat platter with any remaining cabbage salad. Twist and fold the cold cuts and arrange over the salad. Tuck bunches of cress in between. Edge the platter with tomato cups, devilled eggs and sliced cucumber. Top the pyramid with a tomato cup. Serve extra French dressing separately.

Ginger cream trifles
makes 12

2 pkts. soft sponge fingers
apricot jam
225 g (½ lb) stem ginger
1 bottle sherry
852 ml (1½ pints) double cream,
  lightly whipped
25 g (1 oz) almonds, blanched and
  halved

Halve the sponge fingers and spread thickly with apricot jam. Sandwich together and cut into 2·5 cm (1-in.) pieces. Divide between 12 sundae glasses. Finely chop the stem ginger, set aside one-third and mix the remainder with the sponge pieces. Pour about 2 × 15 ml (2 tbsps) sherry into each dish and leave it to soak into the sponge. Spoon the cream

over the sponge mixture and decorate with halved blanched almonds and the remaining ginger.

Menu
serves 20

Quiche lorraine
Rare roast beef
Pâté stuffed chicken
Les crudités
Waldorf salad
Garlic bread
Mousses au chocolat
Winter fruit salad

Timetable
Roast beef, stuff chicken but do not coat with crumbs, and make quiches the day before. Also prepare sweets. Coat and bake chicken, prepare salads and garlic bread on the day. Heat up quiches and garlic bread together just before serving.

Quiche lorraine
make 2

225 g (8 oz) frozen puff pastry,
  thawed
175–225 g (6–8 oz) lean bacon
  rashers, rinded and chopped
175–225 g (6–8 oz) Gruyère
  cheese, thinly sliced
4 eggs, beaten
284 ml (½ pint) single cream or
  creamy milk
salt and pepper

Roll out the pastry thinly and line a 25·5 cm (10-in.) plain flan ring or sandwich cake tin, making a double edge. Cover the bacon with boiling water and leave for 2–3 minutes, then drain well. Put into the pastry cases with the cheese. Mix the eggs and cream, season well and pour into the case. Bake towards the top of the oven at 200°C. (400°F.) mark 6 for about 40 minutes until filling is set and pastry golden.

Pâté stuffed chicken

20 chicken leg portions
1 kg, (2¼ lb) well-seasoned liver
  pâté
6 eggs
6 × 15 ml spoons (6 tbsps) water
1 kg, (2¼ lb) fresh breadcrumbs
salt and pepper
225 g (8 oz) butter

Remove the chicken skin. Using a small, sharp knife, carefully

Spicy ginger cream trifles are easy to make

Pâté stuffed chicken – a soft, rich filling and a crisp outside

work the flesh off the bone from the thigh downwards. Take care not to split the flesh. Stuff each chicken portion with pâté, pushing the filling in from the thigh end. Reshape the flesh and fasten well together, using wooden cocktail sticks. Leave in the refrigerator for at least 1 hour to firm up.

Remove cocktail sticks. Beat the eggs and water together. Dip the chicken joints one at a time in the glaze, coating them evenly, then coat with seasoned breadcrumbs. Pat the crumbs on well. Recoat with egg and crumbs on top of the first coating. Choose 2 ovenproof dishes large enough to take the chicken joints in a single layer. Divide the butter between the dishes and melt. Place the chicken in the hot butter. Bake uncovered at 180°C. (350°F.) mark 4 for 30 minutes. Carefully turn the chicken over and bake for a further 30 minutes. Raise the temperature to 200°C. (400°F.) mark 6 and cook for a further 20

minutes until crisp and golden. Serve hot or cold.

Les crudités

300 ml (½ pint) salad oil
4 × 15 ml spoons (4 tbsps) wine
  vinegar
4 × 15 ml spoons (4 tbsps) lemon
  juice
5 ml spoon (1 level tsp) caster
  sugar
5 ml spoon (1 level tsp) salt
5 ml spoon (1 level tsp) dry
  mustard
freshly ground black pepper
½ kg (1 lb) tomatoes, skinned
450-g (1-lb) pkt frozen broad
  beans or shelled fresh
1 each, red and green peppers
  (capsicums), seeded
½ kg (1 lb) carrots, peeled
bunch of radishes
½ kg (1 lb) celeriac, peeled, or
  celery, scrubbed
225 g (½ lb) salami, thinly sliced
black olives
chopped parsley

Hot French bread with garlic butter is a tasty buffet filler

Whisk together the oil, vinegar, lemon juice, sugar and seasonings. Slice the tomatoes; cook the beans in boiling salted water and remove the outer skin if tough; thinly slice the peppers; coarsely grate the carrots; top and tail the radishes; thinly slice the celeriac and cut into thin strips. Marinade each prepared vegetable separately in a little of the dressing, for a short time.

Arrange the vegetables separately in mounds, on 2 large platters, adding the sliced salami and black olives. Garnish with a little chopped parsley.

Waldorf salad

1 kg (2 lb) crisp eating apples
lemon juice
10 ml (2 level tps) sugar
300 ml (½ pint) mayonnaise
1 head of celery, chopped
100–125 g (4 oz) walnuts, chopped
1 lettuce
few whole walnuts

Peel and core the apples, slice 2 and dice the rest; dip the slices in lemon juice to prevent discoloration. Toss the diced apples with 4 × 15 ml spoons (4 tbsps) lemon juice, the sugar and 2 × 15 ml spoons (2 tbsps) mayonnaise and leave to stand for about ½ hour. Just before serving, add the celery, walnuts and remaining mayonnaise and toss together.
Serve in a bowl lined with lettuce leaves and garnish with the apple slices and a few whole walnuts.

Garlic bread

For each French loaf allow 225 g (½ lb) butter and 2 cloves of garlic, skinned and crushed.
Cut the loaves into thick slices, without completely separating the slices, so that the loaf appears to be hinged. Cream the butter with the garlic and spread bet-

ween the slices. Wrap each loaf loosely in kitchen foil and place in the oven at 170°C. (325°F.) mark 3 for 15 minutes. Raise the temperature to 230°C. (450°F.) mark 8, take out the loaves, fold back the foil and return to the oven for a further 10 minutes to crisp.

Mousses au chocolat

3 small oranges
3 × 15 ml spoons (3 tbsps) orange liqueur
500 g (18 oz) Menier or plain (dark) chocolate
175 g (6 oz) butter
9 large eggs, separated
175 g (6 oz) caster sugar
175 g (6 oz) plain (dark) chocolate for decoration

Cut thin slices of peel, free from all traces of white pith, from one orange and half of another. Cut these into thin strips and blanch them in boiling water until tender. Remove, drain, then macerate them in the orange liqueur. Melt the 500 g (18 oz) Menier chocolate in a basin over a pan of hot water. Cut the butter into small pieces. When the chocolate has melted, remove it from the heat and mix in the pieces of butter. Put the egg whites into a large bowl and chill in the refrigerator. Finely grate the rind from the remaining oranges. Whisk the egg yolks with half the sugar and the grated orange rind, until fluffy. Add the chocolate mixture slowly with 4 × 15 ml spoons (4 tbsps) orange juice and the liqueur drained from the strips of orange peel.
Stiffly whisk the egg whites, gradually adding remaining sugar. Fold the chocolate mixture evenly through the egg whites. Pour the mousse into individual glasses and chill.

Decorate with grated plain chocolate and the shredded orange peel. If you do not have an electric mixer, you will find it easier to make this quantity in 2 lots.

Winter fruit salad

350 g (12 oz) sugar
900 ml (1½ pints) water
rind and juice of 3 lemons
350 g (12 oz) prunes, stewed
350 g (12 oz) dried apricots, stewed
3 bananas, skinned and sliced
6 oranges, skinned and segmented
3 grapefruit, skinned and segmented

Make a syrup by dissolving the sugar in the water over a gentle heat; add the lemon rind, heat gently and boil for 5 minutes. Add the lemon juice, strain the syrup over the prepared fruit and leave to cool.

Menu
serves 12

Melon and Parma ham
Deep fried chicken drumsticks
Tartare sauce
Burgundy beef galantine
Tomato and watercress salad
French bread and butter
Rolla torte

Timetable
for lunch at 1.00 p.m.
Day before: make the Burgundy beef galantine.
Egg and crumb the drumsticks, leave in a cool place. Prepare tartare sauce.
Make Rolla Torten and leave, covered, in a cool place.
Early: Fry chicken joints, drain well, cover and leave in a cool place.

Make up the salad, add French dressing if required.
Slice the galantine.
11.00 a.m. Cut the melons and chill.
12.00 a.m. Remove melons from the refrigerator, add ham and lemon wedges. Set out the food on the table.

Melon and Parma ham

2 large cantaloup (rock) melons
½ kg (1 lb) Parma ham, thinly sliced
lemon wedges for garnish

Cut each melon into 6 portions and remove the seeds. Chill slightly.
Place a slice of Parma ham on each portion of melon. Top with a wedge of lemon and secure with a cocktail stick.

Deep fried chicken drumsticks

12 chicken drumsticks
salt and pepper
2 eggs, beaten
breadcrumbs
oil for deep frying

Season the joints and dip each one in the egg, then coat in breadcrumbs. Leave the joints in a cool place for a while for the coating to 'set'.
Heat the frying oil to 190°C. (375°F.) and fry the chicken joints, 2–3 at a time. When golden brown, remove and drain on absorbent kitchen paper. Allow to cool.
Trim the drumsticks with cutlet frills, which look pretty and give your guests something to hold, to prevent their fingers becoming too sticky.

Tartare sauce

150 ml (¼ pint) mayonnaise
5 ml spoon (1 tsp) chopped tarragon and/or chives
10 ml spoon (2 tsps) chopped capers
10 ml spoon (2 tsps) chopped gherkins
10 ml spoon (2 tsps) chopped parsley
15 ml spoon (1 tbsp) lemon juice or tarragon vinegar

Mix all the ingredients well and leave the sauce to stand for at least 1 hour before serving, to allow the flavours to blend.

Rich mousses au chocolat to tempt your guests

A delicious spread for a buffet lunch

Burgundy beef galantine
make 2

1½ kg (3 lb) chuck steak (in 1 piece)
350 g (¾ lb) back bacon rashers, rinded
salt and pepper
50 g (2 oz) butter
15 ml spoon (1 tbsp) cooking oil
1 large onion, skinned and sliced
1 large carrot, peeled and sliced
1 bay leaf
5 ml spoon (1 level tsp) dried herbs
300 ml (½ pint) red wine, preferably Burgundy
¼ kg (½ lb) button mushrooms, wiped and sliced
15 g (½ oz) powdered gelatine

Trim all the excess fat from the meat and discard. Lay the bacon rashers over the meat to cover it completely and tie into a long roll with string. Sprinkle the roll with salt and pepper.
Heat 25 g (1 oz) butter and the oil in a large flameproof casserole. Add the meat and fry, turning until sealed all over. Add the onion, carrot, herbs, wine and 300 ml (½ pint) water. Bring to the boil, cover and cook in the oven at 180°C. (350°F.) mark 4 for 3 hours.

Remove the meat from the pan and leave until quite cold. Place the stock in the refrigerator; when it is cold, skim off the fat and discard. Make the stock up to 550 ml (1 pint) with water, if necessary.
Melt the remaining butter in a frying pan and sauté the mushrooms; leave until cold.
Cut the meat into thin slices; arrange half of these in a 1·7 litre–2·3 litre (3–4 pint) loaf tin, cover with the mushrooms, then the remaining sliced meat.
Dissolve the gelatine in 2 × 15 ml spoons (2 tbsps) water in a basin held over a pan of hot water, add to the stock and mix well. Leave it to stand and, when beginning to set, pour it over the meat and mushrooms. Leave until completely set.
To serve, unmould and slice.

Rolla torte
make 3

¼ × 2·5 ml spoon (⅛ level tsp) cream of tartar
pinch of salt
3 egg whites
165 g (5½ oz) caster sugar
25 g (1 oz) ground almonds
25 g (1 oz) cornflour

For filling and decoration:
75 g (3 oz) caster sugar
4 × 15 ml spoons (4 tbsps) water
2 egg yolks, lightly beaten
100–175 g (4–6 oz) unsalted butter
50 g (2 oz) chocolate dots
50 g (2 oz) toasted, flaked almonds
icing sugar

Draw 3 × 18 cm (3 × 7-in.) circles on non-stick paper and place on baking sheets. Add the cream of tartar and salt to the egg whites and whisk until very stiff.
Beat in two-thirds of the caster sugar, 15 ml spoon (1 tbsp) at a time. Mix together the remaining sugar, the almonds and cornflour and fold into the meringue mixture.
Using a forcing bag and a 0·5-cm (¼-in.) plain vegetable nozzle, pipe the mixture on to the papers, starting at the centre of the circles and working out to fill the marked area. Take care to see that each ring of meringue touches the next. Alternatively spread the meringue in smooth layers with a palette knife. Bake just below the centre of the oven at 170°C. (325°F.) mark 3 for about 30 minutes, until just coloured and dry. Peel off the paper and cool on a wire rack.
Meanwhile prepare the filling. Place the sugar in a fairly large, heavy-based saucepan; add the water and dissolve the sugar over a very low heat without boiling. When completely dissolved, bring to boiling point and boil steadily for 2–3 minutes, or until a little of the cooled syrup will form a thread when pulled between your wetted finger and thumb (107°C., 225°F.). Place the egg yolks in a deep bowl and pour on the syrup in a thin stream, whisking all the time. Continue to whisk until the mixture is thick and cold. Cream the butter and gradually add the syrup and yolk mixture.
Put the chocolate dots in a small basin with 15 ml (1 tbsp) water; place over a pan of hot water and leave to stand until the chocolate is melted and smooth. Cool slightly and beat into the butter mixture. Sandwich the meringue layers with chocolate filling and coat the torte round the sides Decorate the sides with flaked almonds and dredge the top with icing sugar. Leave the torte in a cool place for 24 hours to mature before cutting; the meringue layers should soften a little.

Coffee

Devoted coffee drinkers tend to be fanatical about their favourite blend and their favourite method of preparing it. However, it is all a matter of personal taste and what is right for one can well be quite wrong for another. There are nevertheless some golden rules about coffee, without which you cannot hope to produce a good, refreshing brew.

The first requirement is that coffee should be fresh. If you have a grinder, buy the coffee beans freshly roasted and store them in an airtight container. Never keep beans for more than a month, and preferably use them up in a shorter time than that. If you do not have a grinder, buy your coffee either freshly ground or pre-ground and packed in a vacuum-sealed package. Once the pack has been opened, only keep it for a week – it quickly gets stale. If you drink so little coffee that you can't use up reasonable quantities in this time, it is much better to keep a jar of a good brand of instant coffee in the cupboard, and buy the fresh only when you know you are entertaining and will require it. Alternatively you might consider the 1-cup size filters with the coffee built in; these come in packs of 8 and, since each is individually sealed, do not get stale quickly. Always keep coffee-making utensils sparklingly clean. This sounds obvious – you always do the washing up – but unless you scrub and rinse the pot thoroughly, as soon as it is empty, the stale coffee will cling and spoil the next brew.

Always drink coffee while it is fresh – never make a bigger quantity than you need and save it for later. Stale coffee becomes bitter-tasting and is unpleasant to drink. Equally, although you should make coffee with freshly boiled water, never boil the coffee itself as this will also make it bitter.

Be sure that the coffee is correctly ground for your particular method. For instance, if you make it in a jug, it is very difficult to make finely ground coffee settle, and the result will be powdery; conversely, if you use coarsely ground coffee with a paper filter, the water stays on the grounds for such a short time that the coffee will be very weak – it needs grinding finely to release its full strength.

Finally, never use boiled milk. Heat the milk to just below boiling point, or serve cream.

JUG METHOD

Warm a jug of which you know the capacity and measure out 30–50 g (1½–2 oz.) medium-ground coffee for every pint of water. Put the coffee in the jug, pour on boiling water, stir and cover. Leave to infuse for 4–5 minutes, then strain the coffee into another warmed jug or straight into the cups.

If you draw a metal spoon across the surface of the coffee just once while it is infusing, the grounds should settle and you may not need to strain it.

CONA OR SIPHON METHOD

For this method a special Cona or similar siphon-type of coffee-maker is needed. Allow 30–50 g (1½–2 oz.) medium-ground coffee per pint of water, and always fill the machine to capacity. Beware of coffee that is too finely ground, as the grounds will creep down the valve into the coffee to be served, making it powdery. Put cold water in the lower container and heat it. Place the upper container, with its valve in position, in the neck of the lower container and add the coffee. When the water boils it will rise on to the coffee. Lower the heat, stir gently once or twice and allow the coffee to infuse for 1–2 minutes, then remove from the heat. The coffee will then filter back into the lower container.

The particular advantage of this method is that the coffee itself is never in direct contact with the heat and therefore cannot boil, however careless you may be. Many people also like the result obtained using a glass container in preference to metal.

FILTER METHOD

For a metal or china filter, allow 30 g (1½ oz.) medium ground coffee per pint of water. For the more modern paper filters, allow 25 g (1 oz.) finely ground coffee.

Warm the coffee pot and place the filter containing the coffee in position. Pour boiling water through the filter. When the water has all gone through, remove the filter and serve the coffee. This method is particularly easy and economical if you are making only 1–2 cups at a time.

PERCOLATOR METHOD

Use a top-of-the-stove percolator, or an electrically heated model. Allow 30–50 g (1½–2 oz.) medium or coarsely ground coffee per pint of water. Pour the cold water into the percolator put the coffee in the metal basket and put this in position. When the water boils it is forced up the centre tube and filters over and down through the coffee grounds. Allow the water to circulate for 8–10 minutes. Most electric percolators can be pre-set to switch off after the required length of time.

ESPRESSO METHOD

Espresso machines make a strong brew. Allow 25 g (1 oz.) finely ground coffee per pint of water. Put the cold water in the machine and the coffee in the special container. When the water boils it is forced under steam pressure through the grounds into a separate jug.

PLUNGER METHOD

Allow 30–50 g (1½–2 oz.) medium-ground coffee per pint of water. Place the coffee in the special jug, pour on the boiling water and insert the plunger. The air escapes through a vent in the centre of the plunger and the coffee is pressed through the filter manually.

PARTY PLANNERS' CHECKLIST
Countdown

A month before

What sort of party will it be? You've a good idea of the numbers by now and have probably decided more or less what to serve, but now you must finalize your ideas.

Food and drink

Order wine and/or spirits from the off licence preferably on 'sale or return'. If you have a freezer, you can start cooking for your party now. Pastry cases, meringues, sauces and pâtés can all be made and packed carefully away.

Extras

Glasses – check if your wine merchant will loan them. If not, compare the price of hiring or buying cheap ones. Will you need extra chairs – china – loudspeakers for your record-player? There's sure to be a firm locally which hires these out.

The week before

All replies will be in by now, and you'll be able to confirm your drinks and glasses orders, as well as anything else you may be hiring. Make a hair appointment for the day of the party, and lash out on a manicure as well.

Non-freezer owners can make meringues and pâtés – both keep happily for up to 5 days. Buy the 'nibblers' – olives, peanuts, crisps, etc., and check you have everything you need in the store-cupboard. Order meat, fish and any special fruit. Make a complete list of other foods you will need, not forgetting coffee, tea and soft drinks.

Order the flowers. Buy in a stock of cigarettes (make sure you have plenty of ashtrays to go round). Buy a quantity of paper napkins and whatever covering you plan to use for the table. Check the linen is all clean and re-iron during the week if necessary. Check your serving dishes and hire or borrow any extras necessary. Buy some candles.

The day before

Clean the house thoroughly. Put away superfluous or precious ornaments to prevent damage. Move furniture away from main traffic areas, but don't let your main room get too bare.

Take food out of the freezer. Prepare pastry and pie fillings. Make up fruit salad (except for bananas) and leave to mature. Order extra milk and cream. Make sure the drink is delivered. Make up the salad dressings; prepare salad stuffs and vegetables as much as possible; cut garnishes. Make up a lot of extra ice cubes – keep them in polythene bags.

Check that you have tissues, cotton wool, safety pins and so on for your women guests. Arrange the flowers. Make up the spare bed – there's always someone who's left at the end. Check that you have enough cutlery – borrow some from a friend if it's too late to hire any. Clean any silver. Collect the meat, fish and green groceries. Don't forget extra bread.

On the day

Remember it's your party and you should enjoy it as well. Clear your dressing table and put out hair spray, tissues, pins and so on for your women guests. A needle and thread might also come in useful. When the family has finished in the bathroom have a tidy-up and put out fresh soap and several guest towels. A clean glass, with drinking water, aspirins and Alka Seltzer would probably be welcome. And don't forget your hairdresser's appointment!

Do as much as possible of the cooking as early as possible. If you're having cold roast meat, this will give your husband a chance to carve it during the afternoon. If anything has a tendency to dry out, wrap it in self-clinging plastic film. Put out the nibblers at the last moment. If you're making a cold wine cup do it in the early afternoon to give it time to mellow. Rice or pasta can be cooked early and reheated by plunging into hot water for 5 minutes if necessary.

Set out the china, glass and cutlery (don't forget to leave room for last-minute serving dishes). Try to arrange your buffet so that you achieve a flow of traffic round the room. Put out *plenty* of ash trays; put out some of the cigarettes, but keep a couple of packets in reserve for late-night desperation. Make sure your record-player and speakers are all functioning properly. Make a note of local all-night taxi services and put it near the phone. Leave yourself time to have half an hour's relaxation – even if it's in the bath.

Festive Cookery

Roast turkey

To help you calculate what size turkey you need, use this chart:

Turkey (oven-ready weight)		Servings
3–4 kg	(6–8 lb)	6–10
4–6 kg	(8–12 lb)	10–20
7–8 kg	(14–16 lb)	20–40

It is useful to know that a 5 kg (10 lb) turkey yields about 1 kg 350 g (2 lb 12 oz) white meat and about the same amount of dark meat. As a straight roast meal, with trimmings, this will serve 8, plus a further 4 servings as cold cuts and should leave you enough for a réchauffé dish as well.

If your turkey is frozen, make sure it arrives in good time. Remove it from the container, cover with muslin and leave it to thaw, preferably in the refrigerator, for 2–3 days. If refrigerator space is not available store in the coldest possible place.

To prepare the bird for the oven, first remove the giblets and use them to make a stock for the gravy. Wipe the turkey inside, then put in the stuffing. Most people use 2 kinds of stuffing in a turkey, 1 at the neck end and 1 at the vent. Allow about 225 g (½ lb) stuffing to each 2½ kg (5 lb) of turkey; do not stuff too tightly. Brush the skin with melted butter or dripping and season with salt, pepper and lemon juice. Either put it in a roasting tin and cover with foil or use plastic film roasting wrap or bag.

Approximate cooking times for the quick oven method using foil wrap, at 230°C. (450°F.) mark 8 are:

3–4 kg	(6–8 lb)	2½ hours
4–5 kg	(8–10 lb)	2½–2¾ hours
5–6 kg	(10–12 lb)	2 hours 50 minutes
6–7 kg	(12–14 lb)	3 hours
7–8 kg	(14–16 lb)	3–3¼ hours
8–9 kg	(16–18 lb)	3¼–3½ hours

If wished, open the foil for the last 30 minutes and cover the bird with rinded bacon rashers. Turn the bird about half-way through the cooking time so that it cooks evenly.

To check if the turkey is cooked, pierce the deepest part of the thigh with a skewer. If the juices are colourless, the bird is ready; if tinged pink, cook it a little longer. Calculate the cooking time to have the bird ready 30 minutes before serving. When ready, lower the oven temperature and keep the bird warm.

If you wish to use the slow oven method, don't wrap the bird in foil, but if it just about fills the oven it is wise to protect the legs and breast. Approximate cooking times for this method at 170°C. (325°F.) mark 3 are:

3–4 kg	(6–8 lb)	3–3½ hours
4–5 kg	(8–10 lb)	3½–3¾ hours
5–6 kg	(10–12 lb)	3¾–4 hours
6–7 kg	(12–14 lb)	4–4¼ hours
7–8 kg	(14–16 lb)	4¼–4½ hours
8–9 kg	(16–18 lb)	4½–4 hours 50 minutes

A tasty risotto makes a change on Boxing Day

Celery stuffing

100–125 g (4 oz) onions, skinned and finely chopped
2–3 celery sticks, scrubbed and finely diced
50 g (2 oz) butter
100–125 g (4 oz) cooking apple, peeled and cored
175 g (6 oz) fresh white breadcrumbs
juice and finely grated rind of 1 small lemon
10 ml spoon (2 level tsps) dried sage
salt and freshly ground black pepper
3 × 15 ml spoons (3 tbsps) concentrated giblet stock

Fry the onion and celery in the butter until transparent. Finely dice the apple, add to the pan and fry a little longer. Stir in the breadcrumbs with the lemon rind, 15 ml spoon (1 tbsp) lemon juice and sage. Season well. Bind together with the giblet stock.

Nut stuffing

50 g (2 oz) shelled walnuts
25 g (1 oz) cashew nuts
25 g (1 oz) shelled Brazil nuts
50 g (2 oz) butter
2 small onions, skinned and finely chopped
100–125 g (¼ lb) mushrooms, wiped and finely chopped
pinch of dried herbs
15 ml spoon (1 tbsp) chopped parsley
175 g (6 oz) fresh white breadcrumbs
1 large egg, beaten
giblet stock to moisten, optional
salt and freshly ground black pepper

Finely chop the nuts. Melt the butter and sauté the onion for 5 minutes until soft but not coloured. Add the finely chopped mushrooms and sauté for a further 5 minutes.
Toss together the nuts, herbs and breadcrumbs. Stir in the mushroom mixture with the beaten egg and, if necessary, moisten with stock. Season to taste.

Mushroom and bacon stuffing

175 g (6 oz) fresh white breadcrumbs
15 ml spoon (1 tbsp) chopped parsley
2·5 ml spoon (½ level tsp) dried thyme
1 clove of garlic, skinned and crushed
50 g (2 oz) butter
100–125 g (4 oz) onions, skinned and chopped
100–125 g (¼ lb) streaky bacon rashers, rinded and chopped
100–125 g (¼ lb) mushrooms, wiped and chopped
salt and freshly ground black pepper
egg yolk
giblet stock (optional)

In a mixing bowl, mix together the breadcrumbs, parsley, thyme and garlic.
Melt the 50 g (2 oz) butter in a frying pan and fry the onion until soft but not coloured. Stir in the bacon, cook for a further 3–4 minutes, then add the mushrooms and mix well. Combine with the breadcrumb mixture. Season well and bind the ingredients together with egg yolk and a little stock if necessary.

Cranberry sauce

175 g (6 oz) sugar
150 ml (¼ pint) water
225 g (½ lb) fresh cranberries, washed or frozen cranberries, thawed
a little sherry

Gently heat the sugar with the water in a pan until the sugar dissolves. Add the cranberries and cook uncovered over a medium heat for about 10 minutes; allow to cool. Add sherry before serving.

Cranberry and bacon balls

makes 16–20

175 g (6 oz) onion, skinned and
    finely chopped
100–125 g (4 oz) streaky bacon,
    rinded and chopped
25 g (1 oz) butter
100–125 g (4 oz) fresh
    cranberries, washed
50 g (2 oz) shredded suet
5 ml (1 level tsp) dried thyme
finely grated rind of 1 orange
175 g (6 oz) fresh white
    breadcrumbs
5 ml (1 level tsp) salt
freshly ground black pepper
1 large egg, beaten
orange juice

Fry the onion and bacon in the
butter until tender. Add the cranberries and cook until the cranberries 'pop'. Cool a little, then
add the suet, thyme, orange rind
and breadcrumbs. Fork through
to blend evenly; adjust the seasoning. Stir in the egg and
enough orange juice to moisten.
Form the mixture into balls.
Heat some lard or dripping to give
0·5 cm (¼-in.) depth in a baking
tin and cook the stuffing balls at
200°C. (400°F.) mark 6 for about
20 minutes.

Turkey risotto

serves 4

175 g (6 oz) onion, skinned and
    finely chopped
25 g (1 oz) butter
100–125 g (¼ lb) lean bacon
    rashers, rinded and diced
225 g (8 oz) cooked turkey meat,
    diced
100–125 g (¼ lb) button
    mushrooms, wiped and sliced
1 small green pepper (capsicum),
    seeded and sliced
225 g (8 oz) long grain rice
celery salt
freshly ground black pepper
4 × 15 ml spoons (4 tbsps) white
    wine
550 ml (1 pint) turkey stock
tomato wedges for garnish

Fry the onion in the butter until
tender, add the bacon and cook a
little longer.
Add the cooked, diced turkey,
mushrooms, pepper, rice and seasonings, stir well and pour in the
wine and stock.
Bring this mixture to the boil,
stirring gently, and turn into a
casserole. Cover tightly and cook
in the oven at 170°C. (325°F.)
mark 3 for about 35 minutes,

until the stock is absorbed and the
rice is fluffy and tender.
Turn on to a hot serving dish and
serve garnished with tomato
wedges.

Turkey cranberry salad

serves 4

2 × 15 ml spoons (6 level tsps)
    powdered gelatine
150 ml (¼ pint) water
4 × 15 ml spoons (4 tbsps) lemon
    juice
198-g (7-oz) can whole berry
    cranberry sauce
300 ml (½ pint) turkey stock
½ × 1·25 ml (¼ tsp) Tabasco
    sauce
5 × 15 ml spoons (5 level tbsps)
    lemon mayonnaise
10 ml spoon (2 tsps) finely chopped
    onion
2–3 sticks celery, scrubbed and
    chopped
1 small green pepper (capsicum),
    seeded and diced
1 red-skinned eating apple, diced
350 g (12 oz) cooked turkey, diced

Sprinkle 15 ml spoon (3 level
tsps) gelatine over the water in a
bowl and dissolve it over a pan of
hot water. Add 2 × 15 ml spoons
(2 tbsps) lemon juice and the
cranberry sauce. Stir thoroughly.
Pour into a 900 ml (1½-pint)
mould and leave to set.
Place the turkey stock in a saucepan, sprinkle the remaining
gelatine over the surface, dissolve
over a low heat but do not boil.
Add the Tabasco sauce and
remaining lemon juice, pour into
a bowl and leave to cool. Gradually whisk in the mayonnaise.
When beginning to set, fold in the
onion, celery, pepper, apple and
turkey. Adjust seasoning. Spoon
the turkey mixture on to the cranberry layer and leave to set.
To serve, unmould and accom-
pany by coleslaw and French
bread.

Turkey broth

serves 4

175 g (6 oz) carrot, scraped and
    coarsely grated
175 g (6 oz) onion, skinned and
    finely chopped
25 g (1 oz) butter
900 ml (1½ pints) strong turkey
    stock
1 bay leaf
50 g (2 oz) small pasta
50 g (2 oz) fresh celery leaves,
    washed and roughly chopped

Fry the carrot and onion in the
butter until soft – about 10

minutes. Pour in the stock and
add the bay leaf and pasta. Bring
to the boil, cover and simmer for
30 minutes. Discard the bay leaf,
adjust seasoning and add the celery leaves.
Served with grated cheese and
hunks of bread, this is almost a
meal in itself.

Roast gammon

serves 10

2 kg (4 lb) gammon joint
100–125 g (4 oz) Demerara sugar
cloves
2 × 15 ml spoons (2 tbsps) honey
2 × 15 ml spoons (2 tbsps) orange
    juice
glacé cherries, canned apricots,
    drained or sliced oranges

Soak the gammon for several
hours in cold water, then drain.
To calculate the cooking time,
allow 20–25 minutes per ½ kg
(per lb) and 20 minutes over.
Place the joint in a pan, skin side
down, cover with water and add
half the sugar. Bring slowly to the
boil and remove the scum.
Reduce the heat and simmer,
covered, for half the calculated
cooking time. Top up with extra
boiling water when necessary.
Drain the joint, carefully strip off
the rind and score the fat into
squares, then stud with cloves.
Blend the remaining sugar,
honey and orange juice and
spread over the joint. Place it in a
roasting tin and roast at 180°C.

(350°F.) mark 4 for the rest of the
cooking time. Baste two or three
times during cooking and, 20
minutes before the end of the
cooking time, raise the temperature to 220C. (425°F.) mark 7.
Serve hot; garnish with apricot
halves and glacé cherries impaled
on cocktail sticks or with slices of
orange.

Christmas pudding

serves 6–8

175 g (6 oz) plain flour
5 ml spoon (1 level tsp) mixed spice
2·5 ml spoon (½ level tsp) grated
    nutmeg
100–125 g (4 oz) apple, peeled and
    cored
75 g (3 oz) fresh white
    breadcrumbs
100–125 g (4 oz) shredded suet
100–125 g (4 oz) stoned raisins,
    chopped
225 g (8 oz) currants, cleaned
225 g (8 oz) sultanas, cleaned
75 g (3 oz) Demerara sugar
grated rind of 1 lemon
grated rind of 1 orange
2 eggs, beaten
200 ml (⅓ pint) brown ale

Grease a 1·1 litre (2 pint) pudding
basin. Sift togther the flour,
mixed spice and nutmeg. Dice
the apple and add to the flour,
along with the breadcrumbs,
suet, dried fruit, sugar, lemon and
orange rind. Mix the ingredients
well. Gradually stir in the beaten
eggs and ale and stir thoroughly.

Traditional Christmas pudding with a fluffy brandy flavoured sauce

If possible, leave to stand over-night.

Turn the mixture into the pre-pared basin, then cover with greased greaseproof paper and kitchen foil or a pudding cloth. Tie the foil or cloth firmly in place with string.

Either place the bowl in a pan with water half-way up the sides and, after bringing to the boil, reduce heat and boil gently for about 6 hours, or place in a steamer and cook for 8 hours. A piece of lemon in the water will prevent discoloration of the pan. Top up with more boiling water at intervals.

To store, leave the greaseproof paper in position, but re-wrap with fresh foil or pudding cloth. On the day, reboil for about 3 hours.

Easy Christmas pudding
makes 2

100–125 g (4 oz) plain flour
5 ml spoon (1 level tsp) cinnamon
2·5 ml spoon (½ level tsp) grated nutmeg
100–125 g (4 oz) fresh white breadcrumbs
50 g (2 oz) soft brown sugar
grated rind of 1 lemon
100–125 g (4 oz) glacé cherries, chopped
50 g (2 oz) nibbed almonds
1 kg 350 g (3 lb) ready-made mincemeat
3 eggs, beaten

Grease 2 × 600 ml (2 × 1-pint) pudding basins and place a circle of greaseproof paper in the bases. Sift together the flour, cinnamon and nutmeg into a large bowl. Add the breadcrumbs, sugar, lemon rind, cherries and almonds, mix together and stir in the mincemeat and eggs. Mix the ingredients well together with a wooden spoon.

Divide the mixture evenly be-tween the 2 basins. Cover tightly with greased greaseproof paper and kitchen foil or pudding cloths. Tie the foil or cloths firmly in place with string.

Place in a saucepan with water half-way up, bring to the boil, reduce heat and simmer for about 4¾ hours. Top up with boiling water when necessary.

To store, leave greaseproof paper in position but cover with fresh foil or pudding cloths.

To reheat, boil gently for about 2 hours.

Home-made mincemeat, with almonds and a little brandy, makes the best mince pies

Fluffy sauce

50 g (2 oz) butter
100–125 g (4 oz) icing sugar, sifted
2 eggs, separated
2 × 15 ml spoons (2 tbsps) brandy
142 ml (¼ pint) double cream

Cream together the butter and icing sugar. Beat in the egg yolks and then gradually beat in the brandy. Add the double cream. Place in a double saucepan and cook over a gentle heat until the mixture is the consistency of thick custard. Beat the egg whites until stiff but not dry. Pour the custard mixture on to the egg whites, whisking all the time. Return to the double pan to keep warm. Stir before serving.

Rum butter

225 g (8 oz) unsalted butter
100–125 g (4 oz) soft light brown sugar
2–3 × 15 ml spoons (2–3 tbsps) rum
icing sugar

Cream the butter in a bowl with a wooden spoon and beat in the sugar.

When the mixture is soft, slowly beat in the rum to taste. Pile into the bowl in which it is to be served and chill.

Just before serving, dredge with icing sugar.

Mincemeat
makes about 3 kg (6 lb)

350 g (12 oz) currants, cleaned
225 g (8 oz) sultanas, cleaned
350 g (12 oz) stoned raisins, cleaned
100–125 g (4 oz) cut mixed peel
350 g (¾ lb) firm, hard cooking apples, peeled and cored
450 g (1 lb) soft light brown or Demerara sugar
450 g (1 lb) shredded suet
5 ml spoon (1 level tsp) grated nutmeg
2·5 ml spoon (½ level tsp) powdered cinnamon or mace
grated rind and juice of 1 lemon
grated rind and juice of 1 small orange
200 ml (⅓ pint) brandy

Roughly chop the prepared fruit, peel and apples. Combine with the sugar, suet, spices, lemon and orange rind and juice and mix all ingredients together thoroughly. Cover the mincemeat and leave overnight.

Next day stir the mincemeat well and put into jars. Cover as for jam. Store in a cool, dry, well ven-tilated place and allow to mature for at least 2 weeks before using. *Note:* 25 g (1 oz) finely chopped sweet almonds may be added to each 450 g (1 lb) of mincemeat just before use.

Mince pies
makes 20

350 g (12 oz) shortcrust pastry – i.e. made with 350 g (12 oz) flour
350 g (¾ lb) mincemeat
icing sugar, sifted

Grease 20 × 6·5 cm (2½ in.) patty pans.

Roll out the pastry about 0·3 cm (⅛ in.) thick. Using a 7·5 cm (3 in.) fluted cutter, cut out 20 rounds for the base and then cut 20 smaller rounds with a 6·5 cm (2½ in.) fluted cutter, re-rolling as necessary.

Line the patty tins with the larger rounds and two-thirds fill with mincemeat, using a teaspoon. Damp the edges of the smaller rounds and place in position. Make a small slit in the top of each and bake towards the top of

No need to pipe elaborate decorations on the Christmas cake – icing 'snow' is just as pretty

Bake in the lower part of the oven at 150°C. (300°F.) mark 2 for about 3½ hours. Cool on a wire rack. If wished, baste with a little more brandy before storing. Wrap in foil or put in an airtight tin and store in a cool, dry place. Decorate not more than 1 week before Christmas.

Snowman cake

225 g (8 oz) butter or margarine
225 g (8 oz) caster sugar
4 large eggs
225 (8 oz) self-raising flour
25 g (1 oz) cocoa
2 × 15 ml spoons (2 tbsps) hot water

For decoration:
2 egg whites
500 g (1 lb 2 oz) icing sugar, sifted
15 ml spoon (1 tbsp) glycerine
5 ml spoon (1 tsp) lemon juice
100–125 g (4 oz) bought marzipan
few drops red colouring
coloured sweets

Grease a 400-ml (¾-pint) and a 1·1 litre (2-pint) ovenproof pudding basin. Line the bases with greased greaseproof paper.
Cream the butter and sugar until light and fluffy, then beat in the eggs one at a time. Fold in the flour. Blend the cocoa with the hot water and stir into the mixture. Fill both basins two-thirds full and put them in the centre of the oven at 180°C. (350°F.) mark 4. The smaller one will take 40 to 45 minutes, the larger about one

he oven at 200°C. (400°F.) mark for about 20 minutes until light golden brown.
Serve pies warm or cold, lightly dusted with icing sugar. If preferred, the tops may be brushed with a little milk before baking, to glaze them.

Yule log pudding
Serves 6

25 g (1 oz) crystallized ginger
75 g (3 oz) glacé cherries
1–2 × 15 ml spoons (1–2 tbsp) brandy
25 g (1 oz) blanched almonds
550–600 ml (1 pint) custard
142 ml (¼ pint) double cream, whipped
1 egg white

Cut the ginger and cherries into small pieces and soak in the brandy for 30–60 minutes.
Chop the nuts roughly. Put the custard into the freezing compartment of the refrigerator, set at its coldest, or a home freezer and leave until half frozen.
Add the fruit, nuts and whipped cream to the custard. Stiffly beat the egg white, fold it into the mixture and freeze until almost set, then beat well.

Pour the mixture into a wetted loaf tin and freeze hard. Turn out, cut into slices and decorate.

Christmas cake

225 g (8 oz) stoned raisins
225 g (8 oz) sultanas
225 g (8 oz) currants
100 g (4 oz) chopped mixed peel
125 g (4 oz) ground almonds
125 g (4 oz) glacé cherries, quartered
225 g (8 oz) plain flour
5 ml spoon (1 level tsp) mixed spice
pinch of salt
225 g (8 oz) butter
175 g (6 oz) soft light brown sugar
4 standard eggs
1½ × 15 ml spoons (1½ tbsps) brandy

Grease and line a 20·5 cm (8 in.) round cake tin.
Check the raisins to make sure all stones are removed; cut large ones in half. Clean the sultanas and currants. Mix the raisins, sultanas, currants, peel, almonds and cherries together.
Sift the flour, spice and salt. Cream the butter until soft, add the sugar and beat until light and fluffy. Beat in the eggs one at a time. Fold in the dry ingredients,

adding the fruit and brandy last. Turn the mixture into the prepared tin. Stand it in a larger tin or line the outside with brown paper. Place on a baking sheet lined with brown paper.

Snowman cake for the children

hour and 15 minutes. Turn out and cool on a wire rack. Brush the loose crumbs off both cakes. Place larger cake on a silver board.

Roughly beat the egg whites in a basin, beat in the icing sugar a little at a time with a wooden spoon. Add the glycerine and lemon juice. The icing should be soft but firm enough to stand in peaks. Using a palette knife, spread the icing over the cake to cover completely and rough up into soft peaks. Place the small cake on top and cover with icing in the same way. Leave to set. Meanwhile, add a few drops of colouring to the marzipan, roll out fairly thinly into a circle and shape into a brimmed hat. When the icing is nearly set, place the hat in position and put the coloured sweets in place to make the eyes, nose and buttons. When the icing is firmly set, secure a coloured ribbon round the snowman's neck to make a scarf.

Marzipan and raisin truffles
makes about 24

225 g (8 oz) plain (dark) chocolate
175 g (6 oz) seedless raisins
15 ml spoon (1 tbsp) rum or coffee
  liqueur
225 g (8 oz) ready-made marzipan
5 ml (1 tsp) coffee essence
75 g (3 oz) chocolate vermicelli
  drinking chocolate powder

Melt half the chocolate in a basin over hot water. Add the raisins and rum or liqueur. Blend thoroughly and, when firm enough, shape into 24 small balls. Chill.

Knead the marzipan until pliable, and work in the coffee essence. Roll out to about 0·5 cm (¼ in) thick and stamp out 24 rounds, using a 5 cm (2 in.) plain cutter. Shape the marzipan round the chocolate and raisins to form balls.

Melt the remaining chocolate in a basin small enough to give a good depth, over hot water. Dip each ball in the chocolate, drain a little, then coat half of them with chocolate vermicelli. Leave the rest to dry on non-stick paper, then roll them in drinking chocolate powder.

Serve in small paper cases.

Christmas Preserves

After Christmas, some special preserves will add to the pleasure of meals. These make good presents, too, if made in attractive jars.

Spiced orange rings

8 thin-skinned oranges
900 ml (1½ pints) water
700 g (1½ lb) sugar
300 ml (½ pint) white distilled
  vinegar
7 g (¼ oz) whole cloves
1½ sticks cinnamon
6 blades of mace

Wipe the oranges, cut into 0·5 cm (¼ in.) slices and discard the pips. Place the sliced oranges in a pan, cover with water, cover the pan and simmer the contents for about 40 minutes, or until the peel is soft. Make a syrup by dissolving the sugar in the vinegar, add the spices and boil for 3–4 minutes.

Drain the oranges, place in a shallow pan and cover with vinegar syrup. Simmer, covered, for 30–40 minutes, until the orange slices look clear. Remove from heat and leave in the syrup for 24 hours.

Drain the orange rings and pack them into sterilized jars. Cover the fruit with the syrup. Do not seal at once, but keep topping up with syrup for the next 3–4 days; then cover as for jam.

Leave to mature if possible for at least 6 weeks.

Brandied peaches

½ kg (1 lb) fresh peaches
225 g (8 oz) sugar
approx. 150 ml (¼ pint) brandy or
  Cointreau

Skin the peaches by plunging them into boiling water, then gently peeling off the skins. Halve the peaches and remove the stones. Make a light syrup by dissolving 100–125 g (4 oz) sugar in 300 ml (½ pint) water and poach the peaches gently for 4–5 minutes. Remove from the heat, drain and cool, then arrange the fruit in small jars.

Add the remaining sugar to the syrup and dissolve it slowly. Bring to the boil and boil to

Christmas preserves – rich or spicy – for cold meats

110°C. (230°F.); allow to cool. Add an equal quantity of brandy or Cointreau to the syrup, pour over the peaches and seal with preserving skin.

Spiced crab apples

3 kg (6 lb) crab apples
900 ml (1½ pints) water
2-3 strips lemon peel
450 g (1 lb) sugar
400 ml (¾ pint) wine vinegar
1 stick cinnamon
1-2 whole cloves
3 peppercorns

Wash and trim the crab apples, then simmer in the water with the lemon peel until just tender; remove from the heat.

Place the sugar and vinegar in a pan and add 900 ml (1½ pints) of the liquid from the fruit. Tie the spices in muslin and add to the liquid. Heat gently to dissolve the sugar, then bring to the boil and boil for 1 minute. Remove the pan from the heat and add the crab apples. Simmer gently until the syrup has reduced to a coating consistency – 30 to 40 minutes. Remove the spices after 30 minutes. Place the fruit in small jars, cover with syrup and seal with preserving skin.

Spiced pears

400 g (14 oz) sugar
20 g (¾ oz) salt
1·1 litre (2 pints) water
3 kg (6 lb) small, hard pears,
  peeled and cored
1·1 litre (2 pints) white vinegar
2 sticks cinnamon
7 g (¼ oz) whole cloves

Dissolve 50 g (2 oz) of the sugar and the salt in the water and bring to the boil. Cut the pears into quarters and add to the boiling water; remove the pan from the heat, cover and allow to cool.

Boil together the vinegar, remaining sugar and spices. Remove the pears from the water and drain, then place them in the syrup and bring to the boil. Take from the heat, allow to cool and bring back to the boil. Repeat this process 3 times.

Finally allow to cool and place the pears in small sterilized jars. Pour the syrup over them, retaining the surplus, but do not seal. Top up each day for the next few days, or until no more syrup is absorbed. Cover with preserving skin.

Brandied pineapple

822 g (1 lb 13 oz) can pineapple
  pieces
3 cloves
5 cm (2 in.) stick cinnamon
150 ml (¼ pint) brandy or Kirsch

Drain the juice from the pineapple and put it into a saucepan. Add the cloves and cinnamon and simmer gently until of a syrupy consistency. Add the pineapple pieces and simmer for a further 10 minutes. Remove from the heat and add the brandy or Kirsch. Leave to cool.

Pack the fruit in a wide-necked bottle, pour in the syrup and seal with preserving skin.

EASTER

Warm hot cross buns on Good Friday,
Easter bread for Sunday breakfast,
simnel cake and Easter biscuits for
tea. In between, all children love a
chocolate egg.

Hot cross buns

makes 12

450 g (1 lb) plain strong flour
*25 g (1 oz) fresh baker's yeast or
   15 ml spoon (1 level tbsp) dried
   yeast*
*5 ml spoon (1 level tsp) caster
   sugar*
150 ml (¼ pint) milk
90 ml (¼ pint less 4 tbsps) water
5 ml spoon (1 level tsp) salt
*2·5 ml spoon (½ level tsp) each
   mixed spice, powdered
   cinnamon, grated nutmeg*
50 g (2 oz) caster sugar
*50 g (2 oz) butter, melted and cool
   but not firm*
1 egg, beaten
125 g (4 oz) currants
25 g (1 oz) chopped mixed peel

For glaze:
2 × 15 ml spoons (2 tbsps) milk
2 × 15 ml spoons (2 tbsps) water
40 g (1½ oz) caster sugar

Flour 2 baking sheets. Place 125 g (4 oz) of the measured flour in a large mixing bowl. Add the yeast and caster sugar. Warm the milk and water to about 43°C. (110°F.), add to the flour and mix well. Set aside in a warm place until frothy – about 20 minutes for fresh yeast, 30 minutes for dried yeast.

Sift together the remaining flour, the salt, spices and 50 g (2 oz) sugar. Stir the butter and egg into the frothy yeast mixture, add the spiced flour, fruit and peel, then mix. The dough should be fairly soft.

Turn it out on to a lightly floured board and knead until smooth. Place the dough in a lightly greased polythene bag, close and leave at room temperature until doubled in size – about 1–1½ hours. Turn risen dough on to a floured surface and knock out the air bubbles. Knead again.

Divide the dough into 12 pieces and shape into buns. Press down hard at first on the table surface, then ease up as you turn and shape the buns. Arrange the buns well apart on the floured baking sheets, place inside lightly greased polythene bags, close and allow to rise at room temperature for 45 minutes (only 30 minutes if the dough has had an initial rising). Make quick slashes with a very sharp knife, just cutting the surface of the bun in the shape of a cross.

Bake just above the centre of the oven at 190°C. (375°F.) mark 5 for 15–20 minutes. Brush the hot buns twice with glaze. Leave to cool.

Buy an Easter egg mould and make your own chocolate eggs

Easter egg cake

90 ml (3½ fl oz) corn oil
*juice of ½ lemon made up to 90 ml
   (3½ fl oz) with water*
2 eggs, separated
150 g (5 oz) plain flour
25 g (1 oz) cornflour
*10 ml spoon (2 level tsps) baking
   powder*
150 g (5 oz) caster sugar
grated rind of 1 lemon

For decorating:
jam or lemon curd
225 g (8 oz) almond paste
175 g (6 oz) glacé icing, tinted
ribbon and sugar flowers
chocolate glacé icing
chicks or small eggs, optional

Grease an oblong tin measuring 23 cm by 12·5 cm by 7·5 cm (9 in by 5 in by 3 in).

Whisk together the corn oil, lemon juice and the egg yolks. Sift together the dry ingredients. Add to the liquid, with the grated lemon rind, then beat to give a smooth, slack batter. Beat the egg whites stiffly and fold in. Turn the mixture into the tin and bake in the oven at 190°C. (375°F.) mark 5 for 50 minutes. Cool on a wire rack. Use a sharp knife to cut it into the shape of an egg. Slice it through lengthwise and sandwich with jam or curd. Brush the outside with sieved jam and cover with rolled out almond paste, moulding it into shape with your hands.

Leave on a wire rack to dry overnight, then coat with tinted glacé icing. When this is completely dry and set, place the cake on a board and tie a ribbon round it. Decorate with sugar flowers, pipe a nest of chocolate glacé icing and add the chicks or eggs.

Simnel cake

*450 g (1 lb) ready-made almond
   paste*
225 g (8 oz) plain flour
pinch of salt
*2·5 ml spoon (½ level tsp) grated
   nutmeg*
*2·5 ml spoon (½ level tsp)
   powdered cinnamon*
225 g (8 oz) currants, cleaned
125 g (4 oz) sultanas, cleaned
75 g (3 oz) chopped mixed peel
*100 g (4 oz) glacé cherries,
   quartered*
175 g (6 oz) butter
175 g (6 oz) caster sugar
3 eggs
milk to mix, if required
1 egg white

Grease and line an 18 cm (7-in.) round cake tin.

Roll out one-third of the almond paste into a round slightly smaller than the cake tin.

Sift together the flour, salt and spices. Mix together all the fruit. Cream the butter and sugar until pale and fluffy and beat in each egg separately. Fold in the flour, adding a little milk if necessary to give a dropping consistency. Fold in the fruit.

Put half the mixture into the prepared tin and place the round of almond paste on top. Cover with the rest of the mixture, spreading it evenly. Bake in the oven at 150°C. (300°F.) mark 2 for 2½–3 hours, until the cake is a rich brown and firm to the touch. Cool on a wire rack. It is not possible to test this cake with a skewer as the almond paste remains soft and may give a false impression. From the remaining almond paste, shape 11 small balls, then cut the rest into a round to fit the top of the cake. Brush the top surface of the cake with egg white, place the almond paste in position and smooth it slightly with a rolling pin. Pinch the edges into scallops with finger and thumb. Score the surface into a lattice with a knife, brush with egg white, arrange the almond paste balls round the top of the cake and brush these with egg white.

Put under a moderate grill until light golden brown.

Easter biscuits

makes 15–20

75 g (3 oz) butter or margarine
65 g (2½ oz) caster sugar
1 egg, separated
175 g (6 oz) self-raising flour
pinch of salt
40 g (1½ oz) currants
15 g (½ oz) chopped mixed peel
*1–2 × 15 ml spoons (1–2 tbsps)
   milk or brandy*
little caster sugar

Grease 2 baking sheets.

Cream the butter and sugar and beat in the egg yolk. Sift the flour with the salt and fold into the creamed mixture, with the currants and finely chopped mixed peel. Add enough milk to give a fairly soft dough, cover and leave in a cool place to become firm.

Knead lightly on a floured board and roll out to about 0·5 cm (¼ in.) thick. Cut into rounds, using a 6·5-cm (2½-in.) fluted cutter. Put on the baking sheets, well spaced, and cook in the oven at 200°C. (400°F.) mark 6 for about 20 minutes, until lightly coloured. After 10 minutes baking, brush the biscuits with egg white and sprinkle with sugar. Cool on a wire rack.

Easter bread

25 g (1 oz) yeast
250 ml (scant ½ pint) milk
*450 g (1 lb) plain strong bread
   flour*
4 egg yolks
175 g (6 oz) caster sugar
50 g (2 oz) butter, melted
*115 g (4½ oz) candied fruit,
   chopped*

dissolve the yeast in the milk, mix with half the flour and leave in a warm place to start to work. Beat the egg yolks and sugar together and when the dough has risen, mix them in, with the melted butter. Add the remaining flour and the candied fruit.

Beat the mixture well, leave to rise again and form it into 2 plaited loaves. Place on a baking sheet, prove for 20–30 minutes and bake at 200°C. (400°F.) mark until well risen and browned – about 30 minutes.

Christenings

Lunch Menu
serves 25

Pâté fleurons
Sardine pyramids
Cheese olives
Hare terrine
Cold roast capon
Salmon rice salad
Tossed mixed salad
Coffee cream flan
Banana and mandarin chartreuse
Christening cake

Pâté fleurons
makes about 50

225 g (8 oz) bought puff pastry, thawed
beaten egg to glaze

For filling:
120 g (4¼-oz) tube liver pâté
50 g (2 oz) butter

Roll out the pastry thinly and using a 4-cm (1½-in.) fluted round cutter, stamp out as many rounds as possible.
Brush with beaten egg and fold over into semi-circles. Place on a baking tray and leave in a cool place for 30 minutes. Brush with beaten egg and bake in the oven at 200°C. (400°F.) mark 6 for about 15 minutes.
With a sharp knife, cut almost through the pastry to allow steam to escape. Leave to cool on a wire rack.

Combine the liver pâté and butter and beat well, or use an electric blender. Spoon the pâté into a forcing bag fitted with a No. 8 star icing nozzle. Pipe in a shell shape down the centre of each fleuron.

Cheese olives
makes 30

225 g (8 oz) full fat soft cream cheese
15 stuffed olives
chopped walnuts

Cream the cheese until well blended.
Using about 10 ml spoon (1 heaped tsp) cheese for each, roll the cheese round the olives to enclose them completely. Lightly toss in chopped walnuts. Chill for about 1 hour. Just before serving, cut in half with a sharp knife.

Hare terrine

1 hare, boned and filleted
1 medium-sized carrot, scraped and grated
1 medium-sized onion, skinned and grated
¾ kg (1½ lb) pork sausage meat
4 egg yolks
300 g (11 oz) raisins
4 × 15 ml spoons (4 tbsps) stock
salt and pepper
bacon rashers, rinded

Reserve the best pieces of hare and mince the remainder. Mix the minced hare with the carrot, onion, sausage meat, egg yolks, raisins, stock and seasonings. Line a terrine with overlapping bacon rashers and fill with alternate layers of sausage mixture and hare fillets. Wrap the bacon over the top to cover and bake in the oven at 180°C. (350°F.) mark 4 for about 2½ hours. Pour off most of the fat and leave to cool. Serve thickly sliced.

Salmon rice salad
make 2

350 g (12 oz) long grain rice
2 × 226-g (2 × 8-oz) cans salmon
½ kg (1 lb) tomatoes, skinned and chopped
8 × 15 spoons (8 tbsps) finely chopped chives
5 × 15 ml spoons (5 tbsps) double cream
12 × 15 ml spoons (12 tbsps) mayonnaise
10 ml spoon (2 level tsp) celery seeds
grated rind of 2 lemons
salt and pepper
lettuce and radishes

Coffee cream and nuts for a delicious flan

Cook the rice in boiling salted water and allow to cool. Drain the salmon, remove the skin and bones and flake the fish; add the salmon, tomatoes and chives to the rice. Whip the cream, fold into the mayonnaise and add the celery seeds, with the lemon rind and seasoning. Fold in the rice mixture and press into a 2·3 litre (4-pint) ring mould. When set, turn out on to a plate lined with lettuce and garnish with sliced radishes.

Coffee cream flan
makes 3

225 g (8 oz) digestive biscuits
75 g (3 oz) butter, melted
2 eggs, separated
75 g (3 oz) caster sugar
1½–2 × 15 ml spoons (1½–2 level tbsps) instant coffee
4 × 15 ml spoons (4 tbsps) water
2 × 15 ml spoons (2 tbsps) Tia Maria
10 ml spoon (2 level tbsps) powdered gelatine

142 ml (¼ pint) double cream
15 ml spoon (1 tbsp) milk
36 hazelnuts, toasted and skinned

Crush the digestive biscuits, blend with the melted butter and use them to line a 25·5 cm (10-in.) French fluted loose-bottomed flan case or a 20·5 cm (8-in.) deeper fluted flan ring placed on a plate. Press crumbs well on to the base and up the sides. Chill the flan case.
Whisk the egg yolks and sugar in a deep bowl until thick and creamy. Blend together the instant coffee, 2 × 15 ml spoons (2 tbsps) water and the liqueur and gradually whisk into the egg mixture.
Dissolve the gelatine in the remaining 2 × 15 ml spoons (2 tbsps) water, in a basin held over a pan of hot water, and add to the coffee mixture. Mix thoroughly and leave in a cool place to set. When this is beginning to set, fold in the stiffly whisked egg

The cake is the centre of the Christening meal

Tasty snacks to serve with pre-lunch drinks

whites. Turn into the flan case and chill.

Before serving, whisk together the cream and milk until light and just thick enough to pipe. Pipe 12 whirls of cream round the flan edge and top each with three toasted hazelnuts.

Banana and mandarin chartreuse

2 lemon jelly tablets
1 orange jelly tablet
juice of 1 orange
juice of 1 lemon
2 × 312-g (2 × 11-oz) cans
mandarin oranges
2–3 bananas
lemon juice

Place the broken up jelly tablets in a large bowl. Pour over 550 ml (1 pint) boiling water. Stir until dissolved.

Pour the fruit juices into a 1·1 litre (2-pint) measuring jug, add syrup from the mandarins and make up to 700 ml (1¼ pints) with cold water. Strain and add to the hot liquid. Spoon enough jelly into a 1·7 litre (3 pint) fancy jelly mould to cover the base; allow to set.

Slice the bananas thinly, dip them in lemon juice. If the mandarins are large, slice them horizontally. Dip the fruit in a little jelly and arrange banana and mandarins alternately in the base of the mould. Leave to set.

Cover the fruit with more jelly and leave to set, then coat the sides of the mould with jelly. To help it set quickly, rotate the mould at an angle over a shallow dish containing water with ice cubes added. Arrange orange and banana alternately round the sides; allow to set. Layer the sides and middle alternately with fruit and then jelly. Chill until firm for at least 2 hours.

To serve, unmould and serve with pouring cream.

Tea Menu
serves 20–25

Open sandwiches
Orange teabread
Almond gingerbread
Cup cakes
Coffee walnut gâteau
Christening cake

Open sandwiches

Danish rye bread, sold in a packet, makes a firm-to-handle base. The butter on the bread provides a useful anchor for the topping, so be generous. Choose both fillings and garnishes with an eye for colour.

Here is a selection of toppings:
Slices of tomato with a good-sized piece of crab, garnished with cottage cheese and black olives.
Slices of salami topped with stuffed olives and tomato slices.
Slices of hard-boiled egg and a sardine, with a few slivers of tomato and stuffed olive.
Luncheon meat topped with a spoonful of potato salad, a few rings of raw onion and slices of radish.
A slice of strong blue cheese, with rings of green pepper (capsicum) and a black olive on top.
A few prawns, with a slice or two of hard-boiled egg.
A slice of luncheon meat, garnished with tomato, cucumber, cottage cheese and a black olive.

Orange teabread
make 2

50 g (2 oz) butter
175 g (6 oz) caster sugar
1 egg, beaten
grated rind of ½ orange

2 × 15 ml spoons (2 tbsps) orange juice
2 × 15 ml spoons (2 tbsps) milk
225 g (8 oz) plain flour
5 × 2·5 ml spoons (2½ level tsps) baking powder
pinch of salt

Grease and bottom-line a 20·5 cm by 10·5 cm (8 in. by 4¼ in.) loaf tin (top measurements).
Beat the butter, add the sugar and beat again until well mixed. Gradually beat in the egg until smooth and creamy. Slowly add the orange rind and juice; don't worry if the mixture curdles. Lightly beat in the milk alternately with sifted flour, baking powder and salt.
Turn the mixture into the tin. Bake in the centre of the oven at 190°C. (375°F.) mark 5 for 40–50 minutes. Turn out and cool on a wire rack. Make 1–2 days before required and wrap in kitchen foil to store. Slice and spread with honey and cream cheese spread or butter.

Almond gingerbread

50 g (2 oz) flaked almonds
350 g (12 oz) plain flour
15 g (½ oz) ground ginger
25 g (1 oz) stem ginger, chopped
75 g (3 oz) lard
75 g (3 oz) soft light brown sugar
350 g (12 oz) golden syrup
100 g (4 fl oz) water
1 egg, beaten
3 × 2·5 ml spoons (1½ level tsps) bicarbonate of soda

Grease a 2·0 litre (3½-pint) plain ring mould. Sprinkle the almonds in the base. Sift together the flour and ginger, add the stem ginger.
Gently heat together the lard, sugar, syrup and half the water, making sure it does not boil. Stir the syrup into the flour, add the egg and beat well. Dissolve the bicarbonate of soda in the remaining water, pour into the mixture and stir thoroughly.
Bake at 170°C. (325°F.) mark 3 for about 50 minutes, until well risen and spongy to the touch. Turn out and cool on a wire rack, nut side uppermost.

Coffee walnut gâteau
make 3

For sponge cakes:
6 large eggs
175 g (6 oz) caster sugar
150 g (5 oz) plain flour
25 g (1 oz) cornflour
15 ml spoon (1 tbsp) glycerine

For crème au beurre:
3 egg yolks
125 g (4 oz) caster sugar
150 ml (¼ pint) milk
15 ml spoon (1 level tbsp) insta coffee
175–225 g (6–8 oz) butter
3 × 15 ml spoons (3 tbsps) coffe liqueur

For topping and decoration:
75 g (3 oz) walnuts, finely choppe
225 g (8 oz) icing sugar
5 ml (1 level tsp) instant coffee
2 × 15 ml (2 tbsps) hot water
sugar coffee beans

Grease 2 × 24 cm (2 × 9½-in sandwich tins, line the bases wit greaseproof paper and sprinkl with caster sugar.
Break the eggs into a deep bow Add the sugar and whisk with a electric mixer or rotary whis until the mixture is thick and pal and leaves a trail when the whis is lifted out.
Sift the flours twice, then tip ha the flour into the sieve and shak it on to the surface of the egg mi ture. Fold in quickly with a met spoon. Spoon glycerine in a thi stream over the surface, sieve the remaining flour and fold until no pockets of flour are lef Pour the mixture quickly into th cake tins. Bake in the oven 190°C. (375°F.) mark 5 for abou 30 minutes.
Meanwhile, whisk together th egg yolks and caster sugar unt light and creamy. Bring the mil and coffee to the boil. Pour th milk into the whisked sugar an yolks, stirring. Return to the pa and cook over a gentle heat, sti ring all the time until the mixtur thickens. Remove from the he and cool, stirring occasionall Beat the butter until light an creamy. Pour the cold coffe sauce in a thin stream into th butter, beating all the time. Sto in a cool (not cold) place unt required.
Sprinkle the sponges with coffe liqueur. Sandwich with one thi of the coffee crème au beurr Coat the sides with another third Press the chopped walnuts on t the sides of the cake with a smal palette knife. Spoon the remain ing crème au beurre into a forcin bag fitted with a medium size sta vegetable nozzle. Pipe stars roun the edge, touching each other.
For the glacé icing, beat togethe the icing sugar and coffe blended with 2 × 15 ml spoons (tbsps) hot water. Add a little mor

water if necessary to give a thick, flowing consistency. Pour into the centre of the cake, tilting the plate slightly so that the top is evenly coated. Before the icing sets, burst air bubbles with a fine skewer or pin. Decorate edge of the cake with sugar coffee beans.

Cup cakes

125 g (4 oz) butter or margarine
125 g (4 oz) caster sugar
2 eggs
125 g (4 oz) self-raising flour
grated rind of 1 small orange

For decoration:
140 (4½ oz) chocolate dots
40 g (1½ oz) butter
4 × 15 ml spoons (4 tbsps) top of the milk
75 g (3 oz) icing sugar, sifted
butter cream

Line about 30 deep bun pans with paper cases – use 2 cases to stop over-browning.
Cream together the fat and sugar until light and fluffy. Beat in the eggs a little at a time. Sift the flour and lightly beat it in with the orange rind. Half fill each of the paper cases with the mixture and bake just above the centre of the oven at 190°C. (375°F.) mark 5 for about 12 minutes, until well risen and golden. Cool on a wire rack and remove the second paper case.
Melt the chocolate, butter and milk in a small bowl over hot water. Beat in the icing sugar. As the mixture cools and thickens, spoon a little over about half the cakes, to come level with the paper cases. Leave to set. Pipe a whirl of butter cream in the centre of each cake. Slice the top off each of the remaining cakes and cut it into 2; pipe a butter cream rosette in the centre of the cake and replace top as wings. Dust with icing sugar.

Savoury open sandwiches

Anniversary suppers

There are no traditional anniversary dishes, but a celebration of this importance merits something special.

Menu
serves 12

Prawn and salmon mousse
Gammon slices with peaches
Boiled rice with almonds
Mixed salad
French bean vinaigrette
Coffee brandy gâteaux
Sunshine fruit salad

Day before: Wash the salad ingredients and pack them in polythene in the refrigerator to keep crisp. Make up the salad dressing and keep it in a screw-top jar.
Cook the beans.
Make the gâteaux and leave them in the refrigerator.
Make the mousse, but do not leave it in the mould overnight if it is a metal one.
In the morning: Make up the fruit salad.
2 hours before: Turn out the mousse and garnish. Turn out the gâteaux and decorate.
1 hour before: Prepare the gammon and put it on to cook. Boil the rice. Toss the salads.

Prawn and salmon mousse

15 g (½ oz) aspic powder
150 ml (¼ pint) hot water
175 g (6 oz) peeled prawns
3 × 226-g (3 × 8-oz) cans red salmon
5 × 15 ml spoons (5 tbsps) lemon juice
salt and freshly ground black pepper
40 g (1½ oz) powdered gelatine
568 ml (1 pint) double cream
4 large egg whites
few extra prawns to garnish, optional

Dissolve the aspic powder in the hot water and pour 3 × 15 ml spoons (3 tbsps) of it into the base of a 2·3 litre (4-pint) ring mould. Leave to set. Arrange the prawns

Coffee brandy gâteau and sunshine fruit salad for an anniversary

on the set aspic and gently pour over the remaining aspic; leave to set.
Drain the salmon, reserving the juice, and discard skin and bones. Mash together the fish, fish juice and lemon juice; or use an electric blender. Season well. Put the gelatine in a bowl with 8 × 15 ml spoons (8 tbsps) cold water and stand it over a pan of hot water until completely dissolved. Whip the cream until thick and stiffly whisk the egg whites. Fold the gelatine and cream into the fish mixture, then lightly fold in the egg whites. Turn the mixture into the ring mould and leave in the refrigerator to set.
To serve, turn out the mousse on to a flat plate and garnish, if wished, with a few whole prawns.

Gammon slices with peaches

50 g (2 oz) butter
3 × 15 ml spoons (3 tbsps) cooking oil
25 g (1 oz) caster sugar
12 gammon rashers, rinded
880 g (1 lb 15 oz) can peach halves
2 × 15 ml spoons (2 tbsps) vinegar
5 ml spoon (1 level tsp) mustard powder
salt and freshly ground black pepper

Heat the butter and oil in a large frying pan and add the sugar. Fry the gammon rashers, approximately 3 at a time, on both sides until golden brown. Remove them from the pan and place in a large shallow casserole, or use 2 if more practical.
Drain the peaches, reserving the juice. Fry them lightly on both sides, and add to the casserole. Pour the reserved juice into the frying pan with the vinegar and

mustard and bring to the boil. Simmer until slightly thickened, season well, and pour the syrup over the peaches and gammon. Cook in the centre of the oven at 200°C. (400°F.) mark 6 for about 30 minutes.
Serve hot with boiled rice, mixed with halved almonds, and mixed salad and French beans in vinaigrette dressing.

Coffee brandy gâteau
make 2

175 g (6 oz) butter
175 g (6 oz) caster sugar
3 large eggs
2 × 15 ml spoons (2 tbsps) coffee essence
15 ml spoon (1 tbsp) brandy
12 trifle sponge fingers
142 ml (¼ pint) double cream, whipped
chopped walnuts

Line the base of an 20·5 cm (8-in.) loose base cake tin with non-stick paper.
Cream the butter and sugar together until light and fluffy and the sugar has lost its grittiness. Beat in the eggs, one at a time. Beat in the coffee essence and brandy. Cut the sponge cakes in half, lengthwise. Arrange 8 pieces in the base of the prepared tin. Pour in half the coffee mixture. Cover with a further 8 sponge pieces, then pour in the remaining coffee mixture. Arrange the rest of the sponge pieces on top.
Press down well. Cover with a small plate, put a weight on the plate. Leave in the refrigerator for about 3 hours, until set.
Shortly before serving, run a round-bladed knife round the edge of the tin. Turn the gâteau out on to a plate, cover the top

with cream and pipe the remaining cream round the top and base of the gâteau, using a large star vegetable nozzle.
Cluster a few chopped walnuts in the centre.

Sunshine fruit salad
make 2

100–125 g (4 oz) caster sugar
300 ml (½ pint) water
juice of ½ lemon
1 medium-sized melon (cantaloupe)
3 oranges
3 grapefruit
225 g (½ lb) strawberries
2 × 15 ml spoons (2 tbsps) Grand Marnier

Make the syrup by dissolving the sugar in the water over a gentle heat and boiling for 5 minutes, allow to cool, then add the lemon juice.
Halve the melon, discard the pips and scoop out the flesh. Chop it roughly. Remove the skin and pith from the oranges and grapefruit, and cut into segments. Discard the hulls from the strawberries and cut the fruit in half.
Put all the fruit into the syrup, add the Grand Marnier and leave to stand for 2–3 hours in a cool place before serving.

Menu
serves 12

Crawfish tails with tarragon dressing
Crumbed lamb cutlets
Beef and pork skewers
Soured cream and garlic dip
Confetti salad
French bread and butter
Tutti frutti ratafia
Cherry flan

Day before: Prepare crawfish but do not slice.
Marinade meats.
Make sponge flan cases; when cold store in polythene bags.
In the morning: Prepare salad dressing.
Cook cutlets.
Prepare soured cream dip.
Finish the cherry flans and make the tutti frutti ratafia.
1½ hours before: Cook the meats and arrange on skewers.
1 hour before: Arrange crawfish and garnishes.
Before serving: Spoon juices over meat.
Add dressing to salad.

Crawfish tails with tarragon dressing

12 crawfish tails, fresh or frozen
2 limes or lemons
2 × 15 ml spoons (2 tbsps)
  tarragon vinegar
300 ml (½ pint) salad oil
thinly pared rind of 1 lemon
2 eggs, hard-boiled
sprigs of parsley
salt and freshly ground black
  pepper
sugar to taste

Cook fresh crawfish tails by placing in cold salted water, bringing to the boil and cooking for 10 minutes. To cook frozen crawfish, plunge while still frozen into boiling salted water and cook for about 8 minutes. Plunge into cold water to cool.
Slit the soft undershell of each with scissors and peel away. Ease out the meat in one piece. Slice thickly and return to the shells. Garnish with wedges of lime or lemon.
Put the remaining ingredients into a blender and mix until creamy (or chop the parsley, roughly chop the eggs and whisk with the remaining ingredients in a basin until creamy).
Serve on a platter with salads such as tomatoes and coleslaw, onions and sweet peppers, marinaded mushrooms and cucumber.

Crumbed lamb cutlets

225 g (½ lb) fresh white
  breadcrumbs
100–125 g (4 oz) streaky bacon,
  rinded and cooked until crisp
50 g (2 oz) onion, skinned and
  chopped
1 sprig of parsley
thinly pared rind of 1 lemon
salt and freshly ground black
  pepper
12 lamb cutlets, trimmed
2 eggs, beaten
6 × 15 ml spoons (6 tbsps) cooking
  oil

Put the breadcrumbs in an electric blender with the bacon, onion, parsley, lemon rind and seasoning. Blend until well mixed. Turn the mixture on to a plate. Dip each cutlet into the egg, then coat with the seasoned crumbs, pressing the crumbs in well. Chill.
Divide the oil between 2 roasting

tins and add the cutlets, turning them in the oil so that both sides are covered. Cook in the oven at 200°C. (400°F.) mark 6 for about 45 minutes, until the meat is tender. Drain and cool on kitchen paper.
To serve, put a cutlet frill on the end of each bone.

Beef and pork skewers

1¼ kg (2½ lb) topside of beef
1¼ kg (2½ lb) middle leg of pork
300 ml (½ pint) red wine
6 × 15 ml spoons (6 tbsps) corn oil
10 ml spoon (2 level tsps) dried
  rosemary
5 ml spoon (1 level tbsp) dried sage
freshly ground black pepper

Cut the beef and pork into large pieces. Place in separate dishes each with 150 ml (¼ pint) wine, turn well and leave covered in a cool place for several hours or overnight.
Drain the meats, add 3 × 15 ml spoons (3 tbsps) oil and the rosemary to the beef, and 3 ml spoons (3 tbsps) oil and the sage to the pork. Turn each to distribute the oil and herbs. Season with pepper.
Place in the baking tins or dishes and cook in the oven at 200°C. (400°F.) mark 6 for 1 hour, then reduce to 180°C. (350°F.) mark 4 for 30 minutes. Baste frequently with the pan juices, add a little of the wine marinade and turn the meat 2–3 times during cooking. When tender, skewer the meats and keep hot. Reduce the juices by rapid boiling, adjust seasoning and spoon over the meats.
Serve with the soured cream and garlic dip.

Soured cream and garlic dip

300 ml (½ pint) soured cream
2 cloves of garlic, skinned and
  crushed
salt and freshly ground black
  pepper

Mix the soured cream and the garlic, and season to taste.

Confetti salad

1½ large cucumbers (or 3 small
  ridge cucumbers)
¾ kg (1½ lb) firm tomatoes,
  skinned and halved
350 g (¾ lb) young carrots,
  scraped
bunch of radishes, trimmed
celery seed dressing

Cut the unpeeled cucumbers in 0·5 cm (¼-in.) slices and then cut each slice into sticks. Remove the seeds from the tomatoes and cut the flesh into strips.
Slice the carrots in rings and cut into sticks as for the cucumber. Slice the radishes thinly.
Combine these ingredients in a large bowl. Add enough French dressing, made with lemon juice and flavoured with celery seeds to moisten.

Tutti frutti ratafia
serves 6

75 g (3 oz) ratafias
3 oranges
¼ kg (½ lb) strawberries (fresh or
  frozen, thawed), hulled and
  sliced
50 g (2 oz) Demerara sugar
142 ml (¼ pint) soured cream
long shred coconut, toasted

A special salad for a celebration supper

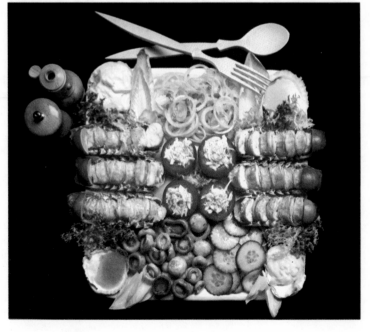

Divide half the ratafias between 6 individual dishes. Peel the oranges, removing all the white pith; divide into segments. Place on top of the ratafias.
Layer up the strawberries, sugar and soured cream on top of the oranges, using half of each. Repeat the layers with the remaining ingredients, finishing with a layer of soured cream. Chill for 1 hour before serving and decorate with toasted, shredded coconut.

Cherry flan
serves 6–8

For flan case:
2 eggs
50 g (2 oz) caster sugar
50 g (2 oz) plain flour

For filling:
396-g (14-oz) can cherries
150 ml (¼ pint) cherry juice (if
  necessary made up with water)
10 ml spoon (2 level tsps)
  arrowroot
3 × 15 ml spoons (3 tbsps)
  red-currant jelly
284 ml (½ pint) double cream,
  lightly whipped

Grease a 21·5 cm (8½-in.) sponge flan tin. Place a round of greased greaseproof paper on the raised part of the tin to prevent sticking. Put the eggs and sugar in a large bowl, stand it over hot water and whisk until the mixture is light and creamy and thick enough to show a trail when the whisk is lifted. Remove from the heat and whisk until cool.
Sift half the flour over the whisked mixture and fold in very lightly, using a tablespoon. Add the remaining flour in the same way. Pour the mixture into the flan tin, spread it evenly with a palette knife and bake above the centre of the oven at 220°C. (425°F.) mark 7 for about 15 minutes. Loosen the edge carefully, turn the flan case out on to a wire rack and leave to cool.
Drain and stone the cherries and place in the sponge flan case. Blend the cherry juice and arrowroot together and add the red-currant jelly. Pour into a saucepan, bring to the boil and cook until it thickens – about 3 minutes. Allow to cool but not become quite cold, then use to glaze the cherries.
Serve with lightly whipped cream.

Planning the holiday weekend

Christmas

Christmas is perhaps the most sociable time of the year. Families gather on Christmas day and both children and adults will have parties to go to throughout the season. There are cards, presents, decorations, the tree. Excitement mounts for 2–3 weeks, reaching a peak when the children break up from school.

Inevitably this causes extra work, but don't be daunted. If you plan carefully and stick to your plan, you can do the shopping and cooking, cater for extra house guests over the holiday weekend and still have time to enjoy it yourself. The first problem to get out of the way is presents.

There are some people who are so well organized they will shop for Christmas presents right through the year. This way the expense is spread. In any case, try to get into top gear at the beginning of October; make comprehensive lists of people, what you are prepared to spend and any ideas that come to mind straight away. Then make a couple of expeditions; the first to buy those presents you are sure about and at the same time to gather ideas for the others; the second to make final purchases. Having bought the presents, wrap and label them as soon as you can, and there is another job finished.

Cards are less difficult, but it pays to buy them early, in November, while there is still plenty of choice. It is then easy to post overseas cards early and to finish the rest in good time. This is a job all the family can help with – many people will be pleased to see the writing of your youngest child on the family Christmas card, instead of yours. Again make comprehensive lists (use a little book which can carry on from year to year) and tick each name off carefully as the card is addressed. With all hands at the mill, writing the cards need only take an evening, or at the most two. Then post them in good time to ease the Christmas rush. School children won't have much time until the end of term, so if your card and present buying is finished you can then give them any help you need.

The cake, puddings and mincemeat should be made in October to give them time to mature.

During the first week in December, decide what parties you'll be having at home, and work out the menus. Send off all your invitations and tick off acceptances as they arrive. Order turkey, ham and any other big joints you may need, specifying the date for delivery. If you are having a frozen turkey you will need early on December 23rd to give it time to thaw. Otherwise, it's better to leave it until Christmas Eve as a turkey is rather big to have around. Next sort out from your menus any foodstuffs that can be bought early. This includes fresh nuts, dried and candied fruits, almonds for the marzipan, dried chestnuts for stuffing, canned fruits and preserves. Your choice will be better early in the month, prices will be lower and it will take some of the load from later.

If you have any holly in the garden with berries at this time, it can be picked now and will keep in a cool place such as a garden shed or garage for the 3–4 weeks until you need to bring it in. The danger with leaving this job until later is that if there is a severe cold spell, the birds will need the berries for food and a whole bush may be stripped in a day. Order your tree now, buy any house plants that will keep and order any cut flowers you want at the last minute, either for the house or as gifts. While you are thinking along these lines, get someone in the family to sort out the decorations and tree lights, check them and buy any replacements necessary. December's first week is a good time to make Christmas bookings, too, whether it be for overseas phone calls, hairdresser or a restaurant table during the holiday period.

The second week of December is the time to sort out your linen for laundering. You may be needing extra tablecloths and bed linen and it will help if this is all checked, laundered if necessary and put away well in advance. Make a list of drinks to be ordered, not forgetting soft drinks for the children together with salted nuts, cocktail biscuits, olives, baby gherkins and crisps. These can be collected straight away if you want. Save your energy at the last moment by listing paper napkins, drip mats, cocktail sticks, candles, Christmas crackers, cooking foil, greaseproof paper, plastic bags and wraps; buy all you need in one shop, now. Check your dishes too, and make arrangements for hiring or borrowing any extras needed.

During this week, you can make a start with the cooking. The almond paste should be put on the cake and you can make mince pies, meringues, brandy snaps and any other cookies, for storing in airtight tins until you want them. Mince pies are best refreshed in the oven for a few minutes before serving. Do extra cleaning now, too. Silver will keep its shine wrapped in polythene bags, especially if it is polished with a long term silver cleaner; if the spare room is cleaned thoroughly now it will need only a quick dust and vacuum at the last minute.

The third week in December is the time to get into top gear. Order all the fresh vegetables and fruit you will be needing, also extra milk, butter and cream from the milkman, and bread. Check carefully through your lists and menus and make sure that you have thought of everything including tea, coffee, sugar and other staple stores. Air the extra blankets and

Painted eggs for the Easter Sunday breakfast table

pillows and make up the spare beds; dust round and remember to put a few flowers in the bedrooms at the last moment. Finish decorating the cake. Collect the tree and, towards the end of the week, ask the rest of the family to decorate it and put up the other decorations. Sit down yourself and make any table decorations or other special bits and pieces you may want.

On 23rd make as much as possible of any food you will want on Christmas Eve; house guests will start to arrive then and there are bound to be people dropping in. Cook any meats for serving cold on Christmas day and make salad dressings. Check that all deliveries are correct; don't assume that all the shops will have made up your order absolutely correctly.

On Christmas Eve you can go all out towards preparing the food for the next day. Prepare the vegetables, make brandy or rum butter, trifle, fruit salads and other desserts. Stuff the bird as near as possible to the time of cooking. Don't try to produce full scale meals today, even if your guests have already arrived – keep them happy with a casserole and cheese. Better still, if it's family only, make do with hot dogs and snacks.

If you have room in the refrigerator, prepare any salad greens and vegetables you will be wanting. After the children have gone to bed, put out the presents and put your feet up.

On Christmas day you are bound to be busy, but by now there should be left only the things which have to be done at the last moment. So that you can look pretty all day, change early and keep an overall in the kitchen to slip on every time you go in there. Find from among the family a reliable second-in-command to help you and make sure you don't put something in the oven and forget it; then relax and enjoy yourself with the rest!

Easter

Easter doesn't take on quite the same social importance as Christmas, so there is less really festive food to worry about. Nevertheless there are usually 3–4 days of holiday for the whole family and for shops and delivery men too.

Breakfast is traditionally the special meal on Easter Sunday and for this there must be Easter bread and eggs, whatever else. For the children it is worth decorating a few eggs – they cannot fail to be delighted. This can be done well in advance and they can be stored in egg cartons out of harm's way until the time comes to show them. Blow the eggs by piercing them with a fine pin at either end and blowing out the insides; work over a basin rather than the sink and you can use the insides for scrambled egg or an omelette. Dye the shells by boiling in a little food colouring mixed in water, paint faces and add hats or ears as your imaginations takes you. As they get older, the children will want to help you do this. Make the hot cross buns in time for Good Friday and heat up those left for Sunday breakfast.

Apart from this there are only normal meals to plan. It is often as well for the holiday period to have a larger joint than usual, so that there will be plenty to eat cold afterwards. The Monday after Easter, particularly, is a time when many of the family will want to either play or watch some kind of sport, and picnic meals will be called for. Prepare salads and desserts in advance, in plastic pots or paper dishes so that they can be packed easily.

If your family is not old enough to plan outings alone, it is wise at this time of the year to plan something for them. March and April do not often provide good weather for playing in the garden, and your own holiday can be ruined if the children are obliged to play indoors all day. Plan an outing together that all will enjoy and make an occasion of it.

Wedding Menu
serves 30

Consommé indienne
Roquefort tomatoes
Salmon and mayonnaise verte
Cucumber chartreuse
Green salad
Potato salad loaf
French bread and butter
Strawberry nut meringues
Wedding cake

In advance: Make and ice cake (see recipe).
Several days before: Make consommé and chill. Make meringues and store in airtight tin. Make mayonnaise and French dressing; store in a screw-top jar.

Day before: Poach salmon. Make cucumber chartreuse and potato salad loaf. Make curry cream for consommé. Prepare salad vegetables. Hull strawberries and whip cream. Prepare the table, except for the food.
In the morning: Prepare Roquefort tomatoes. Dish up consommé and add topping. Unmould cucumber chartreuse and potato salad loaf, but keep covered. Finish strawberry nut meringues. Set food out at last possible minute.

Consommé indienne

make 2 lots

*2·8 litres (5 pints) brown stock,
cold*
*¼ kg (½ lb) lean beefsteak, e.g.
rump*
350 ml (12½ fl oz) water
*2 large carrots, peeled and
quarterd*
*2 large onions, skinned and
quartered*
a bouquet garni
2 egg whites
salt
*5 × 5 ml spoons (5 tsps) sherry,
optional*
*6 × 15 ml spoons (6 tbsps) chopped
fresh herbs (chives, parsley and
tarragon)*
*5 ml spoon (1 level tsp) curry
powder*
*284 ml (½ pint) double cream,
whipped*
25 g (1 oz) flaked almonds, toasted

Remove any fat from the stock.
Shred the meat finely and soak it
in the water for 15 minutes. Put
the meat and water, vegetables,
stock and bouquet garni into a
large, deep pan; add the egg
whites. Heat gently and whisk
continuously with a balloon
whisk until a thick froth starts to
form.
Stop whisking and bring to the
boil. Reduce the heat
immediately and simmer for 2
hours. If the liquid boils too
rapidly, the froth will break and
cloud the consommé.
Scald a clean cloth or jelly bag,
wring it out, tie to the legs of an
upturned stool and place a large
bowl underneath. Pour the soup
through, keeping the froth back at
first with a spoon, then let it slide
out on to the cloth.
Again pour the soup through the
cloth and the filter of egg white.
Adjust seasoning and add a little
sherry if required, to improve the
flavour.
Stir in the fresh chopped herbs
and leave the consommé to cool
and set.
To serve, break up the jellied
consommé and serve in individual dishes. Stir the curry powder into the whipped cream,
spoon a little over each serving
and sprinkle with toasted
almonds.

Roquefort tomatoes

30 large, firm tomatoes, skinned
450 g (1 lb) cream cheese
*350 g (12 oz) Roquefort or Stilton
cheese*
*225 g (8 oz) celery, scrubbed and
finely chopped*
*225 g (8 oz) walnuts, finely
chopped*
568 ml (1 pint) double cream
salt and pepper
chopped parsley

Remove a slice from the round
end of each tomato. Carefully
scoop out the core and seeds with
the handle of a teaspoon. Leave
tomatoes upside down to drain.
Beat together the cheeses and stir
in the celery and nuts. Lightly
whip the cream, stir into the
cheese mixture and adjust the
seasoning.
Pile the cheese filling into the
tomato cases and replace the
'lids'. Garnish with chopped
parsley.

Cold poached salmon

*1 large salmon (or fresh tuna fish),
scaled and cleaned, about 6 kg
(12 lb)*
court bouillon (see below)
550 ml (1 pint) mayonnaise

Prepare the fish. Fill a fish kettle
with just enough court bouillon
to cover the salmon. Bring to the
boil, lower in the salmon and boil
gently for 10 minutes only.
Remove the fish kettle from the
heat, take off the lid and leave
until cold.
To serve, remove the skin and
arrange the fish whole on a long
dish, garnished with radishes and
cucumber, and serve the mayonnaise separately.
Alternatively coat the fish evenly
with the mayonnaise, surround-
ing it with a garnish of salad vegetables.

Court bouillon

900 ml (1½ pints) water
300 ml (½ pint) dry white wine
1 small carrot, peeled and sliced
1 small onion, skinned and sliced
*1 small stalk of celery, scrubbed
and chopped, optional*
*15 ml spoon (1 tbsps) vinegar or
lemon juice*
a few sprigs of parsley
½ a bay leaf
3–4 peppercorns
10 ml spoon (2 level tsps) salt

Place all the ingredients in a pan,

Poached salmon is an impressive central display for a buffet

bring to the boil and simmer for
about 30 minutes. Allow the
liquid to cool and strain before
using.

Mayonnaise verte

watercress leaves
*1–2 sprigs of fresh tarragon or
chervil*
a few parsley stalks
thick mayonnaise
*15 ml spoon (1 tbsp) double cream,
lightly whipped*

Chop the watercress leaves and
herbs very finely. Just before serving, add the mayonnaise and
cream.

Cucumber chartreuse

make 2

2 lime jelly tablets
*550–900 ml (1–1½ pints) hot
water*
300 ml (½ pint) cider vinegar
15 ml spoon (1 level tbsp) sugar
green colouring
*½ kg (1 lb) cucumber, peeled and
diced*
small tomatoes, skinned

Break up the lime jelly tablets and
place in a 1·1 litre (2-pint) measure. Make up to 900 ml (1½ pints)
with hot water and stir until the
jelly has dissolved. Add the cider
vinegar, the sugar and a few drops
of green colouring and leave to
cool until set to the consistency of
unbeaten egg white. Fold in the
cucumber; when it is evenly sus-
pended, pour the mixture into a
1·7 litre (3-pint) ring mould.
Leave in a cool place to set. To
serve, unmould and fill the centre
with tomatoes.

Potato salad loaf

make 3

*¾ kg (1½ lb) potatoes, peeled and
diced*
175 g (6 oz) sliced ham roll
*10 ml spoon (2 level tbsps)
powdered gelatine*
15 ml spoon (1 tbsp) water
*3 × 15 ml spoons (3 tbsps) salad
cream*
*1 small onion, grated or finely
chopped*
3 gherkins or olives, chopped
*5 ml spoon (1 tsp) chopped chives
or parsley*
salt and pepper
1 egg, hard-boiled

Line a loaf tin measuring 21·5 cm
by 11·5 cm (8½ in. by 4½ in.) with
greaseproof paper, letting the
paper extend about 5 cm (2 in.)
above the rim.
Cook the prepared potatoes in
boiling salted water for about 10
minutes until just tender but not
mushy. Drain. Rinse in cold
water. Line the tin with slices of
ham roll and dice the remainder
of the meat.
Put the gelatine and water in a
small bowl and stand it over a pan
of hot water until dissolved. Mix
the gelatine with the salad cream
and pour over the potatoes. Add
the onion, gherkins or olives,
chives or parsley and seasoning.
Mix well.
Place half the mixture in the
ham-lined tin. Cover with diced
ham, add the remaining potato
mixture. Level the top and fold
the paper over. Chill. Just before
serving, unfold the paper, invert
the loaf tin on to a serving dish
and remove the paper. Decorate
with sliced hard-boiled egg.

A loaf-shaped mould will add interest to a potato salad

Strawberry nut meringues
makes 36

400 g (14 oz) icing sugar, sifted
6 egg whites
250 g (9 oz) almonds, blanched
   and finely chopped almond
   essence
568 ml (1 pint) double cream,
   whipped
36 large, whole strawberries,
   hulled

Line 2 baking sheets with silicone (non-stick) paper.
Put the icing sugar in a bowl with the egg whites and place over a saucepan of hot water. Whisk steadily with a rotary whisk or electric beater until the mixture forms stiff peaks.
Remove the bowl from the heat and stir in the nuts and a few drops of essence. Drop spoonfuls of the mixture on to the baking sheets and flatten with a palette knife into small discs about 5 cm (2 in.) across. Bake in the oven at 150°C. (300°F.) mark 2 for about 30 minutes, until the meringue is crisp on the outside and creamy in colour. Remove from the baking sheet and cool on a wire rack. To serve, pipe a border of cream round each and place a large strawberry in the centre.

Wedding cake

This recipe is for a 3 tier cake which will serve approximately 150 people.
For a small wedding a single tier is probably more practical:
a 30 cm (12 in.) cake serves approx. 100
a 20 cm (8 in.) cake serves approx. 30
a 15 cm (6 in.) cake serves approx. 20

For the bottom tier:
1 kg 400 g (3 lb 2 oz) currants
525 g (1 lb 3 oz) sultanas
525 g (1 lb 3 oz) raisins, stoned
350 g (12 oz) glacé cherries
825 g (1 lb 13 oz) plain flour
15 ml spoon (3 level tsps) ground
   cinnamon
3 × 2·5 ml spoons (1½ level tsps)
   ground mace
grated rind of 1 lemon
800 g (1 lb 12 oz) butter
800 g (1 lb 12 oz) light soft brown
   sugar
14 eggs, beaten
250 g (9 oz) mixed chopped peel
250 g (9 oz) nibbed almonds
5 × 15 ml spoons (5 tbsps) brandy

For the 2 upper tiers:
675 g (1 lb 8 oz) currants
275 g (10 oz) sultanas
275 g (10 oz) raisins, stoned
200 g (7 oz) glacé cherries
500 g (1 lb 2 oz) plain flour
3½ × 2·5 ml spoons (1¾ level tsp)
   ground cinnamon
5 ml spoon (1 level tsp) ground
   mace
grated rind of ¼ lemon
425 g (15 oz) butter
425 g (15 oz) light soft brown
   sugar
8 eggs, beaten

100–125 g (4 oz) mixed chopped
   peel
100–125 g (4 oz) nibbed almonds
3 × 15 ml spoons (3 tbsps) brandy
a few drops of prepared gravy
   browning or a little home made
   caramel (optional)

For finishing:
extra brandy
almond paste
decorations
royal icing

Make up and cook the bottom tier first, using a 30·5 cm (12-in.) round tin; prepare the mixture for the 2 upper tiers, divide between a 20·5 cm (8-in.) and a 15 cm (6-in.) round tin. Cook the two smaller cakes together.
Grease the cake tins and line with a double layer of greaseproof paper. Tie a double band of brown paper round the outside or put each tin in a slightly larger tin. Stand the tins on a layer of newspaper or brown paper for cooking. Wash and thoroughly dry the currants and sultanas (unless you are using pre-washed packaged fruit, in which case simply check it carefully.) Chop the raisins, quarter the glacé cherries.
Sift together the flour and spices. Add grated lemon rind. Cream the butter and gradually beat in sugar until light and fluffy. Beat in the eggs a little at a time. If the mixture shows signs of curdling, beat in 1–2 × 15 ml spoons (1–2 tbsps) flour. Fold in the rest of the flour and then the fruit, peel, nuts and brandy. If you wish, add to the smaller cakes a little gravy browning or caramel as they tend to be paler than the larger base. Spoon the mixture into the prepared tins and level the surface. Using the back of a spoon, hollow out the centre of the cake slightly so that it will be level when cooked. At this stage the mixture may be left overnight. Cover lightly with a cloth, leave in a cool place but not in the refrigerator.
Bake on the lowest shelf in the oven at 150°C. (300°F.) mark 2. Cook the 30·5 cm (12-in) cake for about 8 hours, the 20·5 cm (8-in.) cake for about 3½ hours and the 15 cm (6-in.) cake for 2½–3 hours. Look at the cakes half way through the cooking time. If they seem to be browning too quickly, cover the top with a double thickness of greaseproof paper. With a large cake it is often wise to reduce the oven temperature to 140°C. (275°F.) mark 1 after

two-thirds of the cooking time. Cool the cake for a short time in the tin and then turn on to a wire rack. When cold prick at intervals with a fine skewer and spoon some brandy evenly over the surface. Wrap completely in greaseproof paper and then in kitchen foil. Store for at least 1 month, preferably 2–3 months, in a cool, dry place before icing. After icing, wrap and store similarly, but for not longer than 2 months as a mould may form between the cake and the almond paste.
If one tier of the cake is kept for a later occasion such as a christening, remove the icing and almond paste and redecorate it for the second occasion. Directions for almond paste and royal icing are in the 'Cake Decorating' section.

Cake decorating

Most rich fruit cakes for celebration occasions are decorated with almond paste and royal icing. Royal icing is not so easy to handle as glacé or fondant, but the results can be so delightful that it is well worth a little practice. It makes economic sense too, since most confectioners charge quite highly to ice even a birthday cake. Practice on family birthday cakes before you tackle something for a big party; or try out one or two designs on paper (it's cheaper than cake!).

Quantities of icings for a formal cake

Almond paste
Make up a quantity of paste, according to the size of your cake. With a piece of string, measure round the outside of the cake. Take two-thirds of the almond paste and roll it out on a surface dredged with icing sugar to a rectangle half the length of the string and in width twice the depth of the cake. Trim with a knife and cut in half lengthwise. Knead the trimmings into the remaining paste and roll out to fit the top of the cake. Check at this stage that the surface of the cake is absolutely level.
Brush the sides of the cake with apricot glaze. Put the 2 strips of almond paste round the cake and

smooth the joins with a round-bladed knife, keeping the top and bottom edges square. Brush the top with apricot glaze, place the rolled-out top paste in position and roll lightly with a sugar-dusted rolling pin. Make sure the joins adhere well. Run a straight-sided jam jar round the edge to smooth the paste and stick it firmly to the cake. Leave the almond paste for a week before icing, loosely covered.

Royal icing

4 egg whites
1 kg (2 lb) icing sugar, sifted
15 ml spoon (1 tbsp) lemon juice
10 ml spoon (2 tsps) glycerine

Whisk the egg whites until slightly frothy. Stir in the sugar a spoonful at a time with a wooden spoon. When half the sugar is incorporated, add the lemon juice. Continue adding more sugar, beating well after each addition until you reach the right consistency.

It is this initial beating that gives it a light texture; skip it and the result will be disappointing, often heavy and difficult to use. The mixture is right for coating if it forms soft peaks when pulled up with a wooden spoon; it should be a little stiffer for piping and thinner for flooding.

Lastly stir in the glycerine, which prevents the icing becoming too hard. If you use an electric mixer, take care not to overbeat. If royal icing becomes too fluffy, it gives a rough surface and breaks when piped. It helps to allow it to stand for 24 hours in a covered container before using. Gently beat by hand and if necessary adjust the consistency before using.

Note: powdered albumen is available commercially and avoids the problem of large quantities of left over egg yolks.

Equipment

Before starting to decorate with icing you will need the following equipment:

1. A turntable – this enables you to get a smooth finish all over and round the sides of the cake. It is possible to work without a turntable, using an upturned basin instead, but it makes it much more difficult to obtain a good finish.

2. An icing ruler, or a long, straight bladed knife longer than the diameter of the cake – this is for flat icing.

3. An icing nail or a cork fixed to a skewer. This serves the same function as a turntable, in miniature, for piping flowers and other small designs.

4. Plain writing nozzles in 3 sizes, to make lines, dots or words.

5. Star nozzles for rosettes, zigzags and ropes.

6. Shell nozzles.

7. Petal and leaf nozzles.

8. A forcing bag. Preferably make one yourself from grease-proof paper and use with icing nozzles without a screw band. If you use a fabric bag, attach a screw adjustment and use nozzles with a screw band.

Flat icing

To ice the cake, place it on a silver cake board 2–3 in. larger than the cake. With the cake and board on a turntable, spoon on an ample quantity of icing then use a palette knife to work it evenly over the top, using a paddling motion to remove any air bubbles. Roughly level the surface.

Draw an icing ruler (or a knife longer than the width of the cake) steadily across the cake top at an angle of 30° to smooth the surface. Be careful not to press too heavily. Neaten the edges, removing surplus icing by holding the knife parallel with the side of the cake. Leave to dry for about 24 hours.

Cover the sides the same way, still using a paddling motion. Hold a small palette knife or plain edged icing comb in one hand to the side of the cake and at a slight angle towards it. Pass the other hand under and round the turntable so that a little more than a complete revolution can be made. Keeping the knife quite still in one hand, revolve the turntable with the other, smoothly and fairly quickly. Towards the end, draw the knife or comb away without leaving a mark. Remove any surplus from the edge with a knife. If you prefer, ice the sides before the top.

To achieve a really professional looking finish (and this is a must with a tiered wedding cake), give the cake a second coating with slightly thinner icing, about 2 days after the first. Trim off any rough edges from the first coat with a sharp knife or fine clean sandpaper and brush off the loose icing before starting the second coat.

Piping techniques

When using a forcing bag, avoid over filling. Small sized bags are easier to handle especially when using a writing nozzle – it is much better to refill frequently. Insert the appropriate nozzle in the end of the bag, spoon the icing in and fold the top flap down, enclosing the front edge, until the bag is sealed and quite firm. Hold the bag in one hand with the thumb on top, the first finger resting down on the side of the bag and the second finger curved underneath. Use your other hand to steady the bag while you are piping.

To pipe lines use a writing nozzle. Make contact with the surface of the iced cake and squeeze out just enough icing to stick to the surface. Continue squeezing and at the same time raise the bag and pull towards you; hold the bag at an angle of about 45°. Lift the nozzle and the line of piped icing from the surface, to keep a sagging line. The icing can then be guided and lowered into the required design.

To pipe stars and scrolls use a star nozzle. For stars, hold the nozzle almost upright to the flat iced surface, pipe out a blob of icing and withdraw nozzle with a quick up and down movement. For scrolls, hold the bag at an angle, as for a straight line. With the nozzle almost on the iced surface, pipe out a good head and then gradually release the pressure on the bag and pull away with a double or single curve; the whole operation is one movement.

Trellis work can be very effective. Use a writing nozzle to pipe parallel lines across the space to be covered; when these are dry pipe more lines on top of them in the opposite direction. For a really good finish, pipe a third layer, using a very fine nozzle. If any 'tails' are left at the ends of lines, trim them off while still soft.

Break up a spray of artificial flowers to make a delicate decoration

Quantities of icings for a formal cake

Cake size		Almond paste	Royal icing
Square	Round		
	15 cm (6 in.)	350 g (¾ lb)	450 g (1 lb)
15 cm (6 in)	18 cm (7 in.)	450 g (1 lb)	550–75 g (1¼ lb)
18 cm (7 in.)	20·5 cm (8 in.)	550 g (1¼ lb)	700 g (1½ lb)
20·5 cm (8 in.)	23 cm (9 in.)	800 g (1¾ lb)	900 g (2 lb)
23 cm (9 in.)	25·5 cm (10 in.)	900 g (2 lb)	1 kg–1 kg 25 g (2¼ lb)
25·5 cm (10 in.)	28 cm (11 in.)	1 kg–1 kg 25 g (2¼ lb)	1 kg 250 g (2¾ lb)
28 cm (11 in.)	30·5 cm (12 in.)	1 kg 125 g (2½ lb)	1 kg 400 g (3 lb)
30·5 cm (12 in.)	33 cm (13 in.)	1 kg 400 g (3 lb)	1 kg 625 g (3½ lb)

Flowers and leaves Leaves are piped with a special leaf nozzle directly on to the surface of the cake. Flowers are made up in advance on paper and fixed to the cake after they have dried out. Stick 5 cm (2-in.) square of non-stick paper to an icing nail with a small blob of icing (or to a cork fixed to a skewer). Work on this surface and leave the flowers to dry on the paper. When dry, peel away the paper and fix the flowers to the cake with a small blob of icing.

'Run out' designs, may either be piped directly on to the cake and flooded, or on to non-stick paper and fixed on the cake when dry. For separate 'run outs', draw out the design first on card, quite clearly. Cut a piece of non-stick paper to cover it and fix it with a spot of icing at each corner. Trace the outline of the design with a medium-fine writing nozzle; thin the icing to a 'just-flowing' consistency with unwhisked egg white and pour it into a small paper forcing bag. Cut the tip off the bag and flood the icing into the outline; if it is the correct consistency it will run smoothly into place. Leave flat for several days before peeling off the paper. To pipe a 'run-out' directly on to the cake, prick the design out first with a fine pin and work as above.

To decorate our wedding cake

Before starting any piping, place the pillars in position and prick round them with a pin. This will ensure that there is still room for them when everything else is done!

Scallops

For each cake in turn, cut a circle of greaseproof paper the diameter of the cake. Fold the large one into 8, the middle one into 8 and the small one into 6, then for each cake proceed as follows.
Either free-hand or with compasses mark in the scallops (about 2·5 cm (1 in.) deep at the widest point) between the folds in the paper. Place the paper on the cake and secure with pins. Prick the outline of the scallops on to the flat iced surface. Remove and, using the prick marks as a guide, pipe the scallops in with a No. 2 writing nozzle. Pipe a second scallop 0·5 cm (¼ in.) outside the first, using a No. 3 writing nozzle, and a third line using the No. 2 nozzle again.

To make the scallops on the side of the cake, measure the depth of the cake and cut a band of grease-proof paper to size. Place it round the cake and secure with a pin at a point where one of the top scallops comes to the edge of the cake. Mark the points of the scallops right round the cake, remove the paper and draw in the scallops as for the top. At the same time draw corresponding scallops 1 cm (½ in) deep at the base. Secure the paper round the cake and prick out the design. Tilt the cake slightly and rest it on a firmly wedged, shallow tin, so that you can work on the sides. A damp cloth under the tin helps to prevent movement. Pipe in the scallops round the top and base, as for the flat surface.

Lace

Fill in the scallops – top, sides and base – with 'lace'. This is done with a No. 2 writing nozzle, almost resting on the surface. Pipe a wriggly line with no obvious set pattern, but keep it looking neat.

Flowers

The easiest flowers to pipe are daisies. Fix a square of paper to an icing nail or cork and use a medium petal nozzle. Pipe one petal at a time by squeezing out a small amount of icing, withdrawing the nozzle with a quick down and up movement. Pipe 5 petals, almost touching in the centre. Fill in the centre of each daisy either with a silver ball or with a small dot or several tiny dots from a No. 2 nozzle.

Fern shaped lines

The fern shaped lines have to be piped on the side of the cake free-hand. Tilt the cake as for the scallops and pipe the lines 0·5 cm (¼ in.) from the side scallop, using a No. 3 nozzle. Repeat with a No. 2 nozzle 0·5 cm (¼ in.) below the first line. The vertical line is done with a No. 2 nozzle. Finish with a bold dot from a No. 3 nozzle at the apex of the lines. This pattern may be piped as a fine line or as a series of small dots, which are easier to control.

Finishing

Neaten the base of each cake with a series of dots in the angle between the cake and the board; for the large cake using a No. 3 nozzle, for the smaller cakes a No. 2

Piping random lacework to fill in the scallops

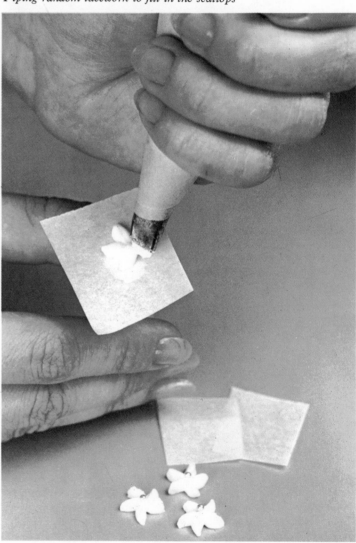

Making daisies separately to be fixed on the cake later

nozzle. Where the scallops meet at the base, bring a line of 3 dots up the side of the cake, with a No. 2 nozzle, using varying degrees of pressure to obtain different sizes. Position the pillars within the guide lines previously pricked out. Check that they are level, to ensure that the tiers stand level when positioned. Ideally use a spirit level for this. Fix each pillar in position with icing, using a lit-

tle extra if the height needs adjusting at all. Ensure that none of the icing creeps out from under the base of the pillars. Allow to dry.
Mount the tiers carefully on the pillars to make sure that everything fits together properly, and decide on the decoration for the top. Then dismantle the cake again and keep the tiers separately until the day.

Flowers For The Table

Flowers bring any table setting to life. Before the meal, when all the linen and tableware are set out but there is no food, the table seems dead until flowers are added. Between courses, flowers help to distract from the bare table mats.

Arranging flowers for the table is a special art, something over and above the normal skills of producing an artistic arrangement. In this context, the choice of flowers is crucial to the success of the arrangement – you can't necessarily just make use of the flowers you have available, as you would in a normal room setting. Just as linen and china are chosen to tone together and to match the mood of the food, the flowers must do the same. Their colours must also tone with or complement the colours of the tableware.

Other considerations also come into your choice of flowers. At a dinner party, or any sit-down meal, the flowers should never be so tall that they obscure one guest's face from another, or that they run the risk of being knocked over as dishes are passed around. Strong-smelling flowers should be avoided as these distract from the pleasure of the food smells and can even conflict with them unpleasantly. On the other hand, flowers for the buffet table benefit from height as the guests are usually standing anyway and the height of a flower arrangement can give shape to an otherwise flat arrangement of foods.

Choose your containers for table flowers carefully. Keep them low, fairly flat and if they have any height at all, be sure they are heavy based and therefore stable. Collect together old pottery dishes, copper or brass pans, large glass ashtrays even – all these are ideal containers for table flowers.

The arrangement shown at the head of this page was made in a copper gratin dish, the handles showing to break up an otherwise rather formal arrangement of red roses, dahlias and briony berries. This particular arrangement is designed for a formal dinner table setting on a white cloth or dark, polished wood surface – the colour is strong, the arrangement low and the shape very compact, the outline broken only by a few straying buds. This red on a coloured cloth could be quite wrong unless it tied in very closely with the colours of the cloth and the china.

Try fixing a small pin holder to one side of a large glass ashtray, using plasticine or florist's clay; make a posy of 2–3 cabbage roses, clematis heads or other wide flowers to cover the pin holder only, leaving the gleaming glass and water exposed alongside. This is an elegant, small arrangement that cannot obstruct the dinner table conversation.

Alternatively, twine a few trailing flowers and leaves round the holder of a tall candle – the candle will be sufficiently firmly wedged not to tip, and the flowers will serve to soften the shape of the holder. (Please don't let the wax drip on them though – there's nothing more dismal than scorched, dying flowers). If you particularly like candles, you may like to buy a special candle holder with a flower holder in the base – these make it much easier to provide the flowers with water.

It is rarely advisable to go for a strictly formal arrangement at the table, even if the setting is a formal dinner. Fine china and silver can become somehow sterile if a stark arrangement of flowers is used, and something soft and casual, added as if an afterthought (but a planned afterthought please) will be more pleasing.

When it comes to choosing flowers, your choice does of course depend largely on what grows in your garden or what you can afford to buy from the florist. Roses are nearly always suitable – either arranged with other flowers as here, or casually plonked in a small pottery jug for the supper table. Daisies of all sorts, marigolds and any small flowers lend themselves well to table arrangements. Don't neglect scabious, Christmas roses or the little early gladioli and even the common nasturtium, with its pretty, round leaves. Large flowers are difficult unless you have a table like a football pitch – guests sit so close to the blooms that the arrangement disappears behind one single flower head. And do be careful to shake dahlias well before you bring them to the table – they are rather prone to hiding earwigs within their curly petals and it is not very appetizing to see an insect emerge and wander across the dinner table.

It is of course possible to use large flower heads by simply floating a single head in a dish of water – take this a stage further and place a small finger bowl by the side of each place, with a flower head floating in it. Big tea roses are ideal for floating in a bowl, though they do need to be fully out to look effective. Hydrangeas also look well in this way and can be used quite late in the year when they are fading to lovely tapestry reds, blues and greens.

Failing finger bowls, use oyster or scallop shells with 1–2 small flower heads fastened with plasticine – pinks and carnations are very good for this but they need a little extra foliage.

To present a striking splash of colour in the centre of the table, arrange a mass of tulip heads in a flattish white, or glass, bowl – cut the heads really short and be generous with the quantity so that they are packed tightly in. Another attractive mass arrangement can be made simply with 4–5 pots of African violets in full bloom, grouped in a shallow, square casserole or similar container. This is not as extravagant as it sounds because the violets will go on as pot plants for months or even years.

At times when flowers are short, use wild berries, hips, spindle, old man's beard, or leaves from variegated plants like peperomia, tradescantia or begonia. Alternatively, use an arrangement of fruit and leaves. Make a base of wide leaves in a dish – ivy, rhododendron, even rhubarb well polished with oil – and make an arrangement of different shapes and colours. Aubergines and grapes go together well, or polished apples and copper beech leaves. Gourds are particularly helpful in this context and it is well worth trying to cultivate an ornamental gourd plant in your garden or on a balcony; they make an extremely attractive base for a table arrangement. Failing this a common marrow makes a good colour base, as long as you cover part of the large shape with something more interesting.

For a buffet table, long stems and an abundance of flowers become an advantage. Tone the colours with the china and linen again but for a buffet you can be much freer with shape. Use either a single, large display or several tiny posies. All the flowers shown in the two biggest arrangements are good buys from the florist as they last well. In the white bowl, spray chrysanthemums, day lilies and chincherinchees with moluccella (bells of Ireland) should keep fresh looking for days. The pink and white arrangement of arctotis (South African daisies), early gladioli, dianthus and chincherinchees should keep similarly well. Remember even for a buffet table to stick with delicately scented flowers – freesias and strongly scented lilies are for the living room only.

If you want an arrangement which does not take up too much room on a buffet table, use tall candlesticks with a special holder that fits where the candle normally goes. The flowers are arranged in the holder, secured in plastic foam and wire, so that they stand above the food while the candlestick itself takes up very little table space. This is a good arrangement for a wedding buffet where the cake takes pride of place. Choose delicate flowers like dianthus, white early gladioli and trails of stephanotis.

Arctotis, early gladioli dianthus and chincherinchees will stay fresh for days

Use height and width for a buffet table arrangement

China, glass, cutlery and table linen can turn a meal into a banquet. They can transform the atmosphere of something quite ordinary into a really special occasion. Perhaps this is why people so love to give them as wedding presents. But to keep them in good condition does require just a little effort.

The easiest to care for is china. Most china and earthenware will keep its good looks with simple washing in hot water and detergent. It is best rinsed in very hot water after washing and left to drain in a plastic covered rack, then put away as soon as it is dry – drying on a tea towel is a miserable job and not terribly hygienic unless you use a clean cloth every time.

Glasses take a little more effort. These really do need polishing with a soft, dry, fluff-free cloth while they are still hot, otherwise they will not have that lovely shine that sets off your table. If your glassware does develop a film – in the bottom of a decanter, for instance – it can be removed with a solution of 1 tablespoon salt in $\frac{1}{4}$ pint ($\frac{5}{8}$ cup) vinegar. When shaken, this acts as a gentle abrasive that will not harm the surface. Stubborn, stuck-on food should be removed from china or glass first by soaking in cold water then, if necessary, rubbing gently with a nylon scourer. Never use a metal scourer, as this will damage the surface.

A dish washer is still regarded as something of a luxury in most households, despite the acceptance of clothes washing machines. But if you have a large family or do a lot of entertaining – or even if you have a small family but are out at work all day – it can save more time than almost any other appliance. The important things to remember if you have a dish washer are to use the correct amount of powder and to stack things carefully in the machine. And don't use it for non-stick pans, or for knives that have bone, wooden or plastic handles that might come loose or warp and discolour in very hot water. If you have any difficulties, such as film forming on the china, try adjusting the amount of powder – this is usually the reason for the film. If the trouble persists contact the supplier of your dish washer, who will usually be able to give you a simple answer depending on the model and type of powder you are using.

Cutlery is very important. Nothing is less inviting than a fork that does not look thoroughly clean – however sure you are that it has actually been washed. Stainless steel is by far the easiest to keep good-looking. All it requires is careful washing in hot water with an ordinary washing up liquid, and drying and polishing to retain its shine. If you leave cutlery to drain you will find it retains the water spots and these cannot be removed once it is dry. Treat stainless steel bowls and vegetable dishes the same way.

If your stainless steel does become marked, perhaps because you have inadvertently left a dish with something in it for too long, use one of the patent stainless steel cleaners, which are usually either a powder or a paste. Never touch it with a tarnish remover intended for silver – this will severely damage the surface. The second common enemy of stainless steel is salt – if allowed to come into contact with stainless steel in hot water it may very quickly

Caring for tableware and linen

There are several proprietary cleaners for silver

Crisp, home-laundered linen

cause pitting. Another is electrolysis – if food is left in a stainless steel dish with a silver or nickel plated spoon in it, or covered with aluminium foil, the two metals set up an electrolytic action and subsequent corrosion that is extremely difficult to remove – and the food is also contaminated.

Silver is much more tedious to keep in good condition, though most people think the result is worth any amount of trouble. Ordinary, everyday cutlery doesn't tarnish as readily as one might think, as the constant washing and drying up polishes it. It will want a thorough clean from time to time though. For any silver there are many proprietary cleaners on the market. Liquid dips are extremely useful in an emergency particularly for items with a difficult

shape like a fork, but silver cleaned this way tarnishes again fairly quickly. Paste or semi-liquid polish or an impregnated pad is more effective for long-term cleaning, and there are some preparations that give a truly long lasting shine. Whatever preparations you choose, do use a very soft cloth – cheese cloth is ideal – or you will risk scratching the silver. For decorative ware a soft brush is useful, to remove the polish from the cracks.

After cleaning always wrap any silver that is not on display in tissue paper and a polythene bag as excluding air delays the tarnishing action (specially treated tarnish preventing cloths are available). Silver cared for like this may need thorough cleaning perhaps only twice a year. Copper, brass and pewter are the same in this respect, and there are special cleaners for all of them.

When it comes to special table cloths and napkins, there is a lot to be said for sending them to a professional laundry. The finish your linen will receive there is much better than you can give at home unless you enjoy ironing and are prepared to spend a lot of time and effort achieving a good finish. Laundries are also experienced in stain removal and are much less likely to damage a badly stained article than you are if you tackle it yourself.

But for everyday cloths and some made from easy-care fabrics, home laundering is just as effective. Courtelle and Terylene are particularly good as they need only light ironing; cotton seersucker is pretty for a breakfast or supper cloth and even looks better for not being ironed! Rayon is difficult to keep looking good however you treat it – it needs as much ironing as linen but will not take starch and loses its 'body' very quickly. The only real disadvantage of synthetic fabrics for the table is that stain removal can be difficult, though some do have a special stain-resistant finish. Most synthetics do not react well to very hot water and some will not withstand the use of chemical solvents. Wherever possible, take some corrective action over a stain as soon as possible, though not at the expense of your guests' comfort and peace of mind! Rinse or sponge any stain with cold water first (hot water will often set a stain like a dye), then soak the cloth in a washing powder solution for several hours before washing.

White linen is usually not much of a problem; normal washing will remove most stains, and a mild solution of bleach can be used for anything that is particularly stubborn. Coloureds are more difficult as the colours may not be fast – whatever treatment you intend using, do test a small corner first. For grease marks use a grease solvent before normal washing – and failing all else send the article to the laundry! Try to keep your tablecloths flat – a special linen cupboard or drawer helps. Nothing is more frustrating than to find that a beautifully laundered cloth has been pushed up to a corner and needs ironing all over again. It helps to preserve the colour of linen that is not used often if you cover it with tissue paper or a piece of sheeting. Do not leave white table linen in the airing cupboard once it is thoroughly dry, either, as the warmth may discolour it.

Cooking
for
Parties

Organising Children's Parties

As a parent, the way you run your children's parties is a tremendous responsibility. If it were your own party and it didn't quite go with a swing, you could just shrug it off and try again next time; but your children will be miserable for days if something goes wrong. It is worth giving it some real thought beforehand.

One of the first decisions is who to ask. On the whole it is best to keep the age groups separate; 8-year-olds don't mix with toddlers, and 12-year-olds are immeasurably superior to the under-10s. It is often better, too, to separate the sexes – boys and girls mix well at nursery school age and again when they get into their teens, but from 6–7 until they are about 13–14 boys are terribly inhibited by the presence of girls, and vice versa, and their interests are widely different.

For a toddlers' party, it is quite in order simply

think round your own friends and invite any children they may have of the right sort of age. But once they get a little older, it is important to invite *only* your child's own friends – outsiders will not be welcome and could be made to feel miserable if those who do know each other decide to turn nasty.

Having decided who to ask, send out invitations. Half the fun of being asked to a party consists in receiving a formal invitation, so don't imagine that a phone call to mother or a verbal message at school will suffice! State on the invitation the time you intend to start *and* finish, and make it clear whether the children are expected to wear 'best' clothes, jeans and T-shirts or fancy dress. It also helps many people if you circulate a list of who else is coming, so that they can join forces to take and fetch the children.

Few people will need reminding to clear the decks properly — remove all breakables from the party area, generally protect anything that needs protection (a good table-top for instance) and lock the doors of all rooms you don't want the children to use. Except in the most reliable of heat-wave weather, you will need a room for coats, raincoats, muddy boots and so on, preferably with space for mothers to manoeuvre as well if the children are young. Don't forget, too, that parents collecting children at, say, 6–7 o'clock will be ready for a drink themselves, but will *not* want it in amongst the kids' chaos – so keep one room civilised for that if possible.

For tiny children, keep the number down and the party short. This isn't just a measure of self-defence – the children themselves will be happier that way. Under-3s simply are not sociable anyway and may be more bothered than entertained by prolonged and unusual activity. Most 3–5-year-olds are starting to make friends and enjoy each others' company, and also to enjoy new experiences, but still 6 or 8 of them will be plenty and 2 hours quite long enough. Don't try to organise this age group into games or anything too much directed, or you will have trouble on your hands. A large room, lots of ordinary, sturdy toys and an adult eye to make sure everyone is happy are all that is required. Provide small quantities of attractive, savoury foods (tiny sandwiches, crisps, sausages) and a few chocolate biscuits – at this age sticky cakes, even jelly, are rather a waste of time.

For the 6–7-year-olds it starts to be worth making a novelty cake, but still keep the portions small as appetites are very limited and children can easily be either put off completely by too much, or else they eat so much that they are sick – to be avoided if possible! This is an age, too, when it helps to have a theme for the party – pirates, or animals, or cowboys and Indians – anything that can be carried through from the guests' clothes and the room decorations, to the novelty cake, the labels on the sandwiches and the games they play. Organized games are a help now too, as without a little control these children can easily get over-excited and out of hand. Boys at this age tend to be particularly wild and you may fear you will have difficulty controlling

Paper tableware is pretty and saves work

Food packs are handy for a picnic party

them at all; in this case try having a series of small tea parties for 2–3 at a time.

8–10 is perhaps the most rewarding party age for the parent. At this age the children have usually developed huge appetites, so you can provide mountains of food and be sure it will all disappear. Provide lots of the usual savouries, sausages, crisps, small rolls with savoury fillings, plus some 'specials' to give it a real feast atmosphere. There are 2 ways of tackling the entertainment side at this age. If you keep them at home, hefty organisation in the shape of games is necessary, preferably with father around for boys; otherwise you will have a riot on your hands and there is danger of serious harm to limbs and property. A popular answer is to take them all out – cinema, pantomime, swimming baths, safari park – anything that is not quite everyday will do, then you bring them all home for the birthday feast afterwards. The main drawback to the latter choice is of course the expense – 12 admission tickets to anywhere will set you back quite a bit; it all depends which you value most, your pennies or your nerves!

One of the most popular parties is a picnic party. Whether you all travel by car, or walk to the field at the bottom of the garden, or whether you simply pack them all off on their bicycles doesn't matter. The easiest and most popular solution for this type of party is individual food packs – each child has a box, marked with his or her name and filled with sandwiches, biscuits, a bag of crisps and so on. They are then all free to eat exactly when they want, without worrying in case they miss anything.

At 11-plus, parties again change their character. This is the age for which it is most difficult to arrange parties because children are becoming self-conscious and there is a great disparity of sizes and interests between children of the same age. One child may be tall, maturing and awkward while the next is still a small child with childish ways. Girls particularly may seem much older than the boys, so it is best to keep them apart still. Keep the party small and perhaps arrange an outing. For girls a theatre party for even 2 guests is probably the most popular.

Gifts and prizes

An essential feature of children's parties is the little gifts that they are clutching when they leave. The actual article is comparatively unimportant – pencils, ballpoint pens, cheap beads, notebooks, balls, toy knives and pistols – the cheap stores are full of suitable knick-knacks. What really matters is the method of distribution. The easiest method is to give them away as prizes – making absolutely sure that everybody wins something, no matter how unlikely it seems. At Christmas you can't go wrong with a Santa Claus sack or a post box for the little ones, or a big tub for a lucky dip. Either way, half the battle is to wrap them prettily so that they really look attractive, no matter how small. Otherwise you can hide the gifts and give each child a set of clues – making the last game into a treasure hunt.

Menu

serves 12

Savoury choux buns
Hot diggety dogs
Cheese pictures
Alaska express
Gingerbread men

Timetable

for preparing the food
Day before: Bake choux buns but
do not fill; bake gingerbread men;
store both in airtight containers.
In the morning: Make cheese
pictures, arrange and cover with
polythene. Cook and stuff
frankfurters, wrap in bacon and
put ready for grilling; split and
butter rolls.
Slice Swiss roll for Alaska
express and place on dish.
Refresh, cool and fill choux buns.
Just before tea: Grill and
assemble hot diggety dogs.
As tea is served finish Alaska
express.

Savoury choux buns

For choux pastry:
40 g (1½ oz) butter
150 ml (¼ pint) water
65 g (2½ oz) plain flour
2 eggs, lightly beaten

For filling:
100–125 g (4 oz) cream cheese
50 g (2 oz) butter
lemon juice
*salt and freshly ground black
   pepper*
chopped parsley

Melt the butter in the water in a
small pan and bring to the boil.
Remove the pan from the heat
and add the flour all at once. Beat
until the paste is smooth and
leaves the side of the pan, forming
a ball. Cool slightly, then gradually beat in the eggs.
Using a fabric forcing bag fitted
with a 1-cm (½-in.) plain nozzle,
pipe the mixture into about 24
walnut-sized balls on greased
baking sheets. Bake in the oven at
200°C. (400°F.) mark 6 for 15–20
minutes, until the buns are golden brown and cooked through.
Make a slit in the side of each bun
to release the steam; if necessary,
put them back in the oven to dry
out; then cool on wire racks.
Beat together the cream cheese,
butter, lemon juice, seasoning

and parsley until smooth. Pipe
into the hollow in each bun using
a 1-cm (½-in) plain nozzle. Pile
the buns in a pyramid on a flat
serving plate.

Hot diggety dogs

12 pairs frankfurters
100–125 g (4 oz) cottage cheese
chopped chives
12 rashers, streaky bacon, rinded
24 long, soft rolls
butter

To cook the frankfurters, bring a
large pan of water to the boil, turn
off the heat and immerse the
sausages in the water for about 5
minutes. Do not boil them or they
will burst.
Slit the frankfurters lengthwise,
almost to the ends, mix the cottage cheese well with the chives
and fill the mixture into the split
sausages.
Cut the bacon rashers in half and
stretch each one with the back of
the blade of a knife. Wrap each
sausage spirally in a piece of
bacon and fasten the ends with
cocktail sticks. Grill until the
bacon is crisp.
Split the rolls, leaving a hinge,
and butter them. Just before serving, remove the cocktail sticks
and place a hot, bacon wrapped
sausage in each roll.

Serve hot diggety dogs with tomato relish and sweetcorn relish
in separate dishes.

Cheese pictures

24 small slices bread
butter
24 slices cold luncheon meat
*12 slices processed Cheddar or
   Cheshire cheese*

Butter the bread and top each
slice with a slice of luncheon
meat. Trim the edges.
Using fancy biscuit cutters, cut
the centres out of the processed
cheese slices. Top half the slices
of luncheon meat with the 12
fancy shapes, using the outsides
of the cheese squares as 'frames'
for the remaining 12 slices.

Alaska express

1 large chocolate Swiss roll
*312-g (11-oz) can mandarin
   oranges*
5 egg whites
275 g (10 oz) caster sugar
*1 litre (35-fl oz) block vanilla ice
   cream*
chocolate polka dots
1 individual chocolate covered roll
cotton wool

Cut the Swiss roll into 10 slices.
Arrange 6 of the slices on a flat,

oblong, ovenproof dish to form
rectangle. Spoon over 2 × 15 m
spoons (2 tbsps) mandarin juic
from the can.
Whisk the egg whites until stif
add half the caster sugar an
whisk again until stiff. Fold i
the remaining sugar with a met
spoon. Spoon the meringue into
fabric forcing bag fitted with
large star vegetable nozzle. Plac
the block of ice cream on th
Swiss roll slices and arrange al
but 3 of the drained mandarins o
top of the ice cream.
Quickly pipe the meringue ove
the ice cream to form an engin
shape to completely enclose th
roll.
Pipe meringue rosettes along th
top and decorate with th
reserved mandarins and polk
dots. Place the engine in th
oven, pre-heated to 230°C
(450°F.) mark 8 for about
minutes, until golden. Th
meringue will be slightly crisp o
the outside and soft inside.
Position the extra 4 slices o
Swiss roll for wheels and use th
small chocolate roll as a funne
with a puff of cotton wool fo
smoke. Serve at once.
Note: The Alaska express, com
plete except for wheels an
smoke, can be packed in a rigi
container and frozen. To serve
remove from the freezer 1 hou

Alaska express is a children's favourite

100

before slicing and keep in a cool place.

Gingerbread men

350 g (12 oz) plain flour
5 ml spoon (1 level tsp)
  bicarbonate of soda
10 ml spoon (2 level tsps) ground
  ginger
125 g (4 oz) butter
175 g (6 oz) soft brown sugar
4 × 15 ml spoons (4 tbsps) golden
  syrup
1 egg, beaten
currants for decoration
white royal or glacé icing for
  decoration

Sift together the flour, bicarbonate of soda and ground ginger. Rub the butter into the sifted ingredients with the fingertips, add the sugar and mix well. Warm the syrup slightly and stir into the rubbed in mixture, with the egg, to give a pliable dough. Knead until smooth and roll out on a floured board to 0·3 cm (⅛-in.) thickness. Draw a gingerbread man about 13·5 cm (5½ in.) high and 11·5 cm (4½ in.) broad on greaseproof or non-stick paper. Cut out the shape and use as a template. Place it on the dough and cut around it with a sharp-pointed knife. Carefully lift the men on to a greased baking sheet, keeping them well apart. On to each man, put 3 currants for buttons and 3 more to represent his eyes and mouth. Bake in the oven at 190°C. (375°F.) mark 5 for 10–15 minutes, until evenly coloured. Cool on a wire rack. To decorate, outline the neck, sleeve ends and feet with piped white icing.

Menu
serves 12

Hot sausages
Pop corn
Chicken puffs
Decker sandwiches
Cheese and cherry
hedgehog
Money cake
Strawberry and orange
cups

Timetable
for preparing food
Day before: Make and decorate the cake; store in an airtight container in a cool place.

Cook the chicken puffs and store in a cool place.
Make the strawberry and orange cups but do not add cream and decoration.
In the morning: Decorate the strawberry and orange cups.
Twist the sausages and put in pan ready for cooking.
Make the sandwiches and chill.
1 hour before: Make the hedgehog.
Just before tea: Refresh the chicken puffs in the oven at 180°C. (350°F.) mark 4 for about 15 minutes.
Cook sausages.
Cut sandwiches into fingers.

Chicken puffs

450 g (1 lb) cooked chicken meat
50 g (2 oz) butter or margarine
100–125 g (4 oz) onion, skinned
  and finely chopped
50 g (2 oz) flour
300 ml (½ pint) milk
lemon juice
salt and pepper
375 g (13 oz) frozen puff pastry,
  thawed
beaten egg to glaze

Discard the skin from the chicken and cut the meat into small pieces. In a saucepan, melt the fat and add the onion; sauté until soft but not coloured. Stir in the flour

and cook for 2 minutes. Off the heat, add the milk, stirring. Bring to the boil, reduce the heat and cook for 3 minutes, still stirring. Add the chicken, lemon juice and seasoning to taste. Turn into a bowl, cover closely with damp greaseproof paper and leave to cool.
Roll out the pastry very thinly and cut out 24 × 10 cm (4-in.) rounds. Brush the edge of each round with egg. Put a teaspoon of the chicken mixture in the centre of each, fold the pastry over, seal and brush with more egg to glaze. Place the puffs on baking sheets and cook in the oven at 200°C. (400°F.) mark 6 for about 20 minutes, until puffed and golden. Serve warm rather than hot.

Decker sandwiches

800 g (1¾ lb) square sandwich
  loaf (preferably a day old)
butter

For first layer:
6 eggs, hard-boiled and sieved
100–125 g (4 oz) butter, softened
salt and pepper

For second layer:
2 × 141-g (2 × 5-oz) cans
  sardines, drained
113-g (4-oz) can pimiento, drained
  and chopped
15 ml spoon (1 tbsp) lemon juice
salt and pepper

For third layer:
225 g (8 oz) pâté
2 gherkins, finely chopped
salt and pepper
For fourth layer:
225 g (½ lb) firm cream cheese
½ bunch watercress, chopped
salt and pepper
Remove the crusts from the loaf. Slice the loaf in half and cut each half into 12 slices, lengthwise. Mix the ingredients for the separate layers in individual basins. Butter and assemble the bread slices with different fillings, in 4 blocks of 6 slices. Wrap in foil and chill until required. Cut into fingers or small triangles.

Money cake

For Victoria sandwich cake:
225 g (8 oz) butter and margarine,
  mixed
225 g (8 oz) caster sugar
4 eggs
175 g (6 oz) self-raising flour
50 g (2 oz) cocoa

For butter cream:
225 g (8 oz) butter
450 g (1 lb) icing sugar, sifted
4 × 15 ml spoons (4 tbsps)
  evaporated milk
a few drops vanilla essence
50 g (2 oz) cocoa blended with a
  little water

For decoration:
foil-covered chocolate coins

Sausage kebabs, with bacon rolls and cheese

Grease and line 3 × 21·5 cm (3 × 8½-in.) straight-sided sandwich tins.

Cream the fats and sugar together until pale and fluffy. Add the eggs a little at a time, beating well after each addition. Sift together the flour and cocoa and fold half into the creamed mixture, using a metal spoon. Then fold in the rest of the flour and cocoa.

Divide the cake mixture between the tins and bake in the oven at 190°C. (375°F.) mark 5 for 20–25 minutes. Turn out the cakes and cool them on a wire rack.

Meanwhile, make the butter cream. Cream the butter and gradually beat in half the icing sugar, with the evaporated milk and a few drops of essence. Then beat in the rest of the sugar. Divide the butter cream into 2 portions, and flavour half with the blended cocoa, mixing well.

When the cakes are cool, sandwich them together with white butter cream. Coat the top and sides with chocolate butter cream and decorate with the foil-covered chocolate coins.

Strawberry and orange cups

6 medium oranges (175–225 g (6–8 oz) each)
1½ pkts orange jelly
350 g (12 oz) cake crumbs
12 fresh strawberries, hulled
200 ml (7 fl oz) double cream, whipped
12 small chocolate peppermint or orange sticks

Halve the oranges and squeeze out the juice, without damaging the skins. Scrape out as much as possible of the white pith. Put the jelly tablets and orange juice in a measure and make up to 900 ml (1½ pints) with hot water. Stir to dissolve the jelly.

Soak the cake crumbs in 300 ml (½ pint) of the liquid jelly and divide amongst the orange halves. Chill until set. Leave the remaining jelly to set. When the jelly is set, chop it roughly and pile it on to the cake crumb base. Pipe a whirl of cream into the centre of each 'cup' and place a strawberry in the centre. Decorate with a chocolate peppermint or orange stick.

For the extras

You will need 700 g (1½ lb) chipolata sausages, each 1 twisted in half. Grill them, or bake in the oven, and spear with cocktail sticks.

Open bags of popcorn and serve it in small dishes.

For cheese and cherry hedgehog, use about 350 g (¾ lb) Cheddar cheese, cut into 1 cm (½-in.) cubes. Spear each cube on a cocktail stick with a stoned black cherry (about 450 g or 1 lb) and spike the sticks into a hard white cabbage. Or make small hedgehogs, using cooking apples instead of the cabbage.

Menu
serves 8

Sausage kebabs
Pinwheel sandwiches
Shoestring potatoes
Knickerbocker glories
Roundabout cake
Owl cookies

Timetable
for preparing the food
Several days before: Make roundabout cake but do not decorate; make owl cookies; store in airtight containers.
Day before: Divide the sausages, make bacon rolls and cut cheese cubes; store in separate polythene bags in refrigerator. Make jellies, leave in a cool place.
In the morning: Make sandwich rolls and refrigerate. Decorate cake.
Before tea: Slice the pinwheel sandwiches, cook sausages and bacon and finish kebab arrangement. Make knickerbocker glories just before serving.

Sausage kebabs

½ kg (1 lb) pork chipolatas
350 g (¾ lb) streaky bacon rashers, rinded
225–350 g (½–¾ lb) Cheddar cheese
potato crisps

Twist each sausage in half and cut into 2 small sausages. Place in a baking tin and cook in the oven at 200°C. (400°F.) mark 6 for about 30 minutes.

On a flat surface, stretch the bacon rashers with the back of a knife; cut each rasher in half and form into rolls. Place in a tin and cook in the oven until beginning to colour. Cut the cheese into cubes and spear with cocktail sticks. Spear the sausages and bacon rolls on sticks and spike all

the kebabs into a cabbage, large apples or a long French loaf. Surround with potato crisps or shoestring potatoes.

The sausages and bacon are best eaten warm.

Pinwheel sandwiches

1 large, square sandwich loaf (preferably a day old)
butter

For sandwich fillings:
*mashed canned salmon and chopped cucumber, mixed
scrambled egg and chopped chives, mixed
cream cheese and diced tomatoes, mixed*

Cut the loaf into slices lengthwise and trim off the crusts. Butter each slice right up to the edges and spread with the fillings.

Roll each slice up like a Swiss roll. Wrap the rolls in polythene or foil and chill for several hours. Just before serving, slice the rolls across into pinwheels and arrange on serving plates.

Knickerbocker glories

½ pkt red jelly
½ pkt yellow jelly
425-g (15-oz) can peach slices, drained and chopped
226-g (8-oz) can pineapple, drained and chopped
1 litre (35-fl oz) block vanilla ice cream
170 ml (6 fl oz) double cream, whipped
8 glacé cherries

Make up the jellies as directed on the packet and allow to set. When set, chop the jellies. Put small portions of the chopped fruit in the bottom of tall sundae glasses and cover this with a layer of red jelly. Put a scoop of ice cream on top and add a layer of chopped yellow jelly.

Repeat the layers, finishing with a layer of cream and topping each with a cherry.

Roundabout cake

225 g (8 oz) butter
225 g (8 oz) caster sugar
4 eggs
225 g (8 oz) self-raising flour
juice of ½ lemon

For filling:
225 g (8 oz) butter
350 g (12 oz) icing sugar, sifted
juice of ½ lemon

For decoration:
225 g (½ lb) orange and lemon slices
1 stick lemon rock
coloured ribbons

Grease 2 × 20·5 cm (2 × 8-in.) sandwich tins and line with paper to come a little way above the rim. Cream the butter and sugar until light and fluffy. Add the egg a little at a time, beating well after each addition. Fold in half the flour using a metal spoon, then fold in the second half. Lastly mix in the lemon juice. Divide the mixture between the tins. Bake in the oven at 190°C (375°F.) mark 5 for about 2. minutes. Cool on a wire rack. Make up butter icing by creaming the butter till fluffy then gradually add the icing sugar and lemon juice. Beat well.

Sandwich the cakes together with a little icing then spread the remainder over the top and sides. Place the cake on a silver board and draw a serrated scraper round the sides.

Using scissors or a sharp knife cut the orange and lemon slices into little boys and girls. Arrange them round the sides of the cake. Fix the ribbons on to the stick of rock with icing, then press the rock into the centre of the cake. Arrange the ribbons so that each figure round the side is holding one.

Owl cookies

150 g (5 oz) plain flour
5 ml spoon (1 level tsp) baking powder
a pinch of salt
75 g (3 oz) butter
90 g (3½ oz) pale soft brown sugar
½ a large egg, beaten
a few drops vanilla essence
25 g (1 oz) cooking chocolate
a pinch of bicarbonate of soda
whole almonds, blanched
tiny chocolate dots

Sift together the flour, baking powder and salt. Cream the butter until pale and light-textured and beat in the sugar; add the beaten egg and vanilla essence.

Melt the chocolate in a small bowl over a pan of warm water, cool it slightly but keep it liquid, and add the bicarbonate of soda to darken it.

Add the dry ingredients to the creamed mixture and stir until evenly blended. Remove two-thirds of the dough to a floured board. Stir the melted chocolate into the remaining third.

Lightly shape both mixtures into sausage shapes. Chill in the refrigerator for ½-1 hour, until the dough is a rolling consistency. Divide the light-coloured dough into 2 portions and roll into an oblong 12·5 cm by 10 cm (5 in. by 4 in.). Divide the chocolate dough into 2 portions and roll each into a 12·5 cm (5-in.) sausage length. Place each chocolate roll on a piece of light dough and roll up. Leave both rolls in the refrigerator for a further 1–2 hours to firm. Cut into slices about 0·3–0·5 cm (⅛–¼ in.) thick. To form the owl's head, place 2 circles side by side and press lightly together. Pinch the top corners of each head to form ears. Cut the almonds diagonally across and place a piece in the centre of each head, for the beak; place chocolate dots for the eyes. Bake the owls in the oven at 180°C. (350°F.) mark 4 for 8–10 minutes. Remove carefully on to a wire rack to cool.

Roundabout cake – allow a ribbon for each guest

Owl cookies can be made well in advance

Menu
serves 6

Sausage beehives
Dip-in salad
Sandwich checkerboard
Chive dip and crackers
Rabbit mousses
Jumbo the clown

Timetable
for preparing the food

Day before: Make cake but do not decorate; store in an airtight container. Make sausage beehives; store in an airtight container in a cool place. Make up jelly for rabbit mousses.

In the morning: Decorate Jumbo the clown. Cut sandwiches and refrigerate, make dips. Prepare rabbit faces and ears.

Just before tea: Reheat sausage beehives if serving warm. Make rabbit mousses — if ice cream is used, do this at the last possible moment.

Sausage beehives

2 × 215 g (2 × 7½ oz) pkts frozen
*   shortcrust pastry, thawed*
½ kg (1 lb) sausage meat
1 egg, beaten

Roll out each piece of pastry into a strip about 51 cm (20 in.) long by 6·5 cm (2½ in.) wide. With a

5-cm (2-in.) cutter, stamp out 2 rounds from each end of each strip of pastry, making 8 altogether. Cut the remainder of each strip into 4 long strips, each 1 cm (½ in.) wide. Brush the pastry strips and rounds with beaten egg. Divide the sausage meat into 8 pieces and shape each piece into a pyramid. Place the pastry rounds on a baking sheet; top each with a sausage pyramid. Then, starting at the base of the pyramid, coil a pastry strip round the sausage meat with the egg side outermost. Slightly overlap each layer to make it look like a beehive.

Brush the finished beehives with beaten egg and bake in the centre of the oven at 200°C. (400°F.) mark 6 for about 30 minutes until golden.

Dip-in salad

2 large carrots
½ small cucumber
2 sticks celery
6 × 15 ml spoons (6 tbsps) bottled salad cream
2 × 15 ml spoons (2 tbsps) sultanas
25 g (1 oz) peanuts

Peel the carrots and cut them into chunky sticks, about 4–5 cm (1½ in.–2 in.) long. Cut the cucumber into sticks about the same size, without removing the skin. Scrub the celery and cut into pieces about 5 cm (2 in.) long. Make small cuts down into the celery to within 1 cm (½ in.) of one end; leave the pieces in very cold water for about 1 hour until the ends start to curl.

Mix together remaining ingredients in a small bowl. Stand the bowl on a plate and arrange the vegetables round it, or serve separately.

Sandwich checkerboard

1 small white loaf
1 small brown loaf
butter
1 egg, scrambled with butter, milk and seasonings
141-g (5-oz) can tuna, drained and flaked
5 ml spoon (1 tsp) lemon juice
bunch of watercress

Cut 9 thin slices of bread from each loaf and butter them. Make egg sandwiches with the white bread. Season the tuna with lemon juice and sandwich with brown bread. Cut off all the crusts

and cut each slice into 4 squares (the 9th slice in each case should be cut and sandwiched to give 2 squares).

Cover a 25·5 cm (10-in.) square board with foil or white paper and arrange alternating brown and white breads to form a square. Garnish with small sprigs of watercress.

Chive dip

100–125 g (4 oz) cream cheese
2 × 15 ml spoons (2 tbsps) chopped chives
15 ml spoon (1 tsp) cream or top of the milk

Blend all the ingredients to a soft cream. Serve in a small dish, surrounded with crackers.

Rabbit mousses

50 g (2 oz) chocolate dots
12 marshmallows
6 individual block frozen mousses or individual dairy ice creams
6 plain chocolate finger biscuits chopped jelly for decoration

Melt the chocolate dots in a small bowl over a pan of hot water. Stir with a teaspoon and then spoon into a paper piping bag.

Dip a pair of kitchen scissors in water and cut 6 of the marshmallows almost completely in half. Snip off the very tip of the chocolate filled bag and pipe rabbit faces on to the 6 whole marshmallows. Leave to set.

Unwrap the mousses or ice creams and place side by side on a flat dish. Decorate each with a rabbit face, using the split marshmallows for ears. Cut the chocolate biscuits in half and position under the faces, for legs. Decorate with chopped jelly. If using mousses, leave them to soften a little; if using ice cream, serve at once.

Jumbo the clown

For cake:
225 g (8 oz) butter
225 g (8 oz) caster sugar
4 eggs, beaten
grated rind and juice of 1 orange
225 g (8 oz) self-raising flour

For frosting:
3 egg whites
500 g (1 lb 2 oz) caster sugar
pinch of salt
6 × 15 ml spoons (6 tbsps) water
pinch of cream of tartar
few drops cochineal or orange colouring

Jumbo the clown is fun to make as well as eat

For decorations:
1 ice cream cone
1 ping-pong ball
1 length of orange ribbon vermicelli

Grease and line 2 × 20·5 cm (2 × 8 in.) straight sided sandwich tins. Cream together the butter and sugar until light and fluffy. Gradually beat in the eggs, orange rind and juice. Sift the flour, fold it into the creamed mixture and mix well. Turn into the prepared tins and bake in the centre of the oven at 180°C. (350°F.) mark 4 for about 30 minutes, or until golden brown. Turn out carefully and cool on a wire rack.

For the frosting, put the egg whites, sugar, salt, water and cream of tartar in a large bowl over a pan of hot water. Beat with a rotary whisk or electric hand mixer until the mixture thickens enough to form peaks – approximately 7 minutes. Colour with a few drops of cochineal or orange colouring; take care not to over-colour.

Sandwich the cakes together with 2–3 × 15 ml spoons (2–3 tbsps) of the frosting. Spread all but 2–3 × 15 ml spoons (2–3 tbsps) of the remaining frosting over the cake and, with a spoon handle, whirl it into a pattern.

Cut the ice cream cone, removing the base for a collar. Fix this in the centre of the cake. Paint a clown's face on the ping-pong ball and fix this to the collar; tie a bow round with the ribbon.

Cover the top of the ice cream cone with frosting, peaking it up and sprinkling with vermicelli. Attach it carefully to the 'face' with the remaining frosting, to make a tall clown's hat. Sprinkle vermicelli on the cake round the base of the collar to make a ruff. Serve on a flat plate or board.

Sausage beehives and dip-in salad

Parties for Young Teenagers

Now is the time for you to leave the youngsters to themselves. If you have a suitable attic or spare room which you can hand over, they may even wish to decorate it to their own taste permanently.

Provide lots of food, preferably hot, plenty of soft drinks and 1 good punch or cup. They will enjoy organising the music and decor themselves, but be around in case advice is needed.

Menu
serves 8

Hamburgers on savoury rice
White cabbage salad
Orange baked apples and cream
Mulled cider

Hamburgers on savoury rice

350 g (12 oz) long grain rice
salt and pepper
100–125 g (4 oz) sultanas
2 × 10 ml spoons (4 tsps) chopped parsley
1 red pepper (capsicum), seeded and diced
1 green pepper (capsicum), seeded and diced
100–125 g (4 oz) cooked ham, chopped
stock
16 frozen hamburgers
olive oil

Boil the rice in salted water for 5 minutes, drain well and place in a large, shallow, ovenproof dish. Stir in the seasoning, sultanas, parsley, peppers and chopped ham; add just enough stock to cover. Brush the hamburgers with oil and place on top of the rice. Cover with greaseproof paper and cook at the top of the oven at 180°C. (350°F.) mark 4 for 45 minutes.

White cabbage salad

700 g (1½ lb) finely shredded crisp white cabbage
2 carrots, peeled and grated
1 eating apple, cored and cubed
1 small green pepper (capsicum), seeded and very finely chopped
15 ml (1 tbsp) chopped onion
2 × 15 ml spoons (2 tbsps) caster sugar
15 ml (1 tbsp) lemon juice
142 ml (¼ pint) soured cream
3 × 15 ml spoons (3 tbsps) mayonnaise
salt and pepper
celery seeds

Toss together the cabbage, carrot, apple, pepper and onion. Blend together the sugar, lemon juice, soured cream and mayonnaise. Check the seasoning. Add the salad ingredients and lightly toss together; sprinkle with celery seeds.

Orange baked apples

8 large cooking apples, wiped and cored
100–125 g (4 oz) butter
100–125 g (4 oz) caster sugar
2 large oranges
284 ml (½ pint) double cream, whipped

Make a cut through the skin round the centre of each apple and place them in a large baking dish. Cream together the butter and sugar until pale and light. Grate the rind from 1 of the oranges and squeeze out the juice; beat the rind into the butter, with as much juice as it will take. Fill this orange butter into the centres of the apples.

Pare the rind finely from the remaining orange, shred it and blanch in boiling water for 5 minutes. Meanwhile remove all the white pith from the flesh and chop the flesh roughly.

Bake in the oven at 180°C. (350°F.) mark 4 for about 30 minutes. Top each apple with a spoonful of chopped orange and a few shreds of rind. Serve hot with whipped cream.

Mulled cider
makes 24 servings

15 cm (6 in) of cinnamon stick
10 ml spoon (2 level tsps) whole allspice
4·5 litres (8 pints) cider
225 g (8 oz) Demerara sugar
1 orange, sliced
1 lemon, sliced
whole cloves

Put the cinnamon stick and allspice in a muslin bag. Heat the cider, sugar and spices in a saucepan and bring almost to boiling point. Remove the spices. Stud the centre of each fruit slice with a clove, float the slices on top of the mull and simmer gently for a few minutes.

Ladle the cider into tumblers or mugs – a spoon in the glasses will prevent them cracking.

Baked apples, stuffed with orange butter and topped with fruit

Menu
serves 12

Brown onion soup
Potato moussaka
Poor man's fondue
Fresh fruit
White wine cup

Brown onion soup

2 × 15 ml spoons (2 tbsps) cooking oil
50 g (2 oz) butter
1 kg (2 lb) onions, skinned and finely sliced
2 cloves garlic, skinned and crushed
2 beef stock cubes
1·7 litre (3 pints) boiling water
salt and pepper

Heat the oil and butter in a large pan and fry the onion over gentle heat for about 20 minutes, until soft but not coloured. Add the garlic, dissolve the beef cubes in the boiling water, add to the pan, cover and simmer for 30 minutes. Adjust seasoning.

Potato moussaka

100–125 g (4 oz) margarine
2 large onions, skinned and finely chopped
2 cloves garlic, skinned and crushed
1 kg (2 lb) cooked lamb, minced
2 beef stock cubes, dissolved in 300ml (½ pint) boiling water
2 × 15 ml spoons (2 tbsps) tomato paste
5 ml spoon (1 level tsp) dried oregano
salt and pepper
100–125 g (4 oz) lard
1½ kg (3 lb) potatoes, peeled and sliced
50 g (2 oz) flour
400 ml (¾ pint) milk
pinch of ground nutmeg
2 egg yolks
50 g (2 oz) Cheddar cheese, grated
2 tomatoes, sliced

Melt 50 g (2 oz) margarine in a large pan, add the onion and fry for 5 minutes, until golden. Add the lamb and garlic, stir in the stock, tomato paste, oregano and season. Melt the lard in a large frying pan and fry the potato slices for about 10 minutes, or until golden. Drain off the fat. Melt the remaining margarine in a pan, stir in the flour and cook over gentle heat for 2 minutes. Remove the pan from the heat, stir in the milk gradually, the bring to the boil, stirring. Cook for 2 minutes. Stir in the nutmeg and season to taste. Beat in the egg yolks, one at a time.

Cover the base of a large buttered casserole with a layer of potatoes, and season. Spread half the meat mixture over the potatoes; top with half the remaining potatoes and half the sauce. Finish with layers of potatoes, meat and sauce. Sprinkle the cheese over the top and bake in the centre of the oven at 190°C. (375°F.) mark 5 for 35 minutes. Garnish with tomatoes.

White wine cup

fresh fruit in season
15 ml spoon (1 tbsp) sugar
4 × 15 ml spoons (4 tbsps) Kirsch or maraschino
1 bottle medium-dry white wine
1 bottle sparkling hock

Slice the fruit (strawberries, peaches, apricots etc.) and place in the bottom of a bowl. Sprinkle with sugar, pour on the liqueur and leave for 30 minutes. Pour on the still white wine and chill for a further 30 minutes. Add the sparkling wine and serve at once.

Poor man's fondue

you may find it easiest to make this quantity in 2 pans

1 clove garlic, skinned and cut in half
75 g (3 oz) butter
4 × 15 ml spoons (4 level tbsps) flour
550 ml (1 pint) medium sweet cider
¾ kg (1½ lb) Cheddar cheese, grated
¼ kg (½ lb) Gruyère cheese, grated
salt and pepper
2·5 ml spoon (½ level tsp) grated nutmeg

Rub the halves of garlic round the sides and base of a large flame-proof pan – this will impart just the faintest garlic flavour. Melt the butter in the pan, stir in the flour and cook for 1–2 minutes. Pour the cider slowly into the flour mixture and bring to the boil, stirring all the time. Simmer for 2 minutes.

Stir the grated cheeses into the sauce and heat gently until it melts. Season lightly with salt, pepper and nutmeg.

Transfer the pan to a table heater for serving, so that it remains hot throughout. Serve with a basketful of French bread cut into small cubes.

Menu
serves 12

Cream of celery and tomato soup
Stuffed jacket potatoes
Hot dogs
Winter fruit salad

Cream of celery and tomato soup

350 g (12 oz) onions, skinned and sliced
175 g (6 oz) butter
1½ kg (3 lb) celery, scrubbed and sliced
1½ kg (3 lb) tomatoes, skinned and sliced
2·3 litres (4 pints) chicken stock
5 ml spoon (1 level tsp) sweet basil
salt and freshly ground black pepper
100–125 g (4 oz) flour
1·1 litre (2 pints) milk
chopped parsley

Fry the onions gently in 50 g (2 oz) butter in a large pan, for 5 minutes. Add the celery and cook for a further 5 minutes.

Add the tomatoes, chicken stock and basil, season well and bring to the boil. Reduce the heat, cover the pan and simmer for about 45 minutes. Sieve, or purée in a blender.

Make a roux by melting the remaining butter in a clean pan and stirring in the flour. Cook over a low heat for 2–3 minutes, remove from the heat and add the milk slowly, stirring until well blended.

Gradually add the vegetable purée, bring to the boil, adjust seasoning and simmer for a further 15 minutes.

Sprinkle in the chopped parsley just before serving.

Stuffed jacket potatoes

12 large potatoes, of even size
cooking oil

For curried egg filling:
4 eggs, hard-boiled and shelled
100–125 g (4 oz) onion, skinned and chopped
25 g (1 oz) butter
5 ml spoon (1 level tsp) curry powder
100–125 g (4 oz) cooking apple, peeled and diced
salt and freshly ground black pepper

For bacon filling:
50 g (2 oz) onion, skinned and chopped
25 g (1 oz) butter
175 g (6 oz) bacon rashers, rinded and chopped
2·5 ml spoon (½ level tsp) marjoram
15 ml spoon (1 tbsp) milk
salt and freshly ground black pepper
100–125 g (4 oz) cheese, grated

Wash, scrub and dry the potatoes. Prick with a fork and brush with oil, then place on baking sheets and cook in the oven at 180°C. (350°F.) mark 4 for about 1½ hours.

For the first filling, sieve 2 of the eggs, fry the onion in the butter until soft but not coloured; add the curry powder and apple and fry for a further 5 minutes, then add the sieved egg.

Cut lids from the tops of 6 of the potatoes when they are cooked and scoop out the centres, leaving a wall of skin. Mix the soft potato with the curried mixture and season well. Replace the mixture inside the potato shells and garnish with the remaining 2 eggs, sliced. Serve accompanied with mango chutney.

For the second filling, fry the onion in the butter until soft but not coloured, and set aside. Add the bacon to the pan and fry until crisp. Stir in the marjoram.

Scoop out the centres from the remaining 6 potatoes, cream the soft potato with the milk, add the onion and bacon and season well. Refill the potato cases. Top with grated cheese and keep warm in a low oven. Brown under a hot grill just before serving.

Hot dogs

1 kg (2 lb) chipolata sausages
½ kg (1 lb) streaky bacon rashers, rinded (optional)
32 long, soft, hot-dog rolls
butter

Grill the sausages alone, or wrap each one first in a piece of bacon. Split the rolls lengthwise, leaving a hinge, and butter them. Insert a sausage in each and serve with sweet corn relish, apple sauce, tomato relish or mild mustard.

Winter fruit salad

juice of 6 large lemons
1½ kg (3 lb) bananas, skinned and sliced
¾ kg (1½ lb) black grapes, pipped
¾ kg (1½ lb) white grapes, pipped
3 × 454-g (3 × 1-lb) cans pineapple slices, drained
12 tangerines, peeled and segmented
900 ml (1½ pints) water
350 g (12 oz) brown sugar
3 × 15 ml spoons (3 tbsps) Kirsch
3 trays ice cubes
426 ml (¾ pint) single cream or 1 litre (35 fl oz) block vanilla ice cream

Potato moussaka is a good filler for young people

Pour the juice of the lemons into a bowl. Add the bananas, grapes, quartered pineapple slices and tangerines. Turn the fruit lightly in the juice. Make up the water to 1·3 litre (2¼ pints) with the juice from the can of pineapple.

In a saucepan, heat the liquid with the sugar until dissolved, then reduce to 900 ml (1½ pints) by boiling rapidly. Cool until there is no steam, then pour over the fruit. Chill, add the Kirsch, and just before serving add the ice cubes. Serve with cream or ice cream.

Menu
serves 8

**West African beef curry
Boiled rice
Sambals
Chicken, rice and corn salad
Fruit salad
Meringue shells
Shandy**

West African beef curry

*2 kg (4 lb) chuck steak
50 g (2 oz) flour
½ × 2·5 ml spoon (¼ level tsp) paprika pepper
½ × 2·5 ml spoon (¼ level tsp) cayenne pepper
½ × 2·5 ml spoon (¼ level tsp) chilli powder
corn oil
½ kg (1 lb) onions, skinned and chopped
2 × 15 ml spoons (2 level tbsps) desiccated coconut
4 × 15 ml spoons (4 level tbsps) curry powder
2 × 15 ml spoons (2 level tbsps) curry paste
1 clove garlic, skinned and crushed
a few drops of Tabasco sauce
1·1 litre (2 pints) stock*

Trim the steak and cut it into serving-size pieces. Toss in the flour seasoned with the paprika, cayenne and chilli powder, using just enough flour to coat the steak thoroughly. Heat 3 × 15 ml spoons (3 tbsps) oil in a large saucepan and fry the onions until evenly browned. Add the coconut, curry powder, curry paste, garlic, Tabasco and stock; bring to the boil.

In a large frying pan, heat enough oil to just cover the base and fry the meat a little at a time, until

sealed and brown. Add the drained meat to the curry sauce, cover and simmer until the meat is tender – about 2 hours. As sambals, serve sliced fruits and raw vegetables, desiccated coconut and pappadums.

Chicken, rice and corn salad

*2 kg (4 lb) chicken, cooked
6 × 15 ml spoons (6 tbsps) French dressing
300 ml (½ pint) lemon mayonnaise
2 × 15 ml spoons (2 tbsps) lemon juice
2 × 15 ml spoons (2 tbsps) single cream
salt and pepper
350 g (12 oz) cooked long grain rice
2 × 312-g (2 × 11-oz) cans sweet corn kernels, drained
2 green peppers (capsicums), seeded and finely diced
1 large lettuce*

Strip the chicken flesh off the bone and cut into 2·5-cm (1-in.) pieces. Toss the meat in French dressing. Put the mayonnaise, lemon juice, cream and seasoning in a bowl. Gently fold in the chicken, rice, corn and green peppers. Adjust seasoning.

Line a large salad bowl with torn lettuce leaves and pile the chicken salad in the centre.

Menu
serves 12

**Sweet and sour meat balls
Noodles
Dutch apple pie
Verandah punch**

Sweet and sour meat balls

*1½ kg (3 lb) minced beef or pork
2 cloves garlic, skinned and finely chopped
125 g (4½ oz) plain flour
50 g (2 oz) fresh breadcrumbs
3 egg yolks
75 g (3 oz) lard
salt and pepper*

For sauce:
*250 g (9 oz) caster sugar
12 × 15 ml spoons (12 tbsps) cider vinegar
12 × 15 ml spoons (12 tbsps) soy sauce*

Sweet and sour meat balls with buttered noodles

*4½ × 15 ml spoons (4½ level tbsps) cornflour
900 ml (1½ pints) water
3 green peppers (capsicums), seeded and sliced
¾ kg (1½ lb) tomatoes, skinned and quartered
3 × 312-g (3 × 11-oz) cans crushed pineapple, drained*

In a large bowl, mix together the meat, garlic, 40 g (1½ oz) flour, the breadcrumbs, salt and pepper. Bind with the egg yolks and form into balls (this quantity should make about 50–60 balls). Toss the meat balls in remaining flour. Melt the lard and fry the balls for 20 minutes, in batches, turning frequently during cooking. Keep each batch hot when cooked.

Meanwhile prepare the sauce. Place the sugar, vinegar and soy sauce in a pan. Blend the cornflour with a little of the measured water and add to the pan with the remaining water. Bring to the boil, stirring, and simmer for 5 minutes. Blanch the pepper and add with the tomatoes and pineapple and simmer for 5–10 minutes.

When the meat balls are cooked divide them between 2–3 large pans, pour the sauce over them and simmer gently for 3 minutes. Serve in large dishes with noodles.

Dutch apple pie
make 3

*¾ kg (1½ lb) cooking apples, peeled and quartered
4–6 15 ml spoons (4–6 tbsps) water
100–125 g (4 oz) soft brown sugar
15 ml spoon (1 level tbsp) cornflour
2·5 ml spoon (1½ level tsp) salt
5 ml spoon (1 level tsp) powdered cinnamon
2 × 15 ml spoons (2 tbsps) lemon juice
25 g (1 oz) butter
2·5 ml spoon (½ tsp) vanilla essence
175 g (6 oz) plain flour
5 ml (1 level tsp) salt
25 g (1 oz) lard
50 g (2 oz) butter
milk to glaze*

Simmer the apples with the water until soft. Mix together the sugar, cornflour, salt and cinnamon and add to the cooked apples. Stir in the lemon juice and cook, stirring, until fairly thick. Remove from the heat, stir in the butter and vanilla essence and cool.

Sift the flour and salt into a bowl. Rub in the lard and butter with the fingertips until the mixture resembles fine breadcrumbs, then add enough cold water to make a stiff dough.

Verandah punch is ideal for a teenage party

West African beef curry

Roll out half the dough and use it to line a 18-cm (7-in.) pie plate, preferably metal; put the apple mixture in the pastry case. Roll out the remaining pastry to make a lid. Damp the edges of the pastry base, cover the pie with the lid and press the edges well together. Knock up and scallop the edges. Brush the top of the pie with milk to glaze and bake in the centre of the oven at 220°C. (425°F.) mark 7 for 10 minutes. Reduce the heat to 190°C. (375°F.) mark 5 and cook for a further 20 minutes, until the pastry is golden.
Serve hot or cold, with whipped cream.

Verandah punch

2 large juicy oranges
3 thin-skinned lemons
150 ml (¼ pint) sugar syrup
300 ml (½ pint) freshly made tea
3 × 175-ml (3 × 6 fl-oz) bottles ginger ale, well chilled
3 × 175-ml (3 × 6 fl-oz) bottles soda water, well chilled
ice cubes and slices of orange to decorate

Squeeze out the fruit juices and mix with the sugar syrup and tea. Cool, then strain into a bowl and chill.
Just before serving, mix in the ginger ale and soda water. Add the ice cubes and sliced orange.

COCKTAIL SAVOURIES

At cocktail time, the food needs to be in small portions, so that guests do not need cutlery, plates or even napkins. Keep to savouries and decorate all your tidbits prettily, so that they look tempting as well as taste good. Allow about 6 per person, plus nuts, crisps and olives for good measure. Provide some snacks that are very light, for those going on to a meal later, but make sure there are 1–2 more substantial items for anyone who is really hungry – remember the drinks will be flowing freely. A good combination would be a few trays of bouchées or other pastries, a cold creamy dip with crackers and crisps, and a hot dip with miniature meat balls, small sausages or fried scampi. Alternatively, supplement the canapés with 2–3 large savoury flans for the hungry people.

Dips

A dip is a soft, well-flavoured mixture which can be hot or cold. A hot dip usually has a base of white sauce to which various seasonings and flavourings can be added, while many of the cold dips are based on cream cheese or soured cream.
For dipping into the mixture, have an assortment of 'dunks' available – crisps, small savoury biscuits, small chunks of French bread, celery curls, or sticks of raw carrot. For something more substantial, offer cooked cocktail sausages with barbecue sauce, fried scampi with tartare sauce, or cubes of grilled marinaded steak with garlic mayonnaise. All should be fixed firmly on cocktail sticks for easy dipping.

Devil's dip

25 g (1 oz) butter
3 × 15 ml spoons (3 level tbsps) flour
2·5 ml spoon (½ level tsp) curry powder
300 ml (½ pint) stock or milk
½ × 2·5 ml spoon (¼ level tsp) cayenne pepper
10 ml spoon (2 tsps) vinegar
142 ml (¼ pint) double cream

Melt the butter in a pan, stir in the flour and curry powder and cook for 2–3 minutes. Gradually stir in the stock or milk, bring to the boil and continue to stir until it thickens; add the cayenne pepper and vinegar. If the dip is to be served hot, pour a little sauce into the cream, blend it smoothly, then return the mixture to the pan and reheat without boiling.
For a cold dip, cool the sauce, whip the cream and fold it in. Serve with carrot sticks, chipolatas or meat balls.

Hot mustard dip

15 ml spoon (1 level tbsp) made mild mustard
10 ml spoon (2 level tsps) made English mustard
2 × 15 ml spoon (2 tbsps) vinegar
25 g (1 oz) butter
3 × 15 ml spoons (3 level tbsps) flour
300 ml (½ pint) stock
15 ml spoon (1 tbsp) cream (optional)

Blend the mustards and vinegar together. Melt the butter in a pan and stir in the flour. Cook for 2–3 minutes, stir in the stock, bring to the boil and stir until the mixture thickens. Remove from the heat and add the prepared mustard Serve hot. If a milder flavour is preferred, stir in the cream just before serving with chipolatas, meat balls or potato crisps.

Chive dip

100–125 g (4 oz) cream cheese
2 × 15 ml spoons (2 tbsps) chopped chives
15 ml spoon (1 tbsp) cream or top of the milk (if necessary)

Beat all the ingredients to a soft cream with a wooden spoon or in an electric blender. Serve with chipolatas, cubed steak, vegetable dunks or French bread.

Cheese butterflies

For pastry:
40 g (1½ oz) butter or margarine and lard
40 g (1½ oz) Cheddar cheese, finely grated
50 g (2 oz) plain flour
pinch of salt

For filling:
100–125 g (4 oz) cream cheese
little milk
finely chopped parsley or paprika pepper

Cream the fat and Cheddar cheese together until soft. Gradually work in the flour and salt with a wooden spoon or a palette knife until the mixture sticks together; with one hand collect it together and knead very lightly until smooth. Cover with greaseproof paper and leave in a cool place to rest.
Roll the pastry out thinly and cut into small rounds with a 2·5 cm (1 in.) plain cutter; cut half the rounds into 2. Put on a baking tray and bake just above the centre of the oven at 200°C.

Prawn bouchées

(400°F.) mark 6 for 10–15 minutes, until a light golden brown.
Mix the cream cheese with a little milk to achieve a piping consistency. Using a large star nozzle pipe a large star on each round Set 2 half-biscuits in the cheese to form 'wings' and decorate with chopped parsley or paprika.

Cherry bacon rolls

makes about 40

225 g (8 oz) thinly sliced streaky bacon
212-g (7½-oz) can maraschino cherries, drained

Rind the bacon and flatten and stretch the rashers with the back of a knife. Cut them in half and wrap each half-rasher round a cherry.
Pierce the cherry and bacon rolls together in groups on thin metal skewers and grill until the bacon is crisp.
Serve the rolls individually on cocktail sticks.

Bouchées

makes 2 dozen

368 g (13 oz) bought puff pastry, thawed
beaten egg to glaze

Roll out the pastry to 0·5-cm (¼-in.) thickness and cut out 24 5-cm (2-in.) rounds, using a plain cutter and re-rolling as required. Place the rounds on wetted baking sheets and brush with beaten egg. Using a 3 cm (1¼ in.) plain cutter, mark a circle in the centre of each, but don't cut right through. Leave to stand in a cool place for 5–10 minutes. Bake above the oven centre at 230°C. (450°F.) mark 8 for about 20 minutes, until well risen and golden brown. Remove the centres,

nd either use the cases hot or ool them on a wire rack and use old.

Mushroom bouchées

lls 24 bouchée cases

0 g (1½ oz) butter
5 g (3 oz) mushrooms, wiped and chopped
5 g (1 oz) flour
42 ml (¼ pt) milk
× 15 ml spoons (3 tbsp) single cream
alt and pepper
Worcestershire sauce

Melt 15 g (½ oz) butter in a small an and sauté the mushrooms. Put them on one side, wipe the an and melt the remaining but-er. Stir in the flour and cook for 1 minute. Slowly beat in the milk nd bring to the boil, stirring; ook for about 2 minutes. Fold in he mushrooms and enough ingle cream to give a thick pour-ng consistency. Season to taste.

Chicken and ham bouchées

Sauté 1 small skinned and finely chopped onion to replace the mushrooms; replace the Worcestershire sauce by Tabas-co, and add 80 g (3 oz) diced cooked chicken and 50 g (2 oz) chopped cooked ham before eheating.

Prawn bouchées

Sauté 125 g (4 oz) shelled prawns instead of the mushrooms and add 1 teaspoon chopped parsley and a squeeze of lemon juice instead of the Worcestershire sauce.

Canapés

Canapés are mouthfuls of savoury food served on small pieces of bread, toast or biscuits. They can be hot or cold, and make a good snack with drinks. The base may be made of but-tered bread – close textured white or brown, sliced about 0·3 cm (⅛ in.) thick and cut into bite-size rounds or fancy shapes; fingers or shapes of toast or fried bread, savoury biscuits, crackers or thin strips of pastry.

Canapés can be more or less elaborate, depending on how much time you may have to pre-pare them. Simple cubes of cheese – Dutch, Cheddar or Danish blue – on cocktail sticks, topped with banana slices, grapes, olives or segments of mandarin orange are very accept-able and have an interesting con-trast in flavour. Slices of hard-boiled egg or ham, with stuffed olives or anchovies on top also present a contrast of the bland and the sharp which goes well on buttered biscuits as an accompan-iment to drinks.

Once you start, you'll find the variations are almost limitless. Here we give a selection of recipes for slightly more elabo-rate canapés.

Blue cheese butter canapés

Blend 50 g (1 oz) soft blue cheese with 100 g (4 oz) butter and spread it on toast or savoury biscuits.

Horseradish butter canapés

Blend 30 ml (2 tbsps) creamed horseradish with 100 g (4 oz) but-ter and pipe it on savoury biscuits. Decorate with half-slices of radish.

Guava cheese spread

Blend 1½ mashed canned guavas and 2.5 ml (½ level tsp) salt with 75 g (3 oz) softened cream cheese. Pipe on top of hard-boiled eggs as decoration, or use simply as a spread.

Tomato canapés

100 g (4 oz) butter
2 × 15 ml spoons (2 level tbsps) finely grated onion
croûtes of fried bread
tomatoes cut in slices
black olives or chopped chives for decoration

Cream together the butter and onion. Spread the mixture on the croûtes. Lay a ring of tomato on each croûte and decorate with

half a black olive or sprinkle with chopped chives.

Camembert canapés

Make and butter some toast and cut into long, narrow fingers about 7·5 cm by 1 cm (3 × ½ in.). Cut fingers of Camembert cheese to the same shape but slightly smaller. Place the cheese strips on top of the toast fingers and cook under a very hot grill for 2–3 minutes, until bubbly and golden brown. Sprinkle the top with pap-rika and serve immediately.

Pâté canapés

Cut rounds of bread about 3 cm (1½ in.) in diameter and fry in butter for 2–3 minutes until gol-den brown; drain on crumpled kitchen paper. Spread or pipe the croûtes with pâté de foie gras and decorate the top of each with a slice of stuffed olive or a gherkin fan.

Devilled crab canapés

15 g (½ oz) onion, finely chopped
15 g (½ oz) butter
100-g (3½-oz) can crab meat
5 ml spoon (1 tsp) Worcestershire sauce or a good dash of Tabasco sauce
pinch of dry mustard
2 × 15 ml spoons (2 tbsps) double cream, whipped
sprig of parsley or a little paprika pepper

A selection of canapés for cocktail time

Fry the onion in the butter for 5 minutes until golden. Drain and add to the crab meat; stir in the seasonings and cream.

Use as a topping for 24 croûtes of fried bread. Decorate each with a sprig of parsley or sprinkle with paprika.

Bacon and egg choux
makes 24

70 g (2½ oz) choux pastry, i.e. made with 70 g flour, etc.

For filling:
300 ml (½ pt) thick white sauce, well-seasoned
2 eggs, hard-boiled and chopped
55 g (2 oz) cooked bacon or lean ham, rinded and very finely chopped

Using a 1-cm (½-in.) plain vegetable nozzle, pipe the choux into about 24 small walnut-sized balls on to greased baking sheets. Bake near the top of the oven at 200°C. (400°F.) mark 6 for 15–20 minutes, until golden brown and crisp. Remove from the oven and cool on a wire rack. If necessary store overnight in an airtight container and refresh the next day before filling.

For the filling, make a well-seasoned thick white sauce and add to it the chopped egg and

bacon. Make a hole in the base of each bun and pipe the filling in with a small plain vegetable nozzle. Alternatively make a slit in the side and spoon the filling in.

Chicken and mushroom choux

24 small choux buns
300 ml (½ pt) thick white sauce, well-seasoned
100 g (4 oz) cooked chicken, finely chopped
50 g (2 oz) fried mushrooms, chopped

Make the choux buns as for bacon and egg choux. Mix the cooked chicken and mushrooms into the white sauce and spoon or pipe a little of the mixture into each bun.

Talmouse

368 g (13 oz) bought puff pastry, thawed
1 egg, beaten

For filling:
185-g (7½-oz) pkt. smoked haddock fillets, cooked as directed
150 ml (¼ pt) thick cheese or white sauce

Roll out the pastry thinly and cut into 7.5 cm (3-in.) rounds with a

plain cutter. Brush the rim of each with beaten egg.

Mix the cold flaked haddock with the sauce and place 5 ml (1 tsp) of this filling in the centre of each round. Draw the pastry up over the filling and pinch to form a 3-cornered shape. Brush with more beaten egg and place on baking sheets. Cook just above the centre of the oven at 200°C. (400°F.) mark 6 for about 20 minutes, until golden brown. Serve hot.

Stuffed grapes

Slit and seed 250 g (½ lb) large black grapes.

Beat 75 g (3 oz) Danish blue cheese until it is smooth. Using a star nozzle, pipe the cheese into the slits in the grapes and serve on cocktail sticks.

Anchovy twists

trimmings of flaky pastry :
55-g (2-oz) can anchovies, drained
1 egg, beaten

Roll out the pastry and cut it into thin finger lengths. Rinse the anchovies in cold water, dry and cut in half lengthwise. Place a half on each piece of pastry and twist the fillet and pastry together. Put on a baking tray, brush the pastry with egg and bake near the top of the oven at 200°C. (400°F.) mark 6 for about 10 minutes.

Creamed kippers
makes about 20

225 g (8 oz) kipper fillets
½ × 2.5 ml spoon (½ level tsp) paprika pepper
dash of lemon juice
pepper
double cream
2.5-cm (1-in.) squares of bread, freshly toasted
radish or gherkin, thinly sliced, or paprika pepper

Grill and skin the kipper fillets. Mash them in a bowl with the paprika, lemon juice and pepper and enough cream to moisten. When sufficiently blended, pile the mixture on the squares of toast and decorate with a slice of radish or gherkin or sprinkle with paprika pepper.
Note: 2 113-g (4 oz) cans of sardines in oil, drained, may be used to replace the kippers.

Cheese aigrettes
serves 4

40 g (1½ oz) butter
150 ml (¼ pt) water
65 g (2½ oz) plain flour
2 eggs, beaten
50 g (2 oz) strong cheese, grated
salt and pepper
cayenne pepper
fat for deep frying

Heat the butter and water in saucepan until the fat dissolve and bring to the boil. Remov from the heat, add all the flour once and beat well until the pas is smooth and leaves the sides the pan. Allow to cool slight then beat in the eggs graduall Add the cheese and season wel Heat the pan of fat and drop teaspoonfuls of the mixture. F until golden, drain well o kitchen paper and serve hot.

Bacon, dates and cheese

Rind some bacon rashers and c each into 2; stone some date Stuff each date with a strip cheese and wrap a piece of baco round. Grill for 8–10 minutes an serve on cocktail sticks.

Miniature meat balls
makes about 24

340 g (¾ lb) lean minced beef (raw)
112 g (¼ lb) minced bacon
half a small onion, skinned and grated
good pinch of mixed dried herb
1 egg yolk
2.5 ml sp. (½ level tsp) salt
freshly ground black pepper
flour

In a bowl, combine all the ingre dients except the flour. Shap into 24 small balls about the siz of a large marble. Dust you hands with flour to help yo shape them. Leave the balls t chill, then lightly oil the base of frying pan and fry them unt cooked – about 7 minutes, turr ing frequently. Drain well an serve on cocktail sticks, with o without a piquant barbecu sauce.

Setting the Scene

Most of us are asked at least once in our lives to organize a social in a club room or public hall. Many people do it regularly, and it becomes a matter of routine, but the first time you are faced with making a very ordinary, if not drab, room convivial enough for a party the task may seem daunting.

If you have a modern hall, purpose built with all the facilities needed for social functions, you have fewer problems; lots of food, flowers, good music and the party is already on the way to being a success. More often than not, though, you will be battling with an ancient tennis pavilion, a sailing club bar or a dilapidated church hall. Even if you have a modern hall, if it is in a multipurpose building with rubber tiled floors and glaring white light in all rooms you still have a problem.

To make your party room a success, it has to have atmosphere and it has to have the appropriate facilities. Before you start, recruit a team of willing, hard workers, including some with special skills such as knowledge of electrical apparatus or flower arranging.

Next make the acquaintance of the caretaker. Check the hall's capacity and how long you may spend there in advance and afterwards. Ask about fire regulations and take these into account when positioning tables, and use any experience the caretaker may have of local hire firms.

Then check the basic facilities, as you may have to arrange hire equipment well in advance. The first is the kitchen. If you are asked to organize a party in a room with no access to a kitchen the most sensible answer is 'no'. If, however, you are forced to manage, use the best camping equipment you can beg or borrow. There are many good stoves which run off bottled gas, and even some ovens. You will need large water carriers and probably an insulated cold store box. A camp table and 2–3 stools will also be useful if you are working in a confined space.

Look at the cloakrooms, too, and if you have any choice at all about where the party is held, take these facilities into account. If you have no choice, work hard to make them as good as possible. Sign-post the cloakrooms and provide a good supply of soap, clean towels or kitchen paper, make sure there is adequate hanging space for coats (coat racks and hangers can be hired), good mirrors and lighting.

Having settled these necessaries, start arranging the room itself. You will need to serve the food fairly near the kitchen, so that those helping have as little manoeuvring through the crowds as possible. Use long trestle tables for serving, covered with full length cloths or paper table cloths. Have one large arrangement of flowers on this table, and small ones on the small tables round the room – the latter are necessary so that the serving area doesn't get over-crowded. In order to avoid a wide expanse of table early in the evening and a huge pile of debris later, it is best to provide a moderate amount of food throughout. This means that there will be food available whenever people need it, an important consideration at a party where people may come and go at irregular times. It also avoids panic in the kitchen as helpers try to get all the food ready at once. Place cutlery, plates and napkins at one end of the table and scatter around an adequate supply of ashtrays.

If you want to serve alcoholic drinks, you will need a bar. Most sports club rooms will

Paper tissue flowers make no pretence of reality but are very pretty

already have a bar, but church or school halls or other hired rooms will not. They may also not have a licence to sell or serve alcohol, and this is another item to arrange early on. Licensing laws are complicated so be sure that any arrangements you make do not contravene the local regulations.

The next thing that requires hard work is the music. The simplest answer here is a tape or cassette player, with somebody detailed to keep it running all evening. An extra speaker is usually necessary, and this is where your man with special skills comes in. If you have hired a discotheque or local group, make sure you know what they are going to bring with them, what they are expecting you to have laid on, and where they will want to set up their equipment. Try to ensure that they arrive at least 30 minutes before the party starts.

Now turn your attention to the decor. At all costs try to resist advice to resort to paper streamers and crêpe paper round the light bulbs. Both usually look makeshift before the party starts and have fallen down before it is half over. As far as the lights are concerned, use coloured bulbs – much more effective than crêpe paper, safer and more reliable. To raise the gloom, though, try 1–2 spotlights, using good desk lights or workshop inspection lamps suitably disguised. Large pots of flowers, leaves or grasses will cover many a dark, dismal corner better than paper streamers, and provide a good subject for spotlighting. Any large pot that will hold water will serve the purpose, and if the party is in winter you may be able to persuade someone to bring in some empty garden urns. Otherwise, perhaps funds will stretch to 3–4 large plastic garden tubs; they are inexpensive and are ideal for the purpose. Alternatively use large paper tissue pom-pom flowers, or tree branches sprayed white, silver or gold and hung with glass baubles.

Pick one of your artistic helpers to take charge of the flowers and give her 'carte blanche' to make the arrangements as large as possible, remembering that grasses from the hedgerow can be used as effectively as expensive flowers from the florist. Using florists' foam, flowers can be arranged 1–2 days in advance.

In general, you will find it easiest to decorate the room if you choose a theme. Where possible, use the materials at hand – in a sports club this usually means sports equipment; sailors probably have the best material handy for draping and making an attractive setting, but even cricket, hockey or tennis equipment can be so arranged that it is decorative. Instead of spotlighting the flowers you could spotlight a display of this kind. If the ceiling is high, lower it with garden netting, or old cricket or tennis nets.

Otherwise, turn to a simple colour scheme. Avoid collecting together all the colours of the rainbow, or the room will resemble a jumble sale. If you choose 2–3 basic toning colours and use them as you would in your home – in table cloths, flowers and any drapes necessary – the effect will be more comfortable. As long as the atmosphere is pleasant the party clothes of the guests will add enough variety to brighten the occasion.

However good your organization, you will be obliged to keep a band of helpers around you all evening to keep the wheels turning smoothly. If appropriate, have someone at the door, to direct those arriving, and make a timetable for the day of the party so that everybody involved knows when they are required. Above all, encourage an informal, helpful atmosphere throughout and your tasks will be made twice as easy.

Socials & Club Parties

Cheese and wine party

This is a particularly good party to have for a large number of people, as most of the food comes straight from the shops with very little to be done to it by you. However, it's well worth the effort to blend some of the cheeses into dips, or even to bake some of your own bread.

Have a good selection of breads, crispbreads and biscuits. Allow about 6 biscuits or crispbreads and the equivalent of 3 chunks of French bread per person. Good breads to choose are French, rye, granary, pumpernickel and baps; biscuits could be oatcakes, water biscuits, digestive, crackers and wheatmeal.

From 454 g (1 lb) butter, you will make about 40 pats.

It is a good idea to label each cheese – not only with its name but also its country of origin and giving an idea of its character (creamy, strong, mild, etc.). This will be invaluable in giving people an idea of what they're eating – and make everyone feel a lot happier.

The food

Allow about 112 g (4 oz) cheese for each guest, excluding the dips, and give them at least 8 varieties of cheese to choose from, including soft, semi-hard and veined types. The flavour of the cheeses will come alive if you match them with fruits, vegetables or nuts.

Radishes, gherkins and onions go well with tangy Double Gloucester or Cheddar and smoked Austrian or German Limburger cheeses are very good with blackcurrant conserve. Some of the cheese can be pre-cut into cubes (about 36 from a 454-g (1-lb) pieces) and set out with plenty of cocktail sticks alongside; Swiss Gruyère and Emmenthal are better cut in wafer-thin slices. Here are some interesting combinations to put together on cocktail sticks.:

Dips for a cheese and wine party

Double Gloucester with pineapple and maraschino cherries; *Caerphilly* with melon and black grapes; *Port Salut* with anchovy fillet; *Samsoe*, or *Havarti* with thick banana slices and halved walnuts; *Danish Blue* with strips of canned pimiento (sweet red peppers) or grapes; *Gorgonzola* with black grapes; *Marc de Raisin* with apple; *Emmenthal* with William pears; *Edam* with melon slices; *Pipo Cream* with walnuts and celery.

The dips should be creamy and light in consistency. Serve them with plenty of crisps, celery sticks, carrot sticks, radishes, pieces of raw cauliflower or spring onions.

Bacon dip

100–125 g (4 oz) bacon
142 ml (¼ pint) single cream
3 × 50-g (3 × 2-oz) pkts. creamy Demi-sel cheese
2·5 ml spoon (½ level tsp) made mustard
freshly ground black pepper

Fry the bacon until crisp; drain, allow to cool and then crumble. Slowly beat the cream into the cheese and mix in the mustard, bacon and pepper to taste.

Blue cheese dip

3 × 50-g (3 × 2-oz) pkts. Philadelphia cream cheese
100–125 g (4 oz) Danish blue cheese
142 ml (¼ pint) soured cream
garlic powder or crushed garlic

Beat together the two cheeses with a wooden spoon. When smooth, slowly beat in the soured cream. Add garlic to taste.

Garlic dip

100–125 g (4 oz) cream cheese
1 clove garlic, skinned and crushed
15 ml spoon (1 tbsp) cream or top of the milk
salt and pepper

Blend the ingredients to a soft cream and season to taste.

The drinks

Two kinds of red wine and two kinds of white should give a sufficient variety to suit all tastes. The white pair could be a Bordeaux, like Mouton Cadet Blanc, and a hock; the red could include the Portuguese Sao Pedro Dão Tinto or Italian Valpolicella or Bardolino. Serve the white wines well chilled to go with the creamy cheeses, the reds for the English and blue cheeses– but leave people free to make their own choice. 1 bottle serves 2 people for this sort of occasion, but order more than this from your merchant, on a 'sale or return' basis; you will need more red than white wine.

Beef and Burgundy party
for 50 people

3 joints of beef – rare, medium and well done
Spiced beef with almonds
Boiled rice
Winter salad
Tomato salad
Cucumber salad
Horseradish sauce
Mayonnaise
French bread and butter

Spiced beef with almonds
make 2

1½ kg (3 lb) lean beef, minced
225 g (8 oz) fresh white breadcrumbs
¼ kg (½ lb) onions, skinned and chopped
salt and freshly ground black pepper
2 eggs, beaten
50 g (2 oz) lard

For sauce and garnish:
100–125 g (4 oz) lard
1 kg (2 lb) onions, skinned and sliced
2 × 10 ml spoons (4 level tsps) curry powder
Tabasco sauce
100–125 g (4 oz) ground almonds
100–125 g (4 oz) flour
2·3 litres (4 pints) stock, made from stock cubes
141-g (5-oz) can pimientos (sweet red peppers), drained and sliced

Mix together the beef, breadcrumbs, onions, salt, pepper and egg; form into 50 balls. Heat the lard in a frying pan and fry the meat balls a few at a time, until golden brown. Place in 2 shallow casseroles, if possible in a single layer. To make the sauce, heat the lard in a saucepan and gently fry the onions until golden brown. Stir in the curry powder, Tabasco sauce, ground almonds and flour. Slowly add the stock, stirring constantly to prevent lumping. Add the pimientos and bring to the boil. Simmer for a few minutes, then pour into the 2 casseroles. Cover and cook in the oven at 180°C. (350°F.) mark 4 for 1½ hours.

Winter salad
make 2

2 kg (4 lb) white cabbage, finely shredded
8 carrots, scraped and sliced wafer thin
2 onions, skinned and finely chopped
225 g (8 oz) seedless raisins
2 celery hearts, scrubbed and finely sliced
100–125 g (4 oz) flaked almonds
284 ml (½ pint) soured cream
300 ml (½ pint) mayonnaise
2 × 15 ml spoons (2 tbsps) lemon juice
salt and pepper

Combine all the salad ingredients. Mix together the soured cream, mayonnaise and lemon juice and season well. Toss the salad in the dressing shortly before serving.

The drinks
Your local wine merchant will usually let you have a large supply of wine on sale or return, so you can afford to cater generously. For 50 people, you should have at least 3 dozen bottles of red Burgundy and 1½ dozen bottles of white.

Pizza and Quiche Party
for 100 people

Pizza with gammon and onion
Pizza napoletana
Cheese and salmon quiche
Cheese medallions
Mixed salads

Pizza with gammon and onion
make 5

For dough:
150 ml (¼ pint) water
10 g (¼ oz) fresh baker's yeast
225 g (½ lb) plain bread flour
5 ml spoon (1 level tsp) salt
10 g (¼ oz) lard
cooking oil

For filling:
½ kg (1 lb) gammon, rinded and cut in 0·5 cm (¼-in) cubes
3 × 15 ml spoons (3 tbsps) cooking oil
½ kg (1 lb) onions, skinned and sliced
10 ml spoon (2 level tsps) dried marjoram
salt and pepper
100–125 g (4 oz) Bel Paese cheese, grated

Grease a shallow rectangular tin measuring about 30·5 cm by 21·5 cm (12 in. by 8½ in). Warm the water, sprinkle on the yeast and leave until frothy. Sift together the flour and salt, rub in the lard and stir in the yeast mixture. Knead, cover with oiled polythene and leave until doubled in size. Roll out the dough on a lightly floured board to fit the base of the prepared tin. Brush with oil. Fry the gammon in oil until sealed. Remove from the pan and fry the onions lightly. Mix with the gammon. Spread the mixture over the dough and

116

sprinkle with marjoram, salt and pepper, then cover with grated cheese. Bake in the centre of the oven at 230°C. (450°F.) mark 8 for 20 minutes, cover loosely with foil and continue to cook for another 20 minutes.

Pizza napoletana
make 7

pizza dough (see gammon and onion pizza)

For topping:
cooking oil
½ kg (1 lb) onions, skinned and chopped
2 × 425-g (2 × 15-oz) cans tomatoes, drained
10 ml spoons (2 level tsps) dried marjoram
salt and pepper
100–125 g (4 oz) Bel Paese cheese, grated
2 × 60-g (2 × 2-oz) cans anchovy fillets
black olives

Grease a 30·5 cm (12-in.) plain flan ring, placed on a baking sheet. Roll out the dough to fit the base and brush it with oil. Sauté the onions in a little oil until soft but not coloured and spread on the dough to within 1 cm (½ in.) of the edge. Arrange the tomatoes on top and sprinkle with marjoram and seasoning. Bake in the centre of the oven at 230°C. (450°F.) mark 8 for 20 minutes. Sprinkle the cheese over, lattice with anchovies and arrange the olives in the lattice. Cover loosely with foil and cook for a further 20 minutes. Serve hot.

Cheese and salmon quiche
serves 20

675 g (1½ lb) shortcrust pastry – i.e. made with 675 g (1½ lb) flour, etc.
8 eggs
1·1 litre (2 pints) milk
salt and pepper
2 onions, skinned and very finely chopped
450 g (1 lb) Cheddar cheese, grated
4 × 198-g (4 × 7-oz) cans salmon, drained
60-g (2-oz) can anchovies, drained or 184-g (6½-oz) can pimientos (sweet red peppers) drained
black olives, stoned

Roll out the pastry and use to line 4 × 20·5 cm (4 × 8-in.) fluted or plain flan rings. Place them on

Try a pizza and quiche party when there are large numbers

baking sheets and bake blind at 200°C. (400°F.) mark 6 for about 20 minutes. Whisk together the eggs, milk, salt and pepper. Then add the onion and cheese and mix well. Flake the salmon and divide between the pastry cases and spoon the cheese custard over. Bake in the centre of the oven at 180°C. (350°F.) mark 4 for 20–30 minutes.
To garnish, cut the anchovies or pimientos into fine strips and place in a lattice over the flans. Place the olives in the lattice.

Cheese medallions
makes about 40 pairs

350 g (12 oz) butter
450 g (1 lb) Samsoe cheese, grated
2 egg yolks
salt
paprika pepper
225 g (8 oz) plain flour

Beat 225 g (8 oz) butter until creamy; gradually add half the cheese, the egg yolks, salt and paprika to taste. Work in the flour. When the mixture is well blended, wrap in foil and put in a cold place for about 1 hour. Knead lightly and roll out on a floured surface 0·3–0·5 cm

(⅛–¼–in.) thick. Stamp into rounds with a 2·5 cm (1-in.) plain cutter and place on greased baking sheets.
Bake in a hot oven at 200°C. (400°F.) mark 6 for 10 minutes, until beginning to colour. Cool on a rack, handling carefully.
Cream the remaining butter and cheese and use to sandwich the medallions in pairs.
Both the cheese discs and the filling can be made the day before. On the day of the party, cream the filling again before use.

Salads
For 100 people you will need the following quantities:

Green salad:
10 lettuces or 8 heads curly endive
5 bunches watercress, optional
10 heads chicory or 5 heads celery
4 cartons mustard and cress, optional
4 green peppers (capsicums)
few spring onions
300 ml (½ pint) French dressing

Tomato and cucumber salad:
3 kg (6 lb) tomatoes
4 cucumbers
1·1 litre (2 pints) French dressing
chopped chives

Spiced beef with almonds, winter salad and tomato salad

Mixing Drinks

All mixed drinks are greatly improved by being really cold, so use plenty of ice, or chill the bottles thoroughly in the refrigerator beforehand. The correct garnish makes all the difference to the appearance of a drink and adds a really professional finishing touch to a cocktail.

Gin

Perhaps the most popular of all bases for mixed drinks. Don't use Dutch gin – this is not really suitable.

Martini

5–6 ice cubes
1 part dry vermouth
3 parts gin
1 large olive

Put the ice cubes in a glass jug, pour in the vermouth and gin and stir vigorously. Strain the drink into a martini glass and decorate with an olive.

Pink gin

2–3 drops Angostura bitters
1 part gin
2–3 parts iced water

Put the bitters into a glass and turn it until the sides are well coated. Add the gin and top up with iced water to taste.

Gibson

5–6 ice cubes
1 part very dry sherry
5 parts gin
1 pearl cocktail onion

Put the ice cubes in a glass jug, pour in the sherry and gin and stir well. Strain the drink into a chilled martini glass and add the onion on a stick.

Negroni

2–3 ice cubes
½ part Campari
1 part sweet vermouth
2 parts gin
1 slice orange
soda water

Put the ice cubes into a tumbler and pour over them the Campari, vermouth and gin. Float the slice of orange on top and then top up with soda water to taste.

Vodka

An increasingly popular drink which can be successfully used as an alternative to gin in many recipes.

Moscow mule

3 ice cubes
2 parts vodka
ginger beer or lemonade
lemon and cucumber slices

Put the ice into a mug or tall glass and add the vodka. Top up with ginger beer or lemonade and garnish with lemon and cucumber. Stir lightly.

Bronx

1 part dry vermouth
1 part sweet vermouth
juice of ½ orange
3 parts vodka

Put 4–5 ice cubes into a shaker and pour in the vermouths, orange juice and vodka. Shake well till a frost forms and strain into a chilled martini glass.

Bloody Mary

1 part vodka
2 parts tomato juice
squeeze of lemon juice
dash of Worcestershire sauce

Put some ice into a shaker with vodka, tomato juice, lemon and sauce. Shake and strain into a tumbler. Tabasco, salt and pepper may be added.

Screwdriver

1 part vodka
juice of 1 orange
Angostura bitters (optional)

Put some ice cubes into a tall glass and pour in the vodka and orange juice. Add the bitters and stir lightly.

Whisky

Scotch, Irish, Canadian, rye or Bourbon all have different tastes. Where necessary we have specified which type should be used.

Old fashioned

1 lump of sugar
1–2 dashes Angostura bitters
1–2 ice cubes
1 part whisky
½ slice orange

Put the sugar cube in a glass and shake the bitters on to it; mix round the glass to dissolve the sugar. Put in the ice, pour over the whisky and float the orange on top.

Whisky sour

juice of ½ a lemon
5 ml spoon (1 level tsp) sugar
5 ml spoon (1 tsp) egg white
1 part rye whisky

Put all the ingredients in a shaker and stir together, then add cracked ice and shake well. Strain into a chilled glass and decorate with a twist of lemon.

Virginia mint julep

9 sprigs of mint
5 ml spoon (1 tsp) sugar or sugar syrup
crushed ice
3 parts Bourbon whisky

Put 6 sprigs of mint into a cold glass. Add the sugar and crush the two together. Fill the glass with crushed ice and pour in the whisky, stirring well.

Tom Collins

juice of 1 lemon
15 ml spoon (1 tbsp) sugar or sugar syrup
3 parts whisky
soda water

In a shaker, mix 6 ice cubes, lemon, sugar and whisky until a frost forms. Pour into a glass and add a slice of orange. Top with soda water and stir.

Rum

A sugar-based drink with a wide range of flavours. There are three basic colourings – dark, golden and white.

Cuba libré

2 parts golden or dark rum
3 parts Coca Cola
juice and peel of ½ lime or lemon

Put 3–4 ice cubes into a tall glass and pour in the rum, Coca Cola and fruit juice. Stir gently and drop in the lemon or lime peel.

Gimlet

3–4 ice cubes
1 part lime juice
3 parts white or golden rum

Put the ice into a jug and pour in the lime juice and rum. Stir well and strain into a chilled martini glass.

Manhattan

4–5 ice cubes
1 part sweet vermouth
3 parts white or golden rum
1 maraschino cherry

Put the ice cubes into a glass jug and pour in the vermouth and rum. Stir vigorously and strain into a chilled martini glass. Drop in the cherry.

Daiquiri

cracked ice
juice of 2 limes
5 ml spoon (1 tsp) sugar or sugar syrup
3 parts white rum

Put lots of cracked ice in a shaker and add the lime juice, sugar and rum. Shake well till a frost forms and then strain into a chilled martini glass.

Many of the cocktail recipes given in our chart can be made with other spirits – in particular, gin and vodka are virtually interchangeable, a vodka martini being a very popular drink. Try making a gimlet with gin or vodka – you'll find it very refreshing. A Collins can be made with any of the spirits as a base and a Rickey or a Manhattan can also be mixed using any of the spirits.

Brandy   Sherry   Wine   Port

Don't use your best brandy for mixed drinks – it should be drunk on its own. Use a younger, cheaper one instead.

The classic before-dinner drink in a new, exciting guise – these recipes may shock the purists but they're delicious.

Ideal for warm days, a wine cocktail, whether based on Champagne or a cheap rosé, is light and refreshing.

Not your favourite vintage port, of course, but a good ruby or tawny one – and white port looks especially refreshing.

Brandy Rickey

1 lime
2·5 ml spoon (½ tsp) sugar
3 parts brandy
maraschino cherry
soda water

Put 4–5 ice cubes in a shaker and add the lime juice, sugar and brandy. Shake well and pour into a tall glass. Drop in the cherry and lime peel and top up with soda water.

Brandy fizz

4–5 ice cubes
juice of 1 lemon
5 ml spoon (1 tsp) sugar or sugar syrup
1 part yellow Chartreuse
2 parts brandy
soda water

Put the ice cubes in a shaker and pour in the lemon, sugar, Chartreuse and brandy and shake until a frost forms. Pour without straining into a tall glass, top with soda and stir lightly.

Brandy Alexander

4–5 ice cubes
1 part cream
1 part crème de cacao
3 parts brandy

Put the ice cubes into a shaker and add the cream, crème de cacao and brandy. Shake until a frost forms and strain into a glass.

Sherry cobbler

(makes 2)

ice
150 ml (¼ pint) sherry
5 ml spoon (1 level tsp) sugar
10 ml spoon (2 tsps) fresh orange juice
slices of orange
few strawberries

Put a few pieces of ice in a glass jug and add the sherry, sugar and orange juice. Stir well. Pour without straining into 2 chilled tumblers and decorate with the fruit. Serve with a drinking straw.

Sherry refresher

(makes 4–6)

3 grapefruit
6 × 15 ml spoons (6 tbsps) sweet sherry
soda water
ice

Squeeze the juice from the grapefruit and strain into a jug. Add the sherry and chill. Serve in goblets with a little ice and soda water to taste.

Sherry cocktail

4–5 ice cubes
1 part dry vermouth
3 parts very dry sherry
1 slice lemon rind

Put the ice in a glass jug and pour in the vermouth and sherry. Stir well and strain into a chilled martini glass. Drop in the twisted lemon rind.

Spritze

(approx. 2 litres – 3½ pints)

1 bottle white wine
1·1 litres (2 pints) soda water

Chill the wine and soda water thoroughly. Just before serving combine in a large glass jug.

Sangria

(approx. 1·4 litres – 2½ pints)

1 bottle red wine, chilled
550–600 ml (1 pint) fizzy lemonade, chilled
1 slice of lemon
1 liqueur glass brandy
slices of apple and orange
caster sugar

Shortly before serving, mix the chilled wine and lemonade in a large bowl and add the lemon slice and brandy (optional). Float the apple and orange slices on top and add caster sugar to taste.

Alfonso

1 lump of sugar
2 dashes Angostura bitters
15 ml spoon (1 tbsp) Dubonnet
Champagne, well chilled

Put the sugar in the base of a champagne glass and drop on the bitters. Add the Dubbonet and, if liked, an ice cube as well. Top up with champagne.

Vin blanc cassis

4 parts dry white wine
1 part crème de cassis

Chill the wine. Pour the crème de cassis into a claret glass and top up with wine.

Port flip

1 egg
5 ml spoon (1 level tsp) icing sugar
1 wineglass port
2–3 ice cubes
nutmeg

Break the egg into a shaker or an electric blender and add the sugar, port and ice. Shake or blend well. Strain into a goblet and sprinkle with a little nutmeg before serving.

Tawny sparkler

(2 litres – 3½ pints)

juice of 1 lemon
1 whole lemon
1 bottle tawny port
4 × 15 ml spoons (4 tbsps) curaçao
soda water

Put the lemon juice in a bowl and add the port and curaçao. Slice the whole lemon, float it on top and leave for 20 mins. Fill glasses two-thirds full and top up with chilled soda water.

Port cocktail

4–5 ice cubes
2 drops Angostura bitters
5 ml spoon (1 tsp) curaçao
3 parts port

Put 4–5 ice cubes in a jug and pour in the bitters, curaçao and port. Stir vigorously and strain into a chilled martini glass.

Note: Whatever you use as a measure, be sure to use the same measure for all the ingredients in a drink, so that the proportion of one ingredient to another is accurate.

HANDY CHARTS

Oven temperatures

Oven	°F.	°C.	Gas Mark
Very cool	250–275	130–140	½–1
Cool	300	150	2
Warm	325	170	3
Moderate	350	180	4
Fairly hot	375–400	190–200	5–6
Hot	425	220	7
Very hot	450—475	230–240	8–9

N.B. To convert Centigrade/Celsius temperatures to Fahrenheit, multiply by 9, divide by 5 and then add 32. Conversely, to turn a Fahrenheit temperature into Centigrade/Celsius, subtract 32, multiply by 5 and divide by 9.

Handy equivalents

Approximate equivalent shown in level 15-ml spoonfuls

Almonds, ground	25g =3½
Breadcrumbs, fresh	25g =7
Breadcrumbs, dried	25g =3
Butter, lard, etc.	25g =2
Cheddar, grated	25g =3
Chocolate, grated	25g =4
Coffee, instant	25g =6½
Cornflour	25g =2¾
Custard powder	25g =2¾
Curry powder	25g =4
Flour, unsifted	25g =3
Suet, shredded	25g =3
Sugar, caster/gran.	25g =2
Sugar, demerara	25g =2
Sugar, icing	25g =3
Syrup or honey	25g =1

Quick comparison

lb	kg
1	0.45
2	0.9
3	1.36
4	1.81
5	2.26
6	2.72
7	3.17
8	3.62
9	4.08
10	4.53
20	9.07
50	22.67

Refrigerator/freezer capacity

Metric Measurement	Approx. Imperial Equivalent
113 litres	4 cu ft
170 litres	6 cu ft
339 litres	12 cu ft

Australian cup measures

1 cup = 8 fl oz

Almonds		
(whole)	6 oz	1 cup
(ground)	4 oz	1 cup
Biscuit crumbs	4 oz	1 cup
Breadcrumbs		
(dry)	3 oz	1 cup
(fresh)	2 oz	1 cup
Cheese (grated)	4 oz	1 cup
Cream	4 fl oz	1 cup
		whipped
Dried fruit	1 lb	3 cups
Flour	1 lb	4 cups
Golden syrup		
or treacle	1 lb	1 cup
Rice	8 oz	1 cup
Sugar		
(brown)	6 oz	1 cup
(caster)	1 lb	2 good cups
(icing)	1 lb	3½ cups
(granulated)	1 lb	2 cups

Metric/Imperial conversion

Metric Measurement	Approx. Imperial Equivalent
25 ml	1 fl oz
50 ml	2 fl oz
150 ml	5 fl oz
300 ml	10 fl oz
400 ml	15 fl oz
600 ml	20 fl oz
1 litre	35 fl oz

Use a 5-millilitre spoon in place of a teaspoon and a 15-ml spoon in place of a tablespoon.

Metric Measurement	Approx. Imperial Equivalent
25 g	1 oz
50 g	2 oz
75 g	3 oz
100–125 g	4 oz
150 g	5 oz
175 g	6 oz
200 g	7 oz
225 g	8 oz
250 g	9 oz
275 g	10 oz

GLOSSARY OF COOKING TERMS

Aspic jelly Savoury jelly used for setting and garnishing savoury dishes.

Au gratin Food coated with a sauce, sprinkled with breadcrumbs (and sometimes grated cheese) and browned under the grill. Usually served in the dish in which it has been cooked.

Bain marie A flat, open vessel, half-filled with water, which is kept at a temperature just below boiling point; used to keep sauces, etc., hot without further cooking. Also a baking tin half-filled with water in which custards and other egg dishes stand whilst cooking to prevent overheating.

Making a sauce in a bain marie

Baking Cooking in the oven by dry heat. The method used for most cakes, biscuits and pastries, and for many other dishes.

Baking blind Baking pastry shapes without a filling. Line the flan case or pie dish with pastry and trim. Line with greaseproof paper and fill with haricot beans, rice or stale crusts of bread. Or press kitchen foil into the pastry case and omit beans, etc. When pastry has set, remove the greaseproof paper or foil and return to the oven to dry out.

Barding Covering the breast of poultry or game birds with pieces of fat bacon to prevent it drying out during roasting.

Basting Moistening meat, poultry or game during roasting by spooning over it the juices and melted fat from the tin, to prevent the food drying out.

Beating Agitating an ingredient or mixture by vigorously turning it over with an upward motion so as to introduce air; a spoon, fork, whisk or electric mixer may be used.

Béchamel A rich white sauce, one of the four basic types of sauce.

Binding Adding a liquid, egg or melted fat to a dry mixture to hold it together.

Blanching Treating food with boiling water in order to whiten it, preserve its natural colour, loosen the skin or remove a flavour which is too strong. Two methods are:–

1. To plunge the food into boiling water; used for skinning tomatoes or to prepare vegetables for freezing.

2. To bring it to the boil in the water; used to whiten veal and sweetbreads or to reduce the saltiness of kippers or pickled meat.

Blending Mixing flour, cornflour and similar ground cereals to a smooth cream with a cold liquid (milk, water or stock) before a boiling liquid is added, as in the preparation of soups, stews, or gravies.

Boiling Cooking in liquid at a temperature of 100°C. (212°F.). The chief foods that are boiled are vegetables, rice, pasta and suet puddings; syrups that need to be reduced are also boiled. Meat, fish and poultry should be simmered – fast boiling makes them shrink, lose flavour, and toughen.

Bouquet garni A small bunch of herbs tied together in muslin and used to give flavour to stews, etc. Usually consists of a sprig of parsley and thyme, a bay leaf, 2 cloves and a few peppercorns.

Braising A method of cooking either meat or vegetables which is a combination of roasting and stewing. A casserole or pan with a tightly fitting lid is used to prevent evaporation. The meat is placed on a bed of vegetables (a mirepoix), with just sufficient liquid to cover the vegetables and to keep the food moist.

Brining Immersing food (mainly meat or fish which is to be pickled and vegetables which are to be preserved) in a salt and water solution.

Browning 1. Giving a dish (usually already cooked) an appetising golden brown colour by placing it under the grill or in a hot oven for a short time. 2. Preparing a dish for stewing or casseroling, by frying to seal and colour.

Caramel A substance obtained by heating sugar syrup very slowly in a thick pan until it is a rich brown colour. Used for flavouring cakes and puddings and for lining pudding moulds.

Casserole A baking dish with a tightly fitting lid, used for cooking meat and vegetables in the oven. The food is usually served straight from the dish. May be 'ovenproof' (for oven use only) or 'flameproof' (suitable for use on top of the stove and in the oven).

Chaudfroid A jellied sauce with a béchamel base, used for masking cold fish, poultry and game.

Chining Severing the rib bones from the backbone by sawing through the ribs close to the spine. Used on joints such as loin or neck of lamb, veal or pork.

Use a special saw for chining

Chopping Dividing food into very small pieces. The ingredient is placed on a chopping board and a very sharp knife is used with a quick up-and-down action.

Clarifying Clearing or purifying fat from water, meat juices or salt.

1. Butter or margarine – Heat the fat gently until it melts, then continue to heat slowly without browning until all bubbling ceases (this shows the water has been driven off). Remove from the heat and allow to stand for a few minutes until the sediment has settled. Pour the fat off gently. It is not usually necessary to strain the fat through muslin.

2. Dripping – Melt the fat and strain into a large basin to remove any big particles. Then pour over it 2–3 times as much boiling water, stir well and leave to cool; the clean fat will rise to the top. When it has solidified, lift it off, dab the underside dry and scrape off any sediment.

Coating 1. Covering food which is to be fried with flour, egg and breadcrumbs, batter, etc.

2. Covering food which is cooked or ready to serve with a thin layer of mayonnaise, sauce, etc.

Coddling A method of soft-boiling eggs: they are put into a pan of boiling water, withdrawn from the heat and allowed to stand for 8–10 minutes. China egg-coddlers may be used.

Compôte Fruit stewed in a sugar syrup and served hot or cold.

Consistency The term used to describe the texture of a dough, batter, etc.

Creaming The beating together of fat and sugar to resemble whipped cream in colour and texture, i.e. until pale and fluffy. This method of mixing is used for cakes and puddings containing a high proportion of fat.

Crimping 1. To remove the skin in strips from cucumber and similar foods, to give the finished slices a ridged appearance.

Use thumbs and fore-fingers to crimp the edge of a pastry case

2. To decorate the double edge of a pie or tart or the edge of a shortbread by pinching it at regular intervals, giving a fluted effect.

Croquettes A mixture of meat, fish, poultry or potatoes, bound together and formed into various shapes, then coated with egg and breadcrumbs and fried in deep fat.

Croûte A large round or finger of toasted or fried bread, about ¼ in. thick, on which game and some entrées and savouries are served.

Croûtons Small pieces of bread which are fried or toasted and served as an accompaniment or garnish to soup.

Curd 1. The solid part of soured milk or junket.

2. A creamy preserve made from fruit – usually lemons or oranges – sugar, eggs and butter.

Dariole A small, narrow mould with sloping sides, used for setting creams and jellies and for baking or steaming puddings, especially castle puddings. Also used to prepare English madeleines.

Devilled Food which has been grilled or fried with sharp, hot seasonings.

Dough A thick mixture of uncooked flour and liquid, often combined with other ingredients. As well as the usual yeast dough, it can also mean mixtures such as pastry, scones and biscuits.

Dredging The action of sprinkling food lightly and evenly with flour, sugar, etc. Fish and meat are often dredged with flour before frying, while pancakes, etc., may be dredged with fine sugar to improve their appearance. A pierced container of metal or plastic (known as a dredger) is usually used.

Dripping The fat obtained from roasted meat during cooking or from small peices of new fat that have been rendered down.

Dropping consistency The term used to describe the texture of a cake or pudding mixture before cooking. To test, fill a spoon with the mixture and hold it on its side – the mixture should fall in 5 seconds, without jerking the spoon.

Egg-and-crumbing A method of coating fish, cutlets, rissoles, etc., before they are fried or baked. Have a beaten egg on a plate and some breadcrumbs on a piece of kitchen paper; dip the food in the egg and lift out, letting it drain for a second or two. Transfer it to the crumbs and tip the paper until the food is well covered. Press in the crumbs, then shake the food to remove any surplus.

Entrée A hot or cold dressed savoury dish consisting of meat, poultry, game, fish, eggs or vegetables, served complete with sauce and garnish.

Escalope A slice of meat (usually veal) cut from the top of the leg. Escalopes are generally egg-and-crumbed and fried.

Espagnole A rich brown sauce, one of the four basic sauces.

Farce, forcemeat Stuffing used for meat, fish or vegetables. A farce is based on meat, bacon, etc., while the basic forcemeat is made from breadcrumbs, suet, onion and herbs.

Fillet A term used for the undercut of a loin of beef, veal, pork or game, for boned breasts of poultry and birds and for boned sides of fish.

Fines herbes A combination of finely chopped herbs. In practice, the mixture is usually parsley, chervil, tarragon and chives, and it is most commonly used in omelettes. When fresh herbs are used one can add enough to make the omelette look green, but when dried ones are used 5 ml spoon (½ teaspoon) of the mix-

ture is plenty for a 4-egg omelette. For other dishes, the blend is sometimes varied.

Flaking Breaking up cooked fish into flakes with a fork.

Folding in (Sometimes called cutting-and-folding). Combining a whisked or creamed mixture with other ingredients so that it retains its lightness. It is used for certain cake mixtures and for meringues and soufflés. A typical example is folding dry flour into a whisked sponge cake mixture. Important points to remember are that the mixture must be folded very lightly and that it must not be agitated more than absolutely necessary, because with every movement some of the air bubbles are broken down. Do not use an electric mixer.

Fricassee A white stew of chicken, veal or rabbit.

Frosting 1. A method of decorating the rim of a glass in which a cold drink is to be served. Coat the edge with whipped egg white, dip into caster sugar and let dry.
2. An icing, especially of the American type.

Iced and creamy desserts look good in a frosted glass

Frying The process of cooking food in hot fat or oil. There are two main methods:
1. Shallow frying A small quantity of fat is used in a shallow pan. Used for steak, chops, sausages, fish steaks and white fish, which need only sufficient fat to prevent them sticking to the pan. Made-up dishes such as fish cakes can also be shallow-fried, but need enough fat to half-cover them. In most cases the food will need to be coated.
2. Deep frying The food is cooked in sufficient fat to cover it completely. Used for batter-coated fish, whitebait, chipped potatoes, doughnuts and made-up dishes such as croquettes and fritters. A deep pan and a wire basket are needed, with fat to

come about three-quarters up the side of the pan; clarified beef fat, lard and cooking oil are suitable. The fat must be pure and free from moisture, to avoid spurting or boiling over, and it must be heated to the right temperature or the food will be either grease-sodden or burnt. If the fat is strained into a basin, jug or wide-necked jar and covered, it may be stored in a cool place for further use. A frying thermometer should always be used with oil for deep fat frying.

Galantine White meat, such as poultry or veal, which has been cooked, rolled and pressed. Sometimes glazed or finished with toasted breadcrumbs.

Garnish An edible decoration, such as parsley, watercress, hard-boiled egg or lemon added to a savoury dish to improve the appearance and flavour.

Glaze Beaten egg, egg white, milk, etc., used to give a glossy surface to certain sweets and to savouries such as galantines. The meat glaze used for savouries is home-made meat stock reduced by rapid boiling. Stock made from a cube cannot be treated this way.

Grating Shaving foods such as cheese and vegetables into small shreds. Foods to be grated must be firm and cheese should be allowed to harden.

Grilling Cooking food by direct heat under a grill or over a hot fire. Good quality, tender meat (steak, chops), whole fish (herring, trout) and fish cutlets are the foods most generally cooked in this way. Some cooked dishes are put under the grill to give them a brown top surface or to heat them through before they are served.

Grinding The process of reducing hard foodstuffs, such as nuts and coffee beans, to small particles by means of a food mill, grinder or electric blender.

Hors d'oeuvre Small dishes served cold, usually before the soup, as appetizers. Hors d'oeuvre are generally small and piquant.

Infusing Extracting flavour from spices, herbs, etc., by pouring on boiling liquid and then covering and allowing to stand in a warm place.

Jardinière A garnish of diced, mixed, spring vegetables, plus green peas, cauliflower sprigs, etc.

Julienne A garnish of fine strips of mixed vegetables.

Kneading Working a dough firmly, using the knuckles for bread-making, the fingertips in

pastry-making. In both cases the outside of the dough is drawn into the centre.

Knocking up Preparing a pastry edge ready for crimping. Hold a round bladed knife parallel with the pastry and knock against the knife, to open up the pastry in ridges.

Larding Inserting small strips of fat bacon into the flesh of game birds, poultry and meat before cooking, to prevent it drying out when roasting. A special larding needle is used for the process.

Liaison A thickening agent, such as flour, cornflour or arrowroot, which is used for thickening or binding sauces and soups.

Lukewarm Moderately warm; approximately 38°C. (100°F.).

Macedoine A mixture of fruits or vegetables cut into evenly sized dice, generally used as a decoration or garnish. Alternatively, the fruits may be set in jelly.

Marinade A seasoned mixture of oil and vinegar, lemon juice or wine, in which food is left for a given time. This helps to soften the fibres of meat and fish and adds flavour to the food.

Masking 1. Covering or coating a cooked meat or similar dish with savoury jelly, glaze or sauce.
2. Coating the inside of a mould with jelly.

Ice helps to set the thin layer of jelly quickly

Meringue Egg white whisked until stiff, mixed with caster sugar and dried in a cool oven till crisp.

Mincing Chopping or cutting into very small pieces with a knife or, more commonly, in a mincer.

Mixed herbs These most commonly consist of a blend of dried parsley, tarragon, chives, thyme and chervil, but other variations using bay, sage or chives may occur in certain recipes.

Mirepoix A mixture of carrot, celery and onion, often including some ham or bacon, cut into large pieces, lightly fried in fat and used as a 'bed' on which to braise meat.

Noisettes Neatly trimmed round or oval shapes of lamb, mutton or beef, not less than 1·25 cm (½ in) thick.

Panada A thick binding sauce using 25 g (1 oz) fat and 25 g (1 oz) flour to 150 ml (¼ pt) liquid made by the roux method and used for binding croquettes and similar mixtures.

Parboiling Part-boiling; the food is boiled for part of the normal cooking time, then finished by some other method.

Paring Peeling or trimming, especially vegetables or the rind of citrus fruits.

A potato peeler makes paring a lemon easy

Petits fours Very small fancy cakes, often iced, and almond biscuits, served at the end of a formal meal.

Piping Forcing cream, icing or butter out of a forcing bag through a nozzle, to decorate cakes, etc. Also used for potatoes and meringues. The bag may be made of cotton, nylon or plastic.

Poaching Cooking in an open pan at simmering point with sufficient seasoned liquid to cover. Used in egg, fish and some meat dishes.

Pot-roasting Cooking meat in a saucepan with fat and a very small amount of liquid; it is particularly good for small and less tender cuts.

Pulses Dried beans, peas, split peas and lentils.

Purée Fruit, vegetable, meat or fish which has been pounded, sieved or pulverised in an electric blender (usually after cooking), to give a smooth pulp. A soup made by sieving vegetables with the liquor in which they were cooked is also called a purée.

Raspings Fine crumbs made from stale bread; used for coating fried foods and for au gratin dishes. The bread is first dried in a cool oven and then crushed.

Réchauffé Reheated leftover foods.

Reducing Boiling a liquid in an uncovered pan in order to evaporate it and give a more concentrated result. Used especially when making soups, sauces, or syrups.

Refreshing 1. After cooking vegetables, pouring cold water over them to preserve the colour; they are then reheated before serving. **2.** Crisping up already-cooked pastry in the oven. **3.** For home-freezing, plunging partly-cooked or blanched vegetables and meat into ice-cold water immediately after removing from the heat.

Rendering Extracting fat from meat trimmings by cutting them up small and heating in a cool oven 150°C. (300°F.) mark 1 until the fat has melted out, or boiling them in an uncovered pan with very little water until the water is driven off and the fat is melted; the fat is then strained into a basin.

Rennet An extract from calves stomachs. It contains rennin and is used for curdling or coagulating milk for junket and for cheese-making.

Rissoles Small portions of minced meat enclosed in rounds of pastry and folded to form a semi-circle, then egg-and-crumbed and fried in deep fat. The term is now loosely applied to a round cake of a meat or fish mixture, egg-and-crumbed and fried.

Roasting In its true sense, roasting means cooking by direct heat in front of an open fire. Thus rôtisserie cooking is true roasting, and the modern method of cooking in a closed oven is really baking. Only good quality poultry, and the best cuts of meat, should be cooked in this way.

Roux A mixture of equal amounts of fat and plain flour cooked together to form the basis for a sauce and for thickening sauces and stews.

Rubbing in Incorporating fat into flour; used when making shortcrust pastry, plain cakes and biscuits, when a short texture is required. Put the fat in small pieces in the flour, then rub it into the flour with the fingertips.

Rusks Fingers or slices of bread dried in a slow oven.

Salmi A ragoût or stew, usually of game.

Sauté To cook in an open pan over a strong heat in fat or oil, shaking the pan to make whatever is in it 'sauter' or jump, to keep it from sticking. The pan used should be heavy, wide and shallow. This may be used as a complete cooking method or as the initial cooking before finishing in a sauce.

Scalding Pouring boiling water over food to clean it, to loosen hairs (as from a joint of pork) or to remove the skin (as on tomatoes or peaches). The food must not be left in the boiling water or it will begin to cook.

Scalloped dishes Food (often previously cooked) baked in a scallop shell or similar small container; it is usually combined with a creamy sauce, topped with breadcrumbs and surrounded with a border of piped potato.

Scalloping A means of decorating the double edge of the pastry covering of a pie. Make close horizontal cuts with a knife round the edge of the pie, giving a flaked effect (see **knocking up**) then, with the back of the knife, pull the edge up vertically at regular intervals to form scallops. Traditionally these should be close together for a sweet pie and wider apart for a savoury one.

Scoring To make shallow, parallel cuts in the surface of food in order to improve its flavour or appearance or to help it cook more quickly (e.g. fish).

Searing Browning meat quickly in a little fat before grilling or roasting.

Seasoned flour Used for dusting meat and fish before frying or stewing. Mix about 2 × 15 ml spoons (2 tbsps) flour with about 5 ml spoon (1 tsp) salt and a good sprinkling of pepper. Either pat it onto the food or dip the pieces in the flour and shake them gently before cooking.

Shredding Slicing a food such as cheese or raw vegetables into very fine pieces. A sharp knife or coarse grater is generally used.

Sieving Rubbing or pressing food (e.g. cooked vegetables) through a sieve; a wooden spoon is used to force it through.

Sifting Shaking a dry ingredient through a sieve or flour sifter to remove lumps and aerate it.

Simmering Keeping a liquid just below boiling point (approximately 96°C. or 205°F.). First bring the liquid to the boil, then adjust the heat so that the surface of the liquid is kept just moving or 'shivering'; continuous bubbling indicates the temperature is too high.

Skimming To take fat off the surface of stock, gravy or stews, or scum from other foods (e.g. jams) while they are cooking. A piece of absorbent kitchen paper or a metal spoon may be used.

Steaming An economical method of cooking food in the steam from rapidly boiling water. There are several ways of steaming, according to the equipment available.

Steeping Pouring hot or cold water over food and leaving it to stand, either to soften it or to extract its flavour and colour.

Stewing A long, slow method of cooking in a liquid which is kept at simmering point; particularly suitable for coarse-fibre foods. The liquid is served with the food, so that flavour is not wasted.

Stock The liquid produced when meat, bones, poultry, fish or vegetables are simmered in water with herbs and flavourings for several hours, to extract their flavour. Stock forms the basis of soups, sauces and stews and many savoury dishes.

Sweating Cooking a food (usually a vegetable) very gently in a covered pan with melted fat until it exudes juices. The food should not colour.

Syrup A concentrated solution of sugar in water, prepared by boiling and used in making water ices, drinks and fruit desserts. Golden syrup is a by-product of sugar refining. Maple syrup is extracted from the North American sugar maple.

Tammy To strain soups, sauces, etc., through a fine woollen cloth.

Tepid Approximately at blood heat. Tepid water is obtained by adding 2 parts cold water to 1 part boiling.

Thickening Giving body to soups, sauces or gravies by the addition of flour, cornflour or arrowroot.

Trussing Tying a bird into a compact shape before cooking.

Vol-au-vent A round or oval case made of puff pastry and filled with diced meat, poultry, game or fish in a well-flavoured sauce.

Whipping or whisking To beat air rapidly into a mixture: **1.** By hand, using an egg beater or whisk. **2.** By rotary beater. **3.** By electric beater.

Zest The coloured part of orange or lemon peel containing the oil that gives the characteristic flavour. To obtain zest, remove the rind very thinly, with no pith, by grating, or use a zester. If it is required for a sweet dish, you can rub it off with a lump of sugar.

Catering Quantities

APPROXIMATE QUANTITIES FOR BUFFET PARTIES

	1 portion	24–26 portions	Notes
Soups: cream, clear or iced	200 ml ($\frac{1}{3}$ pt)	4.75 l (1 gallon)	Serve garnished in mugs or cups
Fish cocktail: shrimp, prawn, tuna or crab	25 g (1 oz)	675 g (1$\frac{1}{2}$ lb) fish 2–3 lettuces 900 ml (1$\frac{1}{2}$ pts) sauce	In stemmed glasses, garnished with a shrimp or prawn
Meat with bone	150 g (5 oz)	3.25–3.50 kg (7–8 lb)	Cold roasts or barbecue chops
boneless	75–100 g (3–4 oz)	2.25–3 kg (5–6$\frac{1}{2}$ lb)	Casseroles, meat balls, sausages, barbecue steaks
Poultry: turkey	75–100 g (3–4 oz) (boneless)	7 kg (16 lb) (dressed)	
chicken	1 joint 150–225 g (5–8 oz)	6 1–1$\frac{1}{2}$ kg (2$\frac{1}{2}$–3 lb) birds (dressed)	Serve hot or cold
Delicatessen: ham or tongue	75–100 g (3–4 oz)	2.25–3 kg (5–6$\frac{1}{2}$ lb)	Halve the amounts if making stuffed cornets
pâté for wine-and-pâté party	75–100 g (3–4 oz)	2.25–3 kg (5–6$\frac{1}{2}$ lb)	Half the amount if pâté is starter course
Salad vegetables lettuce cucumber tomatoes white cabbage boiled potatoes	$\frac{1}{6}$ 2.5 cm (1 in) 1–2 25 g (1 oz) 50 g (2 oz)	3–4 2 cucumbers 1$\frac{1}{2}$ kg (3 lb) 675 g (1$\frac{1}{2}$ lb) 1$\frac{1}{2}$ kg (3 lb)	Dress at last minute for winter salads for potato salads
Rice or pasta	35 g (1$\frac{1}{2}$ oz) (uncooked)	900 g (2 lb)	Can be cooked a day ahead, reheated in 5 min. in boiling water
Cheese (for wine-and-cheese party)	75 g (3 oz)	1.75–2.25 g (4$\frac{1}{2}$–5 lb) of at least 4 types	You'll need more if you serve a cheese dip too
Cheese (for biscuits)	25–35 g (1–1$\frac{1}{2}$ oz)	675–900 g (1$\frac{1}{2}$–2 lb) cheese plus 450 g (1 lb) butter 900 g (2 lb) biscuits	Allow the larger amounts for an assorted cheese board

SAVOURIES AND SWEETS

	Ingredients	Portions	Notes
Sausage rolls	675 g (1$\frac{1}{2}$ lb) shortcrust or flaky pastry 900 g (2 lb) sausage meat	25–30 medium or 50 small rolls	Pastry based on 675 g (1$\frac{1}{2}$ lb) flour, 350–450 g ($\frac{3}{4}$–1 lb) fat
Bouchées	450 g (1 lb) puff pastry 600 ml (1 pint) thick white sauce 275 g (10 oz) prepared filling	50 bouchées	Pastry based on 450 g (1 lb) flour, 350 g ($\frac{3}{4}$ lb) butter. Fillings: chopped ham, chicken, egg, mushrooms, shrimps
Cheese straws	225 g ($\frac{1}{2}$ lb) cheese pastry	100 cheese straws	225 g ($\frac{1}{2}$ lb) flour, 125 g ($\frac{1}{4}$ lb) fat, 125 g ($\frac{1}{4}$ lb) cheese
Meringues	**Meringues** 6 egg whites 350 g (12 oz) caster sugar 400 ml ($\frac{3}{4}$ pt) whipped cream	50 (small) meringue halves	2 halves per head with cream 1 half with fruit and cream, or ice cream
Jelly	3 l (2$\frac{1}{2}$ qrts)	25	
Trifle	2.5 l (4 pts) custard 25 sponge fingers 1 large can fruit	25	Decorate with cream, glacé cherries, chopped nuts, angelica
Fruit salad	3 kg (6$\frac{1}{2}$ lb) fruit 1.75–2.5 l (3–4 pts) sugar syrup 1 l (1$\frac{1}{2}$ pts) cream	25	Can be prepared a day ahead and left submerged in syrup but bananas should be added just before serving

QUANTITIES FOR PARTY DRINKS

Rough guide only, as drinking habits vary.

BUFFET PARTIES

Allow for each, 1–2 shorts and 3–6 longer drinks plus coffee.
Reckon a half-bottle of wine per person.

DINNER PARTIES

One bottle of table wine is sufficient for 4 people.

DROP-IN-FOR-DRINKS

Reckon on 3–5 short drinks each and 4–6 small
savouries besides the usual olives and nuts.

DRINKS BY THE BOTTLE

Sherry and port and straight
vermouths give roughly 12–16
glasses. In single nips for
cocktails, vermouths and spirits
give just over 30 a bottle.
Reckon 16–20 drinks of spirit
from a bottle when serving them with soda,
tonic or other minerals. Liqueurs served in
proper glasses – 30 portions.
A split bottle of soda or tonic
gives 2–3 drinks. A 600 ml (1-pt) can of
tomato juice gives 4–6 drinks.
Dilute a bottle of fruit cordial with
4 litres (7 pts) water for 20–25 drinks.

APPROXIMATE TEA AND COFFEE QUANTITIES

	1 Serving	24–26 Servings		Notes
Coffee ground, hot	200 ml ($\frac{1}{3}$ pt)	225–250 g (9–10 oz) coffee 3.5 l (6 pts) water	1.75 l (3 pts) milk 450 g (1 lb) sugar	If you make the coffee in advance strain it after infusion. Reheat without boiling. Serve sugar separately
ground, iced	200 ml ($\frac{1}{3}$ pt)	350 g (12 oz) coffee 3.5 l (6 pts) water	1.75 l (3 pts) milk sugar to taste	Make coffee (half sweetened, half not), strain and chill. Mix with chilled milk. Serve in glasses
instant, hot	200 ml ($\frac{1}{3}$ pt)	50–75 g (2–3 oz) coffee 3.5 l (6 pts) water	1.25 l (2 pts) milk 450 g (1 lb) sugar	Make coffee in jugs as required. Serve sugar separately
instant, iced	200 ml ($\frac{1}{3}$ pt)	75 g (3 oz) coffee 1.25 l (2 pts) water	3.5 l (6 pts) milk sugar to taste	Make black coffee (half sweetened, half not) and chill. Mix with chilled creamy milk. Serve in glasses.
Tea Indian, hot	200 ml ($\frac{1}{3}$ pt)	50 g (2 oz) tea 4.75 l (8 pts) water	900 ml (1$\frac{1}{2}$ pts) milk 450 g (1 lb) sugar	It is better to make tea in several pots rather than one outsize one
Indian, iced	200 ml ($\frac{1}{3}$ pt)	75 g (3 oz) tea 4.25 l (7 pts) water	1.25 l (2 pts) milk sugar to taste	Strain tea immediately it has infused. Sweeten half of it. Chill. Serve in glasses with chilled creamy milk
China	200 ml ($\frac{1}{3}$ pt)	50 g (2 oz) tea 5.5 ml (9 pts) water	2–3 lemons 450 g (1 lb) sugar	Infuse China tea for 2 or 3 minutes only. Put a thin lemon slice in each cup before pouring. Serve sugar separately

Index

Acknowledgements

*All the photographs in this book
are reproduced by courtesy of
Good Housekeeping except for
the following:*

*Jacket: Bryce Attwell
Endpapers: Paul Kemp
Title: Paul Kemp
Page 97: Melvin Grey*